ELEMENTS OF ETHICS

ELEMENTS OF ETHICS

Adriaan T. Peperzak

STANFORD UNIVERSITY PRESS

STANFORD, CALIFORNIA

2004

To the memory of
Paul Peperzak (1925–2001)

Stanford University Press
Stanford, California

© 2004 by the Board of Trustees of the
Leland Stanford Junior University. All rights reserved.

Printed in the United States of America
on acid-free, archival-quality paper

Library of Congress Cataloging-in-Publication Data

Peperzak, Adriaan Theodor, 1929–
Elements of ethics / Adriaan T. Peperzak.
    p.   cm.
  Includes bibliographical references and index.
  ISBN 0-8047-4769-5 (alk. paper) —
  ISBN 0-8047-4770-9 (pbk. : alk. paper)
   1. Ethics. I. Title.
BJ1012.P418 2003
170—DC21

                           2003007901

Original Printing 2004

Last figure below indicates year of this printing:
13 12 11 10 09 08 07 06 05 04

Typeset in 11/13.5 Adobe Garamond

Contents

Preface

The title of this book indicates that it highlights some—not all—elements of ethics. Its purpose is more limited than the scope of the *Elementa*, *Grundlagen*, *Grundlinien*, or *Principia* in which philosophers from Hobbes to Moore have attempted to replace the foundations of ethics. It concentrates on a few "principles"—including keys, conditions, and perspectives—that should not be forgotten or ignored if ethics is to be true to life.

Thus a certain ambition is not wholly absent from the following pages. Instead of once more explaining the utilitarian, deontological, neo-Aristotelian, or neopositivist doctrines all students of ethics should know, I here examine some of the basic assumptions of any genuine ethics.

Partially motivated by dissatisfaction with the standard treatises, the present study concentrates on a faithful description and analysis of basic experiences from which ethics draws its inspiration. Among the *archai* (beginnings, ruling principles) and *stoicheia* (elements) that provide ethics with a starting point, experience in its most genuine and "archaic" sense is perhaps the most neglected and distorted. Therefore it demands a special rehabilitation, notwithstanding the need of also revising other elements, such as concept formation and thinking.

Making a beginning has always been a problem in philosophy, most explicitly in the modern era. As a philosophical problem, it cannot be resolved without prior involvement in a philosophical practice. Thus, the very question of a good beginning engages thought in a circular—or spiraling—movement. That such a movement is not necessarily vicious is shown by the splendid theories it has generated; but some beginnings certainly are misleading—for instance, those that dogmatically accept the authority of a past or present school. Though no one should be ashamed of following dominant trends, an appeal to such trends is not sufficient to justify a specific starting point. However, no beginning can be justified unless it first has been developed hypothetically.

This book begins with an invitation that seems supported by ancient authority and intrinsic plausibility. "*Know yourself!*" is quoted to suggest an unbreakable connection between philosophical anthropology and the ethical principle of principles: "Be yourself!" Briefly sketching some parts of a justification that must be delayed, the invitation concludes with an announcement of the center to which it would like to direct its readers. This center is called "Correspondence."

The first two chapters (the Introduction and Chapter 2, "From Doing to Living") focus on the question of an appropriate beginning. They situate ethics with regard to its various approaches, philosophy in general, and the ethos of our age. They (re)determine the subject matter of ethics, argue in favor of a fundamental unity of "is" and "ought" against the dominant dualism, and propose a provisional itinerary. With regard to the subject matter, they insist on the unity of each human life from birth to death, the role of life's own experience, and the necessity of accurate descriptions. The conceptual and logical elements of all argumentation are taken for granted and practiced in a manner that owes more to the philosophical classics than to the modern sciences. Though the latter take pride in being "empirical," their abstractions have ignored many conditions of human truth. That these abstractions have enabled the sciences to triumph when concentrating on limited dimensions of their objects warrants admiration. Sometimes, however, the modesty that is appropriate to such self-limitation is replaced by the scientistic (that is, not scientific but dogmatic) conviction that there is no truth other than that of science. When this happens, life, world, and history become poor and dull. Instead of being wonderful and adventurous, they lose their luster. The knowledge achieved in life's own interaction with the most important phenomena is then a priori disqualified, and intuition, sensitivity, refined sensibility, and good taste are deemed irrelevant. Scientism not only blocks the access to the truth of art, morality, and religion; more fundamentally, it distorts the perception of human life as human.

Besides the empirical, descriptive, and phenomenological aspects of the method practiced in this study, a hermeneutical moment is obvious insofar as several classics of philosophy have influenced its analyses. Plato and Aristotle are present on almost every page, but many passages also depend on the work of Plotinus, Augustine, Thomas, Bonaventure, Descartes, Spinoza, Kant, Hegel, Nietzsche, Heidegger, Ricoeur, Levinas, and other heroes of thought. No philosophy succeeds without explicit or implicit retrieval. Those who think the contrary are unaware of the overwhelming extent to which they themselves repeat the past.

Chapters 3 and 4 develop what the first two chapters indicate about the lived experience of human life, paving the way for the central concept, *correspondence*, which will be analyzed in chapters 5 to 7. Chapter 3 ("Affections") focuses on the essence of affectivity and its indispensable role for philosophy in general and ethics in particular, while Chapter 4 ("Desire") narrows this focus by sketching a phenomenology of Desire and desires. The overall perspective is thus radicalized by an examination of the dynamism that mobilizes the emotional, imaginative, practical, intellectual, and referential elements of human activity.

Chapters 5, 6, and 7 explain the "Ought" (or "Should") that constitutes the core of all that is ethical. Although the analysis of Desire given in Chapter 4 indicates that the Kantian contrast between a purely rational imperative and the self-interested desires of human sensibility can be overcome, a more precise analysis is required to understand how the phenomena themselves urge us to appropriately deal with the facts and layers of the human universe.

Chapter 5 ("Correspondence") clarifies the dynamic structure of *responsivity*, a concept that is essential for all forms of "should" or "ought" (or "normativity," as some prefer to say). However, a generic definition of "should" does not do justice to the differences between utilitarian, aesthetic, legal, moral, religious, and other needs or obligations. Therefore, Chapter 6 ("The Analogy of Should") explores how the ethical dimension encompasses various levels and modes of "ought" ranging from consumptive needs to the demands of morality and religion. The result shows a parallelism between the analogy of should and the analogy of being, thus revealing a profound coincidence of fundamental ethics with metaphysics.

A full unfolding of this coincidence, with its twofold analogy, is an urgent task for anyone attempting to overcome the disastrous dualism of "is" and "ought" that has perverted most post-Humean and post-Kantian ethics. But even prior to the completion of that huge undertaking, we must acquire some idea about that which gathers the analogical modes of should (or good) and being into an overarching, though not generic, unity. More concretely, we must clarify to what extent we can still speak of a *universe* or a totality of all beings (as being *and* as demanding) and of an all-encompassing perspective characteristic of the responsive subject. This clarification is broached in Chapter 7 ("Unity and Universality"). As a provisional conclusion of the three central chapters, it leads back to the initial question about the individuality and subjectivity of each human life.

Chapters 8, 9, and 10 seek an answer to that question by focusing on *freedom*. Against the definition of freedom as arbitrary choice or want, but also against its complete identification with the practical side of rational autonomy, these three chapters argue for a definition of freedom that respects the originality of its selfhood, while fully recognizing its situated, culturally and corporeally rooted character and its need of growth, education, conversion, askesis, and purification. Whereas Chapter 8 ("Freedom") focuses on the ethical aspects of determined self-determination, Chapter 9 ("Conscience") reintroduces the old concept of *conscience* as the most original and pure acquaintance with "should" and "good" and argues that this kind of "knowledge" coincides with the "cognitive" side of Desire itself.

Chapter 10 ("Adventures") opens the way for a concretization of conscientious acquaintance. However, it stops short of explicitly engaging in a thorough debate about the assumptions on which most or all forms of "applied ethics" rest.

The last chapter ("Religion") is brief. The reason does not lie in the false assumption that ethics and religion are irrelevant to one another, but rather in my conviction that the relations between religion and ethics deserve much more examination than can be accomplished in a single chapter. While focusing on such an examination in other writings, I here only wish to indicate that loyalty to the world does not exclude authentic religion, but, on the contrary, opens one up to an ultimate horizon that cannot be absorbed by any other dimension. The ultimate cannot be ignored. It demands a response—always and especially when we meditate about justice and injustice, good and evil, meaning, thinking, birth, love, friendship, and mortality.

Many persons have participated in the production of this book—too many to mention all of them by name. I am profoundly grateful to my educators and role models, the illuminating authors from whose work I have borrowed so much, the friends and colleagues who encouraged me, and especially my wife, Angela, who endured my time-consuming concentration on textual production.

I am particularly grateful to Laurel Madison, who meticulously revised several drafts of all the chapters and notes, thus considerably ameliorating the English in which they have been written.

I dedicate this text to the memory of my brother Paul, whose sudden death interrupted our conversation.

Invitation: From "Know Yourself!" to Correspondence

"Know yourself!" At the close of modern philosophy Hegel invoked the "Apollonian command" to summarize not only his own philosophy, but the entire European tradition of thought. In so doing, he presumed that knowledge was the summit of spirituality and that humanity was the embodiment of the Absolute.[1]

When Plato's Socrates appealed to the same oracle, it sounded less theoretical. *Philosophia* still coincided with the erotic search for a good and beautiful life. But even then, *theoria* crowned the search and the Good was approached through contemplation. The tragedies had also emphasized the existential meaning of knowing oneself, but in a different way. Modesty must recognize the boundaries between the gods and the mortals. "Nothing overmuch!"[2] warned against confusion, although at times the gods admitted a hero(ine) to their immortal life.

Pierre Courcelle's admirable erudition has provided us with a survey of the interpretations through which Apollo's injunction has marked our history. His narrative demands a thematic retrieval that cannot be unfolded in the present study, but the awareness that self-knowledge, despite its many transformations, has remained a constant preoccupation is always in the background when we try to thematize the conditions for an ethics of our time. What should we do, how should we act, which kinds of life are desirable, how far does our responsibility go, and so on? All such questions involve us in reflections on a self that remains puzzling or even mysterious.

If an ethics must provide guidance for human lives, its relevance should not require lengthy argumentation. To what extent does ethical guidance presuppose that we *know* what sort of life we live? What kind of self and self-knowledge is required by a good life? Are science, literature, philosophy conditions for living well, or do other forms of knowledge suffice? Can we be good without reflection, in an entirely extroverted and self-forgetful way? If so, the principal commandment would simply state: "Be!"

or "Become good!" (But what and how is "good"?) Although it still could rule philosophy, "Know yourself!" would have lost its existential urgency.

Modern concentration on the human ego has not always respected the self's involvement in its many historical and natural, personal and impersonal adventures. We expected that our intellect would provide us with a satisfactory account of life's essential urgency. Guidance toward wisdom was sought in the law of reason that lay within us, and the autonomy of a rational will was seen as the source of all injunctions. Because reason, as both theoretical and practical, constituted human nature, "Be reasonable!" could be translated as "Be yourself!" or—as Pindar had said in another tone—"Be what you are!"[3] However, since coincidence with one's essence is an endless task, humans never completely "become what they are!" Can they at least get to know what and who they are? And does such knowledge include guidelines for a good life?

Even in its amended, phenomenologically adjusted treatments, concentration on a solitary Ego has governed philosophy. Despite considerable interest in the structures of intersubjectivity, the monological bent of modern thought is still dominant. Neither behavioristic reductions nor proclamations of man's death have eradicated the general desire for knowledge about human destiny. However, we have become more aware of the innumerable connections that involve us in various forms of alterity, from elementary determinisms of nature to various kinds of relationships with neighbors and God.

Is wisdom available only in the form of self-knowledge? Is self-transcendence possible at all? Would we not inevitably transport our very selves to a vantage point from which we could look back on the traditional Ego? A central position within the totality seems inescapable for a philosopher. But at least one can recognize that everyone is preceded, formed, guided, provoked, and responded to by other persons, things, events, elements, structures, and so on. Can I avoid the danger of playing God while analyzing or fashioning my universal "being somehow everything"?[4] Recognition of my finitude will not cure my *hybris* if nothing irreducible confounds my self-consciousness. Unless such irreducibility exists, justice and generosity are impossible. What affects me then, is not a theme; it rather provokes me to a response. Responsiveness overcomes self-reflection. To know who I am refers me to correspondence.

ELEMENTS OF ETHICS

CHAPTER I

Introduction

Beginning

We would not exist if others had not cared for us after we were conceived. Somehow, the beginning of our lives was an experience of moral behavior. Others took care of our survival; apparently, they were concerned about us.

I have used the word *moral* here in a broad and largely indeterminate sense: many motivations are possible for helping someone to survive, but the most obvious meaning of "helping to survive instead of letting die" implies that one has overcome the temptation to kill another demanding and possessive human being.

Although most infants are surrounded by love, they are not grateful for the love that saves them, because they are not aware of the moral difference between caring for others and egoism. Only much later in their formation does such awareness become part of their cultural baggage. Personal awakening to morality is most often the experience of a prohibition: a mother, for instance, forbids her child to realize a wish, thus creating a conflict between a drive and a command. The mother's authority reveals an imperative that contradicts the other's spontaneity. The natural expansion of the latter's vitality runs up against a powerful "No." The child's ethical experience meets with a "Don't!" (don't touch, don't throw, don't cry).

Psychology can show how such elementary experiences evolve into more mature phenomena of moral life, but it cannot explain the essence, the origin, and the meaning of morality. What empirical sciences such as psychology, sociology, ethnology, and history can do is show how specific forms of authority, education, tradition, culture, and civilization stylize and vary the ethos of certain communities and epochs, the behavior of individuals, and the moral convictions by which they are led. Through induction they can also generalize their discoveries, but their generalities do not answer the basic questions of essence and meaning. The immediate transition from empirical descriptions and explanations to philosophical generalizations was one of the great, though misguided, attractions of the nineteenth and twentieth centuries. Biologism, psychologism, sociologism, and historicism are the traps into which a host of intellectuals continues to fall. How often are our time, our education, or our belonging to a particular community forwarded as the reason a certain thesis is upheld? We can no longer believe in such things as "metaphysics," "the Infinite," "essence," "ideas," "prime matter," or "the soul." However, we rarely use "our time" or "our education" explicitly as an argument for positive assertions. For example, it sounds odd to say that we are convinced of the truth that democracy is the best form of government because we are Americans or because we live in the twentieth century. Such an argument too clearly shows that the thesis has no other basis than a contingent belief rooted in a temporary situation. And yet, implicitly, similar arguments (for example, the unproven *doxai* of a certain epoch) are powerfully present in most of the philosophical literature, including some of its most famous specimens. Seldom are the unproven presuppositions of "our time" and "our culture" explicitly stated as such and critically evaluated from a perspective that takes a distance from the contingency of our situation. Some writers even claim that such a perspective is not possible because we are entirely caught up in the particulars of our here and now. If they are right, particularity and contingency have overtaken our universe: essentiality, necessity, infinity, and eternity are illusions, and history, even though it is itself incomprehensible, is the ultimate horizon of reality.

It is not difficult to sketch psychologistic and sociologistic parallels of the historicism referred to here. The fact that I have a conscience (or rather, that I "think" that I have a conscience) is "nothing else than" the result of psychical transformations of an ongoing conflict between drives and the law of "the father." Morality is "nothing else than" a balance of powers whose combats and truces can be detected. And so on.

Two main routes are open to an empiricistic demythologization of morality and ethics. The milder version accepts a certain authenticity and originariness of the ethical while stressing that all existing codes and theories are relative. A broad range of variations are possible on this basis. Though we could hypothesize that all moral codes are variations on a common theme, we could also perhaps defend the idea that they are incomparably different despite a common reference to some very abstract or hidden roots. A radical unmasking of morality—the one Nietzsche attempted, without success—claims that morality, conscience, duties, and so on, are themselves reducible to other, not morally qualified facts, ideas, events, or norms. The facticity of phenomena that are generally called moral or ethical cannot be denied, but the sciences do not have a place for the ethical qualities of those facts. This seduces many of those who believe in science to think that morality, as a secondary or tertiary quality, must be reducible to something more scientifically manageable.

No philosopher, of course, will deny that a philosophical ethics can profit greatly from investigations into the first signs of an individual's moral awareness, the influence of parents on a child's conscience, the relations between the cultural ambiance and personal standards, or the differences between the moral codes of the feudal system, the capitalist bourgeoisie, and the contemporary Mafia. If moral philosophy is possible, however, it begins with the conviction that morality cannot be reduced to anxiety, power play, submission or repression, seduction, attachment to the father or mother, dependence on a factual ethos, the attraction of pleasure, and so on. Nevertheless, all attempts at reducing morality to some nonmoral source are illuminating for at least two reasons: first, by uncovering the nonmoral aspects or relations of moral phenomena, they facilitate a clearer understanding of the moral element in those phenomena, preventing us from basing an ethics on pseudomoral experiences; and second, they urge us to rethink the relations between morality and the moments of power, anxiety, submission, and repression that very often or perhaps always go with it.

If the ethical is irreducible to any other element of the universe, ethics must count on some sort of immediate givenness of the ethical as originary. If this givenness can be shown, it is *in concreto* always caught in a web of interpretative moments. Anticipating later chapters, we can state provisionally that all of our perceptions and descriptions are codetermined by networks of interpretation typical of a particular culture and time and characteristic of the individual lives in which they are appropriated and transformed. Some philosophers see this as a reason for attempting to over-come the particularity of their own perspective by stepping up to a metaethical level from which they can look down upon all particularities, in order to develop a universal, albeit rather formal, theory. The hope that guides this attempt is founded on the supposition that we can isolate a uni-versally valid core within the amalgam of universality and interpretative particularities that make a nonsubjective ethics so difficult.

Kant's *formalism* is an outstanding example of a metaethical theory whose formal character seems to permit application to any particular ethos. Rather than seeking the ethical element of human action in any specific code of obligations, it locates it in the (practical) rationality of human ac-tion. This is not the place to discuss Kant's foundation of ethics or the clas-sical (Hegelian, Marxist, Nietzschean, and Schelerian) objections raised against it. What I do hope to show in the following chapters, however, can be summarized by stating, first, that Kant's formalism is too high a price for its presumed universality, because, although it can detect inconsisten-cies in a proposed ethos, it cannot show what is positively good; and sec-ond, that it presupposes, but does not justify, its presupposition that ra-tionality and retributive justice are the highest standards of "good."

Another, even more popular, attempt at overcoming ethical rela-tivism is *utilitarianism*. Regarding human needs as universal human de-mands and the will to choose as a right, utilitarianism tries to discover the rules that must be observed for a satisfactory economy in which individual and communal drives and choices can be brought into balance or har-mony. Too many presuppositions are involved in this attempt to be fully analyzed here. One of the basic hypotheses is that satisfaction ("happi-ness") and choice are the main constituents of the good. To what extent this hypothesis is true is one of the major questions of this book. Here it suffices to state that neither need nor choice can be isolated from the over-whelming influence of the particular interpretations that mark particular cultures in particular epochs and the individuals that participate in them.

The attempt to reach a level that is exempt from particular and con-flicting interpretations involves itself in particular and conflicting metain-terpretations. Even if there are elements of morality that are universally valid—and this book is a plea for this thesis—these elements cannot be isolated in an independent theory that hovers over the concrete varieties of ethoses and ethics.

Some interpretations, however, are better than others. If we can say this, we somehow "know" or "have" a criterion that guides us in distinguishing the better from the worse. Such a criterion is an orientation or reference to the good. Perhaps the criterion will always remain hidden and obscure (hiddenness and obscurity might even belong to its essence), but that we are guided by some sense or suspicion of it is a necessary presupposition of all ethics. For an ethics to begin, it must start from the concrete situation in which a thinker lives, including his or her already developed and educated life within a specific family, country, language, continent. To a certain extent, our guidance is concretized in a particular ethos and *doxa*, but it also points to a moment of the good that is not narrowed and contaminated by the restrictive and distorting elements of its concrete appearance here and now. Through and in the particular (partly universal and pure, partly narrowed and impure) appearance of the good, we hope to approach the authentic moment of the unrestricted and uncontaminated goodness that alone can give an ethics the basis it needs.

To be ourselves in a philosophical—and thus radically searching and purifying—manner provides the best possibility for a fruitful communication with others who do the same from their own limited and contaminated perspectives within the horizons of their particular and varied cultures. Critical radicality commands us to remain aware and alert with regard to our own unproven opinions and ethos while descending into their depths in search of the hidden presence of the good itself. Such a method presupposes the hope that we will somehow converge with others who practice the same critical radicality from other starting points. Does not the good itself create affinity?

The quest that this book tries to provide a stylized report of is motivated by the conviction that conscience, despite admixtures and distortions, reveals the originary reality of the ethical. If ethics is possible at all, its point of departure must be given in an irreducible—that is, immediate and originary—way, even if the first, second, and following encounters with the ethical are mixed experiences in which the ethical itself is not yet clearly distinguished. *If the ethical is real, it cannot be proved, because it is either nothing at all or an irreducible origin.*

From the perspective of science and scientific philosophy, this point of departure must be seen as an unwarranted hypothesis, a risky wager, or an arbitrary form of antiscientism. Their own operations, however, are also motivated by unproven convictions, as the theory of science has made clear. Scientists can proudly refer to the theoretical and technical results of their work: "if you do not believe my hypotheses, recognize at least the marvelous products they made possible." Can a philosopher provide similar products? An ethics is the unfolding of an initial perspective and principle into a theory that is or is not recognized by people whose ways of life are thematized in that theory. Their own lives are the issue of a reflection in which their thoughts about this issue are presented in a more or less clarified and systematic form. Recognition demands not only the ability to decipher that form, but also an affinity between the conscience of the reader and the conscience described and analyzed in that ethics. If a reader does not recognize his or her own conscience in an ethics, the cause of this failure may lie in the ethics or the reader's conscience, or both. The product of an ethics cannot be as easily demonstrated as scientific results: more is required than complicated observations and theoretical skills. A refined sensibility is demanded for an appropriate evaluation of the degree to which an ethics tells the truth about a good human life. Again, we confront the question of how we can know that the evaluators themselves are conscientious enough to evaluate the (in)correctness of an ethics. We turn in circles. This is an indication that we are in the presence of something that is either void or is so originary that it, although unprovable, can only be experienced, believed, or postulated as preceding all provable facts and theses. The authenticity or inauthenticity of such assumptions can be experienced—but these experiences can and must be tested. The methodology of ethics includes a theory of such testing. Life is an experiment with itself—not only to discover a good way of living, but also to reveal appropriate criteria and manners of evaluating and guiding it. The guiding thread of ethics cannot be imported from the outside; it exists in the lived, experimental, and self-evaluating life of people who are moved by the good, in competition with other, wrong and bad attractions. Conscience itself is the beginning, but it is often seduced by illusions, distortions, or rationalizations.

Doing Philosophy

Doing philosophy is thinking through an issue from A to Z. Even if you are explaining the work of a dead philosopher, you must rethink its basic principles, the experiences from which they emerged, and the perspectives that guided the author's writing. If a commentary does not bring the text once again to life, the philosophy it contains remains a fossil, still good, perhaps, for a review of former opinions or "ideas," but not a part of the history of living thought.

Doing philosophy is participation in the ongoing discussions of an epoch. Most often this means that one participates in the work in progress of a school or a trend, focusing on a set of standard questions, using a common terminology, referring to the same manuals, dictionaries, journals, authors, classics, and established theses. One has then adopted the characteristic framework and basic assumptions of a specific tradition within the history of philosophy. If your school is recognized as the mainstream or thodoxy and if you master the generally approved convictions and skills, you can make a career. If the situation remains the same for an extended period of time, you can lead a peaceful and productive life, at home in a commonly recognized pattern of thinking.

The classics of philosophy practiced philosophy differently. Though well aware of the mainstream thought of their times, they transformed it— sometimes in a revolutionary, but always in a refreshing, way—by re- thinking its basic questions, and often changing the questions themselves. They introduced a new perspective and tried a new approach. Once the re- sistance of the traditional majority was overcome, the innovators were rec- ognized as new authorities and quoted as classics instead of or in addition to former ones. Philosophy was rejuvenated. A new field of exploration lay open for elaboration; once again a mainstream of thought could develop. Neoplatonism, Neostoicism, Neoepicureanism, Neokantianism, Neo- hegelianism, Neothomism, and so on, testify to the fertility of philosoph- ical revolutions while also showing that most philosophers spend their lives in a less original unfolding or application of perspectives and principles in- troduced by their heroes. We could call them epigones, but we cannot deny that their work is important insofar as it shows the consequences and configurations made possible by the classics. Without their assiduous elab- orations, we would neither fully appreciate the relevance of their master's revolution nor discover to what extent even the classics need amendments and transformations. However, the danger of being a mere follower is scholasticism. Once you are so impressed by a particular framework and style that you are no longer able to compete with it by rethinking your own basic tenets, you have surrendered to authority; you then restrict yourself to further analyses and applications of principles and perspectives that are taken for granted once and for always. This surrender, expressed in the rep- etition of fundamental assumptions without renewed efforts to connect them with the roots of experience, description, imaginative conceptualization, and faithful interpretation, is the germ that kills philosophy. Hosts of intelligent and assiduous professionals are dedicated to developing the tradition of their schools or fashions without looking back in suspicion; but what we need more than ever is to reexamine the main questions and basic assumptions themselves. Scholasticism tends to stifle philosophical wonder. Boredom is a healthy reaction to its pseudo-obvious repetitions, but it is a sign of decadence and imminent death. Agonies can take a long time, however.

The Situation of Ethics

The greatness of the modern revolution was its courageous decision to abolish all beliefs in order to take complete responsibility for all that can be said in philosophy. By proclaiming the autonomy of thought as the critical unveiling of the first and last grounds of the entire universe, modern thought declared itself emancipated. It became the master and proprietor of the world and the potential engineer of its intelligible reconstruction. Instead of the heir to ancient or medieval wisdom, modern thinking would be the creator of its own universe on the basis of an all-encompassing knowledge of the structures and materials available or producible.

The modern project is still an inspiring symbol for all philosophers who believe that philosophy is a lie if it is not radical enough to continually search for the primordial, the roots, the ground(s). However, who among us still believes in the real possibility of fully becoming "masters and owners of the world"?[1] And who can still maintain that the classics of modernity were wholly independent of their predecessors in ancient, early Christian, and medieval times, after so many historical studies have shown the contrary?[2] Modern philosophers, too, relied on unproved assumptions and traditions; despite their revolution, they too continued a particular history. Even philosophers cannot create ex nihilo. Their originality remains hermeneutical.

Modernity itself has generated schools and scholasticisms. Besides (Neo)Spinozist, (Neo)Kantian, and (Neo)Hegelian trends, analytic philosophy is a clear case in point. Its adherents enjoy a commonly shared set of perspectives, assumptions, terms, questions, and convictions, but they are in danger of losing touch with the genuine experience of the reality from which all those elements have been taken.

More than a century ago, phenomenology came to the fore as a reminder that "the issue" (*die Sache*) itself should neither be forgotten nor
prematurely stylized by hasty adaptations to "natural" or scientific treatments. It is a rather enigmatic fact of twentieth-century philosophy that the
phenomenological impulse has not been more successful and is practically
ignored outside the circle of its adherents. Even within phenomenology
there is hardly any unity that would justify characterizing it as a school.
Scholastic developments are not absent, although the thrust of Husserl's devices have prompted most phenomenologists to rethink their point of departure. It is mainly the development of a hermeneutical view that has become critical of the conception according to which it is not only required,
but also possible, to get in touch with things as they are in themselves.

So-called continental philosophy is a mixture of very diverse trends.
Besides the Anglo-American "analytic" continuation of eighteenth-century
philosophy, a more continental style, exemplified by Habermas, testifies
that modernity is not yet dead. Empiricism and hostility toward metaphysics are dominant in these schools; Kant is celebrated, but his metaphysical project is most often ignored. In contintental philosophy, phenomenology and hermeneutical retrievals of the past are the ruling
tendencies. The history of philosophy has become an integral part of thematic philosophy, and the human sciences, masked as philosophy, have in-
vaded the scene. Metaphilosophical considerations show how problematic
the concept and the praxis of philosophy have become, occasionally de-
claring or announcing the end of philosophical thought itself. Relativism,
widespread awareness of ubiquitous ambiguity and ambivalence, skepticism, and surrender to scientific empiricism seem to confirm this diagnosis, but many attempts at conserving the classical past through ever more
accurate reconstructions or re-creative retrievals testify to the strength of
immortal heroes and traditions. Divided by nostalgia and expectation, we
waver between gratitude and hope on one side, and rejection or despair on
the other. Is it not presumptuous, in this situation, to venture a new beginning? Yes, if someone hopes or promises to lay an entirely new foundation. No, if a new beginning means that philosophers should always pierce
the surface of scholastic traditions and all-too-familiar texts of others and
their own, in order to discover again and again what, in the end and at the
beginning, really matters. Then perhaps they will be visited by a few simple but illuminating insights for which a long commerce with founders,
schools, and traditions is not too high a price.[3]

Philosophy in Search of Wisdom

In the preceding sections, I have taken for granted that ethics, as a philosophical discipline, should continue the academic, more or less scientific, style it has acquired in the modern university. The great masters of *ethica*—not only the premodern ones, but also Descartes, Spinoza, Leibniz, and Kant—demanded more than academic rigor; they saw their endeavors as ways to wisdom. Since Plato, the relations between *epistēmē* and *sophia*, *scientia* and *sapientia*, *knowledge* and *wisdom* have been discussed in many meditations on the nature, the end, and the use of philosophy. To what extent does and should philosophical theory, besides displaying skillful thought, contribute to the practice that is necessary and sufficient for leading a wise and good life? Some have answered that experience, not philosophy, makes one wise, whereas others have argued that wisdom requires dialectics. One cannot say that most philosophers of our century are models of wisdom or even that they see the facilitating of wisdom as their task. However, many students eagerly turn to philosophy in the hope of learning lessons for life, and some professors do not discourage them in their desire to discover a contemporary version of Plato's Academy.[4]

That modern science has become the paradigm of thought is one of the factors that has caused a rupture between philosophical knowledge and wisdom. Another, not unrelated, factor lies in the breach of philosophy with theology, faith, and spirituality. As long as the Jewish, the Christian, and the Muslim faiths expressed themselves through the integration of Greek and Roman philosophy into a theologically reflected spirituality, philosophical endeavors served the unified goal of a contemplative wisdom in close connection with the attempt to lead a religiously and morally good life. The modern divorce of philosophy from theology and faith has created a situation in which philosophical seekers of wisdom must look to other sources for orientation. In the meantime, however, modern philosophy developed a basic attitude and a spirituality of its own, which do not allow for certain kinds of conviction and orientation. This situation created tensions, or even conflicts, between loyalty to the orthodox way of modern philosophizing and sympathy for certain kinds of (true or false) wisdom. Some students turn away from philosophy because of their disappointment; others continue to insist that the fundamental reflection it engenders must not withdraw before the *really* interesting questions, all of which are somehow existential.

It seems obvious that questions of the (ultimate) truth, the meaning of human life, the validity of personal conscience, the possibility of happiness, and so on can neither be ignored nor relegated to other disciplines than the one that prides itself on its all-encompassing thoroughness. It has become equally obvious, however, that the modern idea of rationality, as practiced in mainstream philosophy, is overburdened when urged to answer those questions thoroughly. The project of Descartes, Spinoza, Kant, and Hegel has failed. Is its inspiration exhausted, as widespread relativism and skepticism, especially in ethical questions, suggest?

The unfulfilled promises of modernity turn many students away from logos to mythos, religion, superstition, or faith. Such forms of wisdom are less rational than they would be if it were possible to integrate the logically won insights of modern thought into a well-thought and wise philosophy (or theology). The leap from reflection to unreflective surrender repairs neither the breach between *epistēmē* and *sophia* nor the inner duality that haunts most scholars of our time. A new form of internal and external reconciliation is necessary. Such will not be possible unless the basic categories of philosophy are rethought in their relation to wisdom, praxis, spirituality, belief, and faith. Intellect and reason, experience and rationality, respect for the given, and recognition of the facts as they appear must be experienced anew as elements of a desired gnosis that has remained the goal of all seekers, including those who choose philosophy as their profession in the belief that it promises living, not lifeless, truth.

Obviously, a renewal of the philosophical search for wisdom demands an insight into the causes and conditions of the modern rupture, and such an insight demands a diagnosis of modernity in general. Which ideas and attitudes prevented modern thought from achieving wisdom? Why did the epoch in which mathematics, science, and technology reached such heights leave us without a rigorous theory of how human life ought to be lived? Why do so many great scholars lack wisdom?

Before even attempting to diagnose modernity from the perspective of wisdom, we need to intensify our amazement. Wisdom, as a blend of sensibility, serious contemplation, and genuinely lived experience, including personal adventures and experiments, is not a privilege of some learned, priestly, or prophetic elite. To some degree, it is everybody's task to acquire wisdom in order to live a sensible life. How can we live meaningfully if we are ignorant with respect to eating and drinking, health and sickness, education, family life and friendship, speaking and dealing with others, making decisions, procreating and welcoming newborns, accepting suffering and death? All people are urged by life itself to become knowledgeable about the key issues of living. If philosophers, as specialists of the search for fundamental truth, have a task, it certainly includes the clarification of those and other existential issues. The problems of Everyman cannot be ignored or dismissed by the philosophers, even if they find them too difficult for the logic that rules their profession today. If, for example, concern for methodological purity impedes them from treating the central and universal questions of all humans, to whom then should these questions be addressed? Even if philosophers—or, for that matter, theologians (who cannot speak without appealing to philosophy)—are reluctant to speak out because of their high standards for conclusive rigor and precision, would they prefer to relinquish those questions to the domain of fundamentalist beliefs or the easy promises of salvation by false prophets?

If the search for wisdom, together with questions of ultimate meaning, is excluded from philosophy, philosophers condemn themselves and others to a lack of reflective insight. This does not necessarily impede them from becoming very clever, scientific, sophisticated, and rigorous within the limits of their (unexistential and thus very abstract) science and logic. Their attachment to the satisfaction of a restricted rigor can be so strong that the pleasure of the game, as it is played with fellow philosophers, becomes obsessive and exclusive. Like fanatic chess players, they no longer pay attention to needs that are at the same time epistemological and existential. Philosophy has then become one of the many disciplines whose relevance is neither fundamental nor decisive.

The preceding sections simplify the situation of ethics and philosophy in general by focusing on one type of contemporary philosophy. The injustice of such a simplification should be counterbalanced by a more refined description and by the reminder that Pascal, Hamann, Kierkegaard, and other exceptional thinkers are still evoked as supplemental to the main trends of modern philosophy. However, the recognition of many modern voices does not abolish the modern schism between scientifically rigorous and existentially sensitive thought. The experience of life and logical reflection have not come together in a convincing pattern that we could spontaneously adopt as a framework for our reflections.

Is my plea for a new union of *epistēmē* and *sophia* anything else than a defense of existentialism, which briefly conquered the European scene in the 1940s and 1950s? My answer is short. Without entering into a critique of such diverse authors as Husserl, Heidegger, Jaspers, Marcel, Buber, and

Sartre, I only wish to state that their success, even now, suggests a widely felt need and that a return to the most genuine experiences of human life itself seems prima facie to be an obvious condition for any theory that discovers how, in truth, life should be understood and lived. If there is something suspect about philosophical abstractions, the only possible safeguard consists in a renewed recourse to the basic experiences that orient and mark existing lives. In order to avoid infidelities, we must, from the beginning, remain as close as possible to the skin of the earth where the real life is lived by average people without philosophical preoccupations. Escaping all contamination by the historical factuality is hardly possible because most people have already incorporated the premises of the ruling culture. However, it is not necessary to recover a completely naive life in order to determine whether our conceptions do or do not do justice to the essential occurrences of human life. To begin, it is perhaps sufficient—although already difficult—to test the cultural and philosophical patterns that rule us by evaluating whether and how much they do justice to the possibilities of a fully human existence.

Life, as it is lived by humans, is neither a biological nor a psychological or sociological category. Rather than possessing or mastering it, we are possessed by life. It allows us to live while urging that we live it in a way that is neither random nor arbitrary but—at least to some extent—meaningful. If life itself demands that we be good, wisdom includes a sort of feel or sense for its desires and needs. Would it not be marvelous if philosophy could contribute to the understanding of that urgency?

Diagnosis of Our Time

If philosophy can neither be performed nor understood in isolation from the more general search for wisdom that characterizes all civilizations, a metaphilosophical understanding of any ethics presupposes an insight into the cultural context from which it emerges. An interpretation and diagnosis of our culture and its patterns, traditions, differences in style, contradictions, conflicts, doubts, and crises is such an enormous task that it cannot be accomplished even in several volumes. Even if we restricted ourselves, as many philosophers do, to the philosophical productions of the last decades, the variety of tendencies and traditions is too extensive and our distance too limited to allow for a broad enough perspective and an adequate portrayal of the actual situation. Most overviews of contemporary philosophy and its relations to the philosophies of other epochs still borrow simple schemas of classification and periodization from some fa-mous—rationalist, empiricist, scientist, Kantian, Hegelian, Marxian, Ni-etzschean, Heideggerian, Wittgensteinian, or other—perspective of the past; the use of such names as "postmodernism" and "postmetaphysical thought" further neglects the existing polymorphism and its many inter-pretations. Little profit is drawn from such simplifications. We do not even agree on the question of whether we, as philosophers, are somehow united by a shared affinity, inspiration, or "spirit," or rather are so scattered into monads, chapels, and schools, that we can no longer understand each other's languages and methodical demands.

The situation of philosophy resembles a museum of ethnology. If the visitor does not immediately identify with one of the exhibited forms of life (including imagination, thought, and other symbolisms), the many possibilities that are practiced and displayed can only create confusion or else present a difficult challenge to which each must respond by discover-ing and constructing his or her own way of thinking (that is, perceiving, approaching, feeling, questioning, distinguishing, and pondering).

Although it may seem that a treatise must begin by clarifying how the method it practices relates to other methods—a task that presupposes a diagnosis of the entire history of philosophy—the very impossibility of fulfilling such a requirement here releases me from that (seeming) obliga-tion.[5] The simple use of epithets such as "dialectical," "phenomenological," or "existential" would likewise not help to clarify in advance what sort of argumentation a reader of this book may expect. The best clarification might be found in a procedure that combines the actual (and partially naive) development of a thought process that is accompanied by lateral or retrospective explanations of the steps that it will have made.[6]

Mapping Ethics

The composition of a treatise reveals what the author deems basic, important, secondary, accidental, or marginal. Unity and structure, analy-sis and synthesis are unavoidable; but there are various modes of display-ing elements, and each mode provides a different picture of the reality. For example, the beginning contains important decisions with regard to the shape of the entire field; the division of the parts shows how the writer re-constructs the skeleton of the subject.

Few manuals discuss the systematic division and composition ac-cording to which an ethics should be structured. Yet the overall structure of a philosophical discipline determines the framework and the perspective of the entire approach practiced within it. By contextualizing all its sections and sentences, a systematic whole is part of the meaning that is expressed in the parts; these would be isolated fragments with no conclusive meaning if they did not function as elements of a whole. Casuistry and concentration on propositions easily lead to the neglect of methodological questions of composition and division. However, such questions cannot be relegated to metaethical considerations that would follow a "first-order" ethics; the meaning of the very first parts of the treatise would have already answered those questions in an uncritical way. Are we then caught in a circle? In order to compose and divide a treatise, we must already be acquainted with the subordinate sections; but in order to "place" the sections and understand their relevance, we must know how they fit together as moments of a totality. Indeed, we must take up both ends simultaneously and hold them together as inseparable elements of a circular, or perhaps a spiraling, *movement*. No one can write an ethics unless one already has an—albeit vague—"Idea" of the overall structure that will develop out of the first sections. Some sort of encompassing project is required from the outset, but each realization demands a critical re-view of the project itself.

No project is possible without at least a preliminary idea of the entire field and some—albeit provisional—answer to the question of how the particular issues fit into the whole. The structure of "the hermeneutical circle" (or spiral) dominates all interpretations in literature, art, religion, morality, science, and philosophy. That this is often forgotten or even denied may be because many ethicists take certain frameworks for granted without critically reflecting on their validity. Scholastic traditions can be recognized by the repetition of standard questions and generally accepted theses, and by the canonical arrangements through which these questions and theses are connected. The adherents of such traditions hardly question such arrangements; at home in the inherited systematics, they typically try to refine the customary questions and to solve remaining puzzles without questioning the problematic framework. Revolutions in philosophy occur when a framework itself is changed. Then it is no longer possible to repeat fragments of the inherited tradition, as if nothing had happened to their justification; even though they may still be recognizable, they have been fundamentally transformed.

The hermeneutical spiral creates a perpetual movement. In a first, still naive, stage of reflection, we develop obvious questions within a traditional and naively accepted framework. Once we have developed a theory, we look back: how did we proceed, what did our method reveal, did our approach do justice to the phenomena, and were our questions on target? A critical view of the work accomplished might lead to a revision of our points of departure: perspective and method may need to be adjusted; some questions that seemed basic may now appear derivative; the outline may need to be modified, and so on. A second attempt led by a different plan can now begin, and the process continues.

The division and composition of a treatise present an overview of the connections by which the elements of a certain universe are distinguished and united according to an understandable order. Such an overview can be either naive or sophisticated, but it is never completely original; tradition and former, less reflective attempts play a role in all new beginnings.

As a consequence of the preceding statements, we must state that a thorough methodology cannot precede ethics or—for that matter—metaphysics and philosophical anthropology. On the contrary, in a critical and transformative way, methodology looks back to a preceding, more naive development, in order to adjust the approach that was used, indicating how the next development of the same matter should be guided by a more appropriate approach. Epistemology is particularly necessary between two phases of philosophy, as practiced in (for example) metaphysics or ethics. The proper time of epistemology (including methodology) is that between a more or less achieved past and a more desirable future in philosophy. An epistemology of ethics thus represents an intermediary stage between two stages of ethics. As an exercise in methodological revision, it announces a better ethics, which has not yet been unfolded. The development of the announced ethics must then show to what extent the methodological rules practiced in it have succeeded in being more appropriate than the former ones.

Looking Back

When concentrating on ethics, we can learn about the relevance of divisions by comparing some classical treatises. To sketch in an all too brief and prescholarly fashion an example of such a comparison, I will present the ethics of Aristotle, Aquinas, and Kant, without denying that a more scholarly comparison should also bring in other ethics, such as those of the Stoics, Epicurus, Bonaventure, Hume, and Nietzsche.

Aristotle presents the *Nicomachean Ethics* as the first part of a treatise that encompasses the entire field of social and political philosophy. Ethics centers on *eudaimonia* as self-sufficient perfection, full flourishing of human beauty through the free actualization of logos in an impassioned but well-proportioned life. An analysis of human perfection and its conditions—logos, deliberation, choice, habituation—lays the foundation, after which the particular forms of excellence ("virtues") and human relations (especially friendship and justice) are investigated. The combination of splendid behavior and philosophical contemplation constitutes *eudaimonia*. Ethics thus reveals what it means to be fully and beautifully human.

Full insight into the relevance of ethics presupposes an insight in the tripartite division of philosophy that, since Aristotle, has dominated western thought. *Logic* (including all formal disciplines), *Physics* (including metaphysics), and *Ethics* (including social and political philosophy) divide the philosophical universe into one methodical and two "material" parts. Most often the logic has been developed in close connection with physics and metaphysics, which represented the theoretical side of philosophy, while ethics was treated as secondary. A typically ethical logic was not developed; even the need for it was rarely perceived.

Aquinas's ethics, on the other hand, is part of a universal theology. It treats the return (*reditus*) of the soul to God, which, according to a Neoplatonic schema, must follow the *exitus* of the finite universe from God. At the same time, however, it is a systematic retrieval of Aristotle's ethics.[7] Its setting transforms the Greek *kalokagathos* into a Christian saint by arguing that *beatitudo* cannot be perfect unless it is motivated and permeated or "informed" by Christian love. The unifying framework of the Greek polis is replaced with the worldwide communion of divine *caritas*. The indwelling of a good *daimon* (*eudaimonia*) becomes the *beatitudo* of Jesus' blessings. The analysis of free actions is systematized and refined while the passions (*pathē*) are systematically classified and characterized. The treatment of natural and supernatural virtues retrieves almost everything found in Aristotle, but at the same time shows how much a Christian saint differs from Aristotle's ideal citizen-philosopher.[8]

In Kant's foundation of ethics, *eudaimonia* and *beatitudo* are replaced by a very different notion: *Glückseligkeit*, which is more or less equivalent to "happiness." This notion belongs to the realm of natural inclinations, which are comparable to Aristotle's *pathē* and Thomas's *passions*. However, it has lost the "logical" or rational character of their virtue theory. As a result of the Cartesian separation of body and spirit, the inclinations, and with them happiness, have fallen back into the chaotic mess of irrational, hedonic material. Only the will, as practical reason, can make human behavior good or bad. Human "autonomy" must rule our intentions. Striving for happiness is not rejected, but it is ethically indifferent: as a natural necessity, our desire for happiness must be disciplined; although it does not contribute to the goodness of a life, and is in fact a hindrance, it allows us to earn rewards by observing the rigorous duties prescribed by our own rationality. To be fully human is to always honor human dignity, which consists of being rational. Rationality—not beauty or sanctity—is the ideal. This thesis guides the entire composition of Kant's works on ethics. Instead of the *polis* or the *communio sanctorum*, the framework is the realm of all beings that are led by the a priori universality of reason.

The sketches above are schematic. Besides the three classics mentioned, many other approaches should be analyzed and critically retrieved, and the same is true of the standard divisions practiced in the contemporary literature. More refined analyses would then show that the composition of each treatise on ethics expresses the basic theses defended in it. Before we read any of its arguments, the table of contents has already informed us which notions are fundamental and relevant and how they are connected. As philosophers, we cannot take this structure for granted until we have pondered the question of its justification. A critical review of its structure must accompany the study of any ethics if we want to examine its presuppositions. Although the layout is certainly a decisive part of its argument, it is often presented as obvious, and few authors bother with an explicit justification of their approach.

Is such a justification even possible at all? Is not every framework rather an experiment that begins more or less intuitively or by way of trial and error, with its possible fecundity shown only afterward? Is it possible to justify the structure of a treatise without circularity? Modern philosophy sought to establish the one true system, but can we not think of radically different philosophies equally good and true but irreducible to one synthesis? In art, variety is not a problem. Why should the truth of finite, inevitably perspectival, persons be confined to one systematic whole?

The Initial Overview

Well aware of the partially or wholly subjective, intuitive, unconscious, emotional, traditional, archaic, and otherwise contingent elements that may interfere with my attempt at integrating the many lessons I have received from teachers, writers, students, and colleagues, I take the risk of presenting an overview from which this book developed. If the process of its elaboration led in fact to something other than I had hoped for, this might point to another and preferable way of structuring the field of morality. Whether this indeed is the case must be (re)considered at the end of the attempted development (which always is also a readjustment and sometimes the [partial] refutation or conversion of a position that dominated the beginning).

The approach will be (1) phenomenological, (2) analytical, (3) dialectical, (4) hermeneutical, and (5) contemplative.

I. Point of departure

"What should I do?" In order to answer this question, we must first understand it. This presupposes that we acquire an insight into the following topics.

"What." A deed ("doing") is part of an action, and actions are parts of plans, adventures, a course of life. A life has a style or "way" of its own. This style is an individual variation on social and cultural patterns that precede the actor. These patterns are marked by spatial (geographic, climatic, linguistic, imaginative, emotional, national and continental) and temporal (historical, traditional, genealogical, familial, scholastic) factors. "Doing" cannot be understood in isolation from the situation and the life story in which it is done.

"What" or *"how"*? Is the central question of ethics "*What* should I do?" or "*How* should I act, behave, endure, feel, suffer, be hospitable, die?" The style of behavior shows a certain attitude. Good behavior has a good style and testifies to a good attitude; it is virtuous. A good life encompasses but is more than a collection of virtues.

"Doing" or *"undergoing"*? To live is not only action, activity, planning, taking initiative, and executing decisions; it is also, and primarily, receptivity, consent, acceptance. Suffering, death, and birth are the clearest proofs of our passivity. How do we receive what cannot be planned? How should we accept this passivity? Life demands a skillful interweaving of passivity and activity.

"Should." What is the ethical sense of "should"? The word possesses many meanings, from divine command and absolute obligation to the suggestion that we behave in conformity with a group code. Does every meaning correspond to a different ethics, or does ethics privilege a specific meaning? In any case, the variety of meanings must be clarified by determining the borderlines between them.

"*I.*" Who is the "*I*" of "What should I do/receive/accept/act/plan?" and "How should I do it?" It is a yearning I (II), which experiences its own existence as a given and a task (III).

II. Desire and Correspondence

1. A life is full of needs, wants, wishes, and desires, but is there not one ultimate and all-encompassing Desire that rules all we do? If so, we must describe and analyze

(a) what this Desire desires (*eudaimonia*? happiness? success? a good, beautiful, meaningful life?).

(b) how it is structured.

(c) how it is/can be/should be awakened, unfolded, met, satisfied and dissatisfied, enriched.

(d) how it can/should relate to the reality of the world, history, its own existence, and others.

2. The Desired demands an appropriate responsivity. Correspondence realizes the unity of "value" and "fact" of all things. The analogy of being coincides with the analogy of being good. Ethics and metaphysics are inseparable because they express two aspects of the same reality.

3. Responsivity is basically affective: I am affected, touched, impressed (etc.) in various ways by the existing phenomena. They are telling and demanding. They also reward appropriate responses by pleasure and punish inappropriate ones by pain. To what extent has hedonism seen some elements of truth? Is utilitarianism defensible as an ethical theory, or is it the expression of an immoral, or even vicious, attitude?

III. Life as Task and Liberation

1. If I ought to act, behave, live well (compare I), I experience myself as a task. How does the experiencing I and the experienced I relate? The "should" of "How should I love?" (I) must be determined through an analysis of various kinds of "ought": invitation, demand, appeal, duty, obligation, vocation.

2. "Ought" reveals "can." All ethical phenomena presuppose and imply freedom. Freedom implies responsibility; it is not the same as the possibility of choice, but what exactly is the difference? Be and become what

you are and therefore have to be (and allow all things to be and become what they are).

3. To achieve the task of being good implies the overcoming of obstacles inside and outside the I that I already am. To become good is a combat with all kinds of evil that assail me, and it presupposes *katharsis* (purification).

4. If to be good is to become good, a moral life is a journey from stage to stage. Ascent, descent, exodus, conversion, adventures, and transformations qualify the temporality of morality. The method of ethics is hodological.

IV. The Social Dimension

1. Commerce and conversation constitute the intersubjective and social space-time of morality and ethics. This aspect of the situation (compare I) must be analyzed before we know who "I" is/am.

2. *Ethics* cannot be separated from *politics*. How is the task of my life related to the world and history of my family, school, tradition, language, nation, church, humankind? To what extent can/should I have a private life?

V. Ethics and Religion

1. Whether members of a religious community or not, all humans possess a basic trust and are guided by some appeal to the good. What are the consequences of this fact for the basic questions of ethics? Can, for example, the question of good actions or virtues be separated from the most basic commitment of a life?

2. What, then, can be learned from the tradition of Christian spirituality as documented in the religious literature of Jews and Christians?

CHAPTER 2

From Doing to Living

The Question

Questions evolve in the process of thinking. If ethics is seen as an on-going operation for which our predecessors have laid the foundations and accomplished a good deal of work (that is, if we cherish a scholastic conception of ethics), we inherit the layout of this discipline; but even then, our reflection, if thorough, transforms the traditional questions, at least through selection and reformulation. If moral philosophy has the higher ambition of discovering the foundations of ethics by taking a critical stance with regard to all preceding attempts, it must decide which questions to pose as the most originary. It cannot simply restate the questions asked in existing manuals or long-standing traditions, but neither can it authoritatively declare that this or that question is most fundamental. It is improbable that an ethicist can even begin with a question whose originary character he or she can vouch for. The distinction between fundamental and secondary questions already presupposes a thorough familiarity with the entire field of ethics. The process of ethical thinking itself might reveal that certain questions, initially held to be fundamental, are secondary with regard to questions whose primary relevance was ignored. The beginning of philosophical thought is always more or less contingent; it is, for example, largely dependent on the situation in which the thinker is introduced to philosophy. Only thorough reflection on questions already suggested by others to be basic or central can lead to a beginning, which, as philosophical, is always a new beginning.

Many ethicists accept the standard questions and perspectives of authors or schools that have acquired power—in the academy, in politics, in journalism, or in the average opinions of "the many." It is obvious that such forms of power deserve suspicion and critical investigation. But a standpoint free of *doxa* from which to test such questions is not immediately available; if it is accessible at all, it must be established by critically reflecting on opinions forwarded as authoritative.

"What Should I Do?"

"What should I do?" often functions as the paradigm for moral questions.[1] Can we develop an ethics by unfolding and answering this question? Let us first try to understand the question and detect some conditions of its meaning.

Similar to the epistemological question "What can I know?" and the ontological question "What is X?", the question "What should I do?" suggests that something should be done. To be done, it must be doable; if it is done, it is a doing or a deed. The words *deed* and *doing* can be understood in two ways: either we can think of a concrete deed that is done or can be done at some point in time and space, or we can focus on general characteristics, asking what kinds of deeds ought to be done in determinate places and times. Let us here concentrate on a concrete individual deed.

Such a deed is always part of a more complicated action, and actions are parts of plans. The thought of an isolated deed is an abstraction: any doing is part of an activity that occurs within specific circumstances, that is, in a qualified space and time. Actions are situated in a particular context, and they belong to chains or courses of action that develop over periods of time. Some periods can be determined as time spans during which a certain action plan is being accomplished.

When we concentrate on one specific deed, a certain here and now is involved: "What should I do here and now?" A particular situation is given, which I must change by my intervention. The question concerns both the situation in which I am involved and my own existence (for I myself change by acting). "Should" refers to a future: the near or far future of a later present in which the deed or action should take place. Changes in the present situation and in ourselves, as involved in it, are events that constitute history: the history of a period, a life, a group, a culture, a language, a country, a continent, the world. My involvement in situations implies that I am not the creator of my deeds: most often they are suggested to me by the situation itself or by others present or past—for example, my parents and teachers, my peers, my role models or heroes. Even in those cases where my intervention is original and surprising, it is a variation or transformation rather than something completely new. Moreover, not all deeds are possible in given circumstances: some are appropriate and others may be strange or even mad, but their meaning is never independent of the configuration that precedes and follows their achievement.

The situation determines me before and after I change it. I am not a toy or an instrument, but I am engaged and involved, even without seeking or wanting it. The place and time (the here and now) of my acting are continually changing together with me. My life is on the move as part of an historical constellation; my doing begins, or rather continues, as already involved and caught up in a part of the changing space-time, which I cannot refuse or avoid but must accept. Even if I am able to extricate myself from a particular situation—for example, from citizenship in a specific country or from my native language—this does not liberate me from the rule of situatedness: one configuration is replaced by another as particular as the first.

If we say that human actors are unavoidably "parts" of unchosen contexts and that they must accept this, we risk underestimating the moment of selfhood equally constitutive of our doings. I am not just a part, because I experience my unchosen engagement as a constellation that, while restricting my possibilities and thwarting my wishes, provides me with opportunities for initiatives. I can respond to this situation by indulging in a bitter mood, by criticizing or swearing at anyone whom I meet in it, by scapegoating, or by making myself important as victim. Even if I cannot change the situation in which I find myself, I can still refuse to accept it, for acceptance is more than the passive reception of unavoidable factuality—it presupposes that I take, grasp, and embrace the facts, including the circumstances of my life as they are. It is possible to deny the facts even if they are irresistible. Denial is not the same as factual destruction, but rather the resistance of something in us (the will? desire?) that, by awakening to life in the world, is forced and at the same time invited to live this factuality. To live is not ipso facto to accept living; it is to be allowed and invited to live this unique, unchosen, already situated, and to that extent predestined life. The difference between refusing or embracing this life as it is given (with its limited possibilities of transformation) reveals the basic meaning of human selfhood. I can loathe my being-here-and-now, but I can also accept and enjoy it, exploit it as an opportunity, or celebrate it as a feast. The possibility of denial (necessarily followed by an at least partial self-destruction) or affirmation (which, as *Jasagen*, is always a confirmation), reveals human freedom as a fundamental possibility of choice. If we can show that the acceptance of life-as-it-is-here-and-now has the character of an ethical "should" (that is, if the undeniable fact of my concrete existence is at the same time a demand to accept it as my destiny), we have found a hard fact that includes the basic "ought" of ethics. Be what you are! Be the life that is yours! Live your life! The objection that we cannot negate hard facts is here invalid because human life presents itself as something "to be accepted and lived," which entails the possibility that we may not obey this order. For some mysterious reason, we at times refuse or even destroy it. It is true that nobody can escape from enacting his or her life, not even someone who prepares a hasty or a slow suicide (although suicide is precisely the contradictory practice of living for death).

We must return to the fact of a situated life as a primordial command to engage in it, but at this stage of reflection, it is sufficient to understand that all doing presupposes a basic acceptance of the individually concrete condition in which existence is given to human actors.

"What?"

Since Socrates taught us to ask "What is justice, piety, courage, etc.?", we also ask, "What is that (move, change, event, deed, thing) which I must do, cause, achieve, or perform?" Most often, our question points to the active solution of a problem: an intervention, a response to a challenge, an action in conformity with the law, or a service done for some cause. Less frequently, we think of acceptance, letting go, endurance, suffering, or holding back, although such seemingly passive attitudes likewise demand a real effort. Doing is always the bringing about of some change in the existing situation, but its result is not always a new product. The situation and I myself also change when I respond to chaotic or confusing surroundings by silently observing them and letting things take their disorderly course. Such a response is part of the ongoing situation, but it simultaneously determines the person who lets things go. When someone describes the new situation by stating that some person did nothing to change the chaos, this statement is correct, but that person's nonintervention has nonetheless transformed the situation. The new situation may be described as "disorder observed by a passive observer" or as "passive observation of chaos." "Passivity" here includes the activity of observation, response, and motivation. We must establish whether the observer is motivated by enjoyment, indifference, despair, or interest. If such motivations have a phenomenal aspect, each of them codetermines the concrete character of that situation, and a complete description must include the specific mode in which the "inactive" observer integrates the other elements.

Doing (including the seeming passivity of observation and letting go) is always an interaction with the surroundings, involving other persons, animals, plants, instruments, and objects that happen to determine the here and now of the actor. This interaction includes my body and all the automatisms, customs, patterns, and processes that characterize me as a socialized, educated, inculturated, and historical human being. In a sense that must be clarified, my doing is thus also an interaction with my body, character, and historical having-become-what-I-am-here-and-now. Acting is evolving self-involvement—the transformation of my existence in conformity with what I have been in the past. I continue to become what I will be as a result of many influences and my own way of taking up, having, living, and being my already determined life. At the same time, I respond to the unavoidable fact of my having become such as I am now by responding to other beings appearing in my space and time. Acting is the ongoing transformation of my involvement in a concretely individualized universe, the continual retrieval of a past that my present changes into a future. The course of each life has its own characteristic style of referring back to what it has been and forward to modifications that will constitute a different life, and all deeds share in the style of the life to which they belong.

Work

It is as if the question of what we must do escapes us time and again by continually referring us to human life as such: as a course, a dynamic process, or, perhaps, a whole. But can life be a whole at all? Does not death condemn it to be a fragment only? Can life ever be complete, as one overall task, plan, or work?

There is a tradition in ethics, according to which work is the central paradigm for ethical considerations of human activity. "Work" is often conceived of as the result or product of some kind of making. Doing would be synonymous with making or producing. Such a paradigm fits well into the modern, scientific, utilitarian, and technological perspective. It has also served as a leitmotiv in Plato's analyses of *praxis* and *theoria*. But can this paradigm capture the task or "work" of living a good life, of living well? Does living resemble any making?[2]

Birds make nests, but we do not know whether they have intentions or plans while doing so. Although normally the making of a chair or a cup is planned, it is not unthinkable that humans make things without planning, for instance, during sleep, or as a result of habituation. A certain, albeit vague, provisional, and changeable, image of a chair or cup can precede the formation of some appropriate material in conformity with that image. During the process, the shape of the product can be changed: the rough preliminary form is evaluated, then adjusted or modified into a more satisfactory or pleasing form. The process of formation contains an element of experimentation; unless the plan is a very detailed blueprint or prescribes the exact reproduction of an already existing cup, the original image leaves open the possibility of modification.

Can a human life be compared to a work? Can we "make" our lives? Can we plan or program them? A life might be a success or a failure, but we must wait until it is finished—and thus has disappeared—before this can be determined. What remains of a life is not a work, but a corpse, and—to a very limited extent—a memory; or perhaps some poems or paintings of the deceased. Can the course of life then be an ongoing work, a work in progress that ends in disappearance?

It is true that to live demands effort: one must "work" at it. It is also true that living a human life is an experiment full of trials and errors, adjustments, new beginnings, transformations, luck, frustrations, plans, and adventures. But can a life be planned as a work for which we prepare the appropriate material, skills, and conditions? Such a technological conception would follow from the conviction that the productive possibilities of the natural sciences are paradigmatic for human activity. If that conviction is right, human lives can be assessed by evaluating their products: persons have value or meaning insofar as they leave behind statues, scores, texts, inventions, or monuments. Apart from its works, a life then does not have any value, except insofar as parts of a corpse can be made useful for others. By observing today's society, full of busy and overburdened people bent on productive outputs, we might be inclined to agree with a technological explanation of human behavior. If this view adequately explains what human beings live for, the decisive question is, why are products and productivity desirable, good, and meaningful? What can motivate an ethics of work?

Means and Ends

When planning to make some product, one must procure materials and means: a blueprint, a sketch or outline, tools, instruments, machines, computers. These means are most often produced in their turn, but somewhere at the beginning of all production processes, there is an immediate encounter of human hands with wild nature. This beginning underlies all civilization, although it is difficult, if not impossible, to still discover places where such a beginning can be observed. The wilderness changes into cultivated land as soon as human intervention occurs. The world in which we are born is a mixture of nature and culture; we are embedded in historically grown fashions and patterns that ask for transforming continuation.

The means employed in the making of a product gain significance from their utility: they are useful for the successful production of the end they serve. Yet besides their value as means, they may have other valuable qualities. For example, they are pleasing to the touch, or they are beautiful, well-shaped, and a work of art in themselves. Insofar as they are means, however, they refer us to ends; we use and appreciate them for the sake of something other. They would not be used, or even exist, if we did not desire the ends. They are caught, and we with them, in referential frameworks that structure the process of planning and making.

What, however, are our ends? What motivates production, hard work, preparation for the future, and a desire to be other than we are? Is it pleasure, consumption, beauty, meaning, aristocracy of the mind? What is at stake, and what is the issue of human life as such? This question cannot yet be answered. But if we will be able to answer it, and if that which is no end can only be a means, we must concede that means as such do not have any value in themselves. They are necessary conditions for the acquisition of the ends, but that is all. Illustrations of such a theory can be found in the kinds of labor whose only meaning lies in a product that is never enjoyed by the laborer. Many people suffer from the meaningless operations they must perform to earn their salary. Are these operations wholly meaningless? Poor in meaning, certainly, but are we able to perform actions without any meaning at all? Should there not be at least some aspect of enjoyment in handling things or being in the company of other workers doing the same things?

Another illustration of the teleological explanation sketched above can be found in a conception that views our earthly life as a mere preparation for life in heaven or paradise or utopia. The latter would be the ultimate end, whereas all preceding activity would have only an instrumental character. Such a conception correctly emphasizes the ongoing dynamics of human life and the impossibility of completing all the tasks with which it is involved before death destroys it; but interpreting life's activity as a chain of means without intravital ends contradicts the idea that life, despite mortality, is desirable and lovable for its own sake. If all temporal events and actions are only instrumental, we are incessantly running toward an event that will never happen. How can we maintain our dynamism without being already (within the time span of a mortal life) in touch with that which ultimately and originally is at stake in being human? If we must maintain the teleological pattern, "the end" must somehow be present in "the means." The main issue of life must be present in our planning for its future.

If human existence is a mere succession of instrumental activities, the future is a hunt without prey; fatigue will be the only reward, and only a transmortal faith will save us from cursing the futility of life's concerns. The products of life do not compensate for its final failure. To be accepted as a meaningful task, life must have its own meaning; we cannot wait until all instrumental operations have been performed. No one thing, act, or event within the span of life is itself the central issue, but this issue is always a part of what we do. Human time cannot be divided into times of preparation and times of arriving at the end; to be alive is to enact the passage from past to future in the restless presence of a hidden Meaning.

Poiēsis and Praxis

Since Aristotle, the distinction between making (*poiēsis*) and acting (*praxis*) is found in all good manuals on ethics.[3] Production of a work (for example, a poem or a building) is different in kind from an action that, instead of changing something in the world, changes the agent. Making a table is a different sort of activity than dancing or meditation. Doing has at least these two different meanings.

To make distinctions is helpful, but to leave it at that is dangerous, because a distinction often hides the affinity and unity that it also includes. The analysis remains superficial if we take the above distinction for granted without examining its presuppositions, the examples that might blur it, and the essential unity of "immanent" and "transcendent" ways of doing. For example, the distinction sets the external world in opposition to the actor by distinguishing activities *ad extra*, which realize something outside of the agent, from activities that concern the agent herself. But is the agent not a part of the world—at least in a certain respect? And is not the world a part of the agent's possibility of existing, acting, surviving? Can we do anything without changing at least some details of the "outer" world? Can we change anything in "the world" without thereby changing our situation and thus our bodily self? By dancing, we change the space and the time of our surroundings as much as we change ourselves and one another. Even meditation makes the space silent and sedate; this is obvious as soon as you enter a Buddhist temple or an abbey where monks are gathered in prayer. Although we are not just elements of the world, like stones and plants, there is a kind of osmosis that forbids clear-cut distinctions between inner and outer. The world resonates in human agents and is permeated by their sounds and traces, even if they are occupied primarily with their own concerns. Productivity is always also self-transformation, and every movement of my body or mind leaves its mark upon the world.

The distinction between production and self-transformation is useful to indicate different aspects that belong to all activity. It can, for instance, introduce the contrast between a business that is preoccupied with the production of works and the enjoyment of living as such and for its own sake.[4] Whereas works, as belonging to "the world," can survive me to be enjoyed by others, the enjoyment of my life disappears with me, although traces of it might survive in others' memories. The enjoyment of life—my contentment with being alive—does not seem to be an activity at all. Is it not rather a mood, a passive resonance in me, which is not necessarily shared by others? "Enjoyment" can be understood in a more active sense, however, and even in the most passive examples, a certain appropriation and reaction is required. This is the reason why some persons have a joyful and others a bitter relationship with their own life. Enjoying life involves eating and drinking; walking; breathing the air; bathing in sunlight and rain and water; feeling the wind, the heat, the cold; meeting with surprises in the adventures of a lifetime; conversing with others; participating in family and social life, in politics, history, and philosophy—just for the sake (and the "fun") of being part of it, and feeling the vitality, the energy, the surprising movement and the thrill of it. Obviously, this enacting of life contains a great deal of passivity, as I am neither the initiator nor the master of what is happening to me. I am not wholly passive, however, even though the basis of enjoyment is a fundamental passion. If a certain love of life, or at least a fundamental acceptance of and agreement with it (as it is given here and now), were entirely lacking, we could not produce or do anything. The very act of caring about my life or any of its needs would be impossible if I truly hated it. The beginning of vital wisdom seems to lie in an agreement that unfolds in experiencing this given life as enjoyable and living it passionately. At the same time, it is obvious that this life in this world and history is not pure pleasure. Pain, evil, and crimes are everywhere, within and without my mind, body, and surroundings, but I experience them as secondary and extraordinary—as a problem rather than as the primary given reality of my being given here and now.

Basic enjoyment, although mixed with detestable pain and evil, makes it possible to work toward goals, make plans, and produce a more satisfactory world. But if life as such is enjoyable, what sorts of goals and works and products can be attractive to us? This question is the big question of Desire: What do we as humans want? Is maintenance of vitality enough? Do we—should we—want more than just to live? Does not life contain a whole range of promises on various levels and to different degrees? The question of human ends demands that we analyze the varieties of Desire. A few examples of desirable ends may suffice in order to make "doing" somewhat more concrete.

If I enjoy living as such, survival will give me pleasure: I feel good because I feel alive. But I also feel threatened because my life is fragile; many dangers and hostile factors lurk in the background. To stay alive and to intensify the pleasure, I need to secure protection against heat and cold, destructive elements of nature, the power of wild animals and enemies. Life itself urges us to build up an economy of survival and well-being. We produce tools and structures of exchange in order to survive and live well. A world of utility emerges from the passion of life that makes us accept and foster it. An ethics that would concentrate on this aspect of our passion would be exclusively utilitarian.[5]

There are motivations for human action other than utility, however—for example, aesthetic motivations. One can produce a monument in order to earn money or make a clever financial move by investing in a

Madonna of Memlinc, but works of art primarily invite appreciation of their beauty. One can spend time, money, and energy on works of art without expecting any use from them. Even pleasure is not necessarily the goal, although it might accompany our admiration. Why do we travel, stand in line, pay money, and spend time to look at the paintings of Vermeer? What do we "get" from it? Nothing else than the viewing of an image. Economy cannot capture such fascination; it can only make use of the fact that some people are ready to sacrifice useful things for an encounter with art. People who have not discovered such incomparable beauty may try to reduce all art to something that fits into their utilitarian brains and hearts, but that is then precisely their condemnation: beauty hides itself from their economy.

The difference between the useful and the aesthetic is not confined to productive activities; it is also found in praxis. Singing or dancing, for instance, can be done as a means of survival or out of pure love for its own fun or splendor. Different motivations can of course be combined, but if the first is overarching, the others risk becoming inauthentic. This example shows that an end (singing well) can at the same time be a means (for earning money). The financial motivation is revealed as decisive when a singer stops singing because nobody offers the required honorarium. Because utilitarianism does not have ears or eyes for beauty, it undermines civilization by reserving the most appreciated forms of art for those who are wealthy enough to pay for them.

Can we extend the contrast mentioned above to the entire course of a life? Is it possible to accept and enact life not so much for utilitarian reasons, but primarily for the beauty of it? Some people indeed seem to live and die for beauty. To live beautifully, *kalōs*, has even been proclaimed as the highest standard of ethics.[6] A beautiful death is then proof of a successful, although antiutilitarian, life. To ridicule such a death shows how uncivilized the laugher is.

A beautiful life does not concentrate on a work that is to be produced; its main question is not "What should I do?" but rather "How should I live, act, move, change, and die?" Must the central question of ethics be transformed into a question about the mode or style of acting? If living disappears with death, and if works cannot capture the meaning of the life whose products they are, is the way or form of life itself then not the main issue? If so, we must not focus on the "what," the products or effects that emerge from human lives, but rather concentrate on the style, taste, nobility, goodness, or splendor of its course.

The Course of a Life

The passion with which we live our lives motivates our plans. As soon as we have become aware of what and who we are, life presents itself as something "to be lived." This opens up the future and forces us to prepare for it by some sort of planning. However, as mentioned before, much of our past and future has already been decided and determined by factors outside of our power and will. My life, as it has become, such as it is now, cannot be replaced by a life in another time or space with other familial and social ties and other cultural allegiances. I have to accept what I have become, and this largely predestines the continuation of my life story. With it, I have received the characteristic patterns, customs, and institutions of an entire social and cultural world. As embedded and involved, I must make plans that fit into the existing universe, although some originality and variation is possible.

I share in the convictions and the ethos of the groups to which I belong: my parents and educators have formed me according to the norms and customs of their culture; twenty-first-century nature, politics, and economics structure my activities; the complicated network of technical and scientific automatisms predetermines the framework of my planning. And yet, it is *I* who am involved and must "make it." Since I am unique, some kind of originality must be possible. Appropriation, personal style, and individual transformations testify to my—relative, but real—independence. If planning is more than mere repetition of what "everybody" does, it is *my* manner of wanting to continue this given life, my preparation for a unique future, my stylization and personal transformation of the here and now into a "tomorrow and afterward" for me. Such activities demand that I adapt myself to the world as it has become, discover its possibilities for continuation, calculate my chances, choose or invent appropriate techniques and strategies, and accomplish my plans, adjusting them when I encounter unforeseen problems or obstacles.

If I were only a factor within a world entirely ruled by alien forces (that is, if a rigid determinism were true), our lives would be governed by Fortuna, Fate, *Moira*, Destiny. No interference would be possible in the course of a destiny that would possess us rather than urge us to a responsible search for meaning. The question of how we should live would then wrongly suggest that we are capable of determining the adventure of our own life. Ethics would be an empty enterprise because the ethical question itself would be an illusion.

However, is it thinkable that we are wholly determined by the inexorable course of things inside and outside ourselves, with the only exception that we are forced to choose an attitude with regard to this fate? Such would be the universalization of certain extraordinary situations (such as the death of a friend or the outbreak of a war) in which we have no other choice than to adopt an attitude of our own toward the inevitable. In response to such situations, we might become bitter or find peace, flee into resignation or hate the universe. Only our mode of relating to the unavoidable (our "interiority") would then depend on us; in this respect, we would still be "free."

As we said before, our interiority is always conveyed to the "outer" world through the expression of our eyes, our smile or frown, the gracious or harsh gestures of our hands, the plans and deeds into which we translate our moods. If it is impossible to separate our interiority from our body and the world, the opposition between inner freedom and outer determinism does not seem to be coherent. It follows that the death of a friend, for instance, cannot be described adequately if the reactions it provokes in others are not taken into account. This death changes not only the world, but all persons related to the deceased as well.

The attempt to distinguish the inner from the outer aspect of determinism is important because it points to the fact that our choice is very often narrowed by the "work" of adopting a more or less appropriate attitude toward things and events that cannot be changed unless they are first accepted as they are, although they may be loathed at the same time.

Suffering is a normal consequence of our being involved in a body and a world not chosen by us but being-there, factually given. This life in this universe here and now, as it has become what it is, is given to me; I am the dative who must "work" with it—not with another life that might better correspond to my wishes. The difference between what is factually given, and what I would like to have, do, experience, or be, is a source of suffering insofar as it is difficult and painful to accept the limited and deficient factuality of my being. I want to be and maintain who and what I am—do not call me by the wrong name!—but I would also like to have better health, a sharper intelligence, a warmer heart, a friendlier character. Who is entirely at peace with what he or she has become? The realism demanded for total agreement is rare. This is understandable because our wishes reach further than the less-than-ideal factuality of our present. And yet we cannot ameliorate this present unless we accept it as it is, without at the same time giving up the desire to transform it into a better mode of life. To bear with yourself, to tolerate your past and "present perfect" without denying its shortcomings and imperfections, is the difficult first step of "planning." Enjoyment of life includes endurance. Because I want to live this unique life here-and now-as-it-is, I also have to embrace the difficulties and pains that are inseparable from the enjoyment it promises. Enjoyment of life includes suffering.

Birth and Death

The passivity constitutive of human life finds a clear expression in birth and death. Although death has received much more attention, birth might be more radical; nonetheless, both must be considered to discover the real condition of human activity.

Birth

We have no direct experience or memory of our birth. We are told about it, and we may have observed another person's birth. Thus we imagine the reality of our being born. What I experience is the gratuitous givenness of all things and events and experiences: the amazing fact of the universe and my own part in it. My entire existence is given—a fact that cannot be deduced but only accepted. Why should I exist? It is certainly not experienced as a necessity. Even if I could prove the necessity of my existence, its pure givenness to me—that is, my complete lack of responsibility for this existence—would remain an undeniable experience. The image of my birth, the quasi-memory through which I reach back to the temporal beginning of my entire universe summarizes the givenness of my life and world. Nothing escapes this beginning. All of its transformations are later developments in which I myself have played some role, but their basic possibility precedes my choice and knowledge. Even my consciousness comes later, as awareness of a past that has already been there before I became aware of it. I have been given to myself, but consciousness forces me to receive this gift. Apparently, I am capable of receiving what I have not chosen—what I have not even chosen to receive. Some form of acceptance is inevitable, even for abolishing my existence. My birth itself cannot be denied (although it could have been denied me by others who might have decided that my birth or conception did not please them or was not a good idea).

Having received life in birth, I can live it in amazement, gratitude, bitterness, enthusiasm, or other moods, but I cannot efface its appearance in human history. Unable to deny or erase this fact, I am necessarily a combination of passivity and activity: I can only receive my life in a specific (bitter, reluctant, joyful, grateful, puzzled, desperate) way. My acceptance is qualified by the mode of my response to my existence. Among the surprises, adventures, or wonders in human life or history, the greatest surprise is that we are born. All wonderment begins with this event. The rest is elaboration. That I exist—and my world with me—is the source of all amazement.

As the beginning of my social history, my birth precedes my involvement in human interaction. I reach my birth by going back imaginatively through the chain of events of which I retain some memory, aided by stories or pictures that others offer me. However, in some sense, the source and "beginning" of my universe is contemporary with all the moments of my experiencing it. My completely unchosen givenness is not confined to today and yesterday; it continues to carry me in every experience and adventure. I am aware of the nonnecessary character, the contingency or gratuity of my being this living human here and now. What I do with it constitutes variations on a unique but contingent theme.

Death

Death has been thematized as the impossibility of all my possibilities and as phenomenal proof of my finitude.[7] Death is not directly given, as Epicurus knew, who remarked that I am not there when death presents itself, and that death is not there as long as I exist.[8] However, like birth, death is continually operative within the course of each human life. We are aware of fatigue, pain, weakness, sickness, and diminishing vitality as well as the limits of our energy—all forebodings of our nonexistence after a time of unfolding and discovery. Although birth symbolizes universal openness for surprise and adventure, death closes off the future. The certainty of the final arrest (when and where?) restricts the givenness of life: it is only given for a certain—and uncertain—time. No insurance against death is possible; destruction continually threatens the living of a life. Death and birth are thus contemporaneous with the presence of my here-and-now. The intermingling of passivity and activity is most concrete in the form of a born-but-already-dying life.

The presence of death—our mortality—is hidden from our consciousness by many factors. Fear and anxiety are powerful forces in suppressing our awareness of death's inexorability; there is an unwillingness to recognize our crucial defeat as signified by death's ascertained victory. The gigantic system of contemporary health care, including thousands of centers for cancer and heart research, manifests a collective will to postpone that defeat, to lengthen life, to extirpate sickness, to conquer vulnerability. The modern war against death is waged through technological control of physiological structures and processes. Control of vitality is one of the victories by which the technological project of modernity tries to prove its utility. The branches of Descartes' philosophical tree are paradigmatic for the modern era: did he not present mechanics, medicine, and ethics as the applied sciences through which true metaphysics would show its indirect fecundity?[9]

Technological control of death is possible only in the sense of some mastery of time: we can hasten and sometimes delay the destruction of a human life. The fight against cancer, for example, seldom yields more than a delay. (But so does life in general.) We can alleviate the pains that accompany our sicknesses, which makes the delay perhaps less exasperating, but it does not alter our mortality. We have more power over the other end of human lives: it seems that birth, at least, can be controlled. Not, of course, in the sense of bringing ourselves to life or preventing ourselves from coming into existence—our own birth is an indestructible fact—but we can prevent the birth of other humans or occasion their production in laboratories. We cannot create ourselves—a human *causa sui* (even a divine one) is impossible—but we are capable of destroying ourselves. We are very good at destruction: not only are we able to prevent the generation of new lives, we also are able and even eager to destroy many lives before they get the chance to participate in our (joyful and sad) world. The billions of promising humans that are destroyed before they are born express a generalized reluctance to welcome newcomers. Does it perhaps even manifest a growing hatred of life itself? This would seem to contradict our own attachment to life. It also seems to contradict the hospitality to victims of persecution that we profess—at least in words.

The systematic organization of abortion, birth control, biogenetic experimentation, modern health care, euthanasia, and so on cannot be understood if we do not first understand the technological culture of which they are the symptoms.[10] The modern dream of autonomy, which burdens humanity with the universal providence that formerly was attributed to God, must end in universal mastery, planning, experimentation, control. The systematic slaughter of three million Cambodians, organized by semi-intellectual fanatics is—in its willful and technical character—similar to the (quasi-)systematic killing of millions and millions of unborn humans in totalitarian and "democratic" countries of our time. Death and birth are interpreted and handled as technical problems to be solved by scientifically trained hands. This is the basic mistake; human coming into existence and passing away are not scientific facts or objects for engineering minds. They appeal to us in a radically different way: as amazing secrets that refute the universality of our mastery. Whether welcome or unwelcome, they essentially surprise us, unless we suppress their mystery by means of scientific and technological objectivity.

Birth and Death

Birth and death together constitute an aspect of our finitude, but perhaps not the only or the most essential one. In any case, "mortality" is not the best way to characterize human finitude; it not only fails to differentiate the mortality of gods, humans, animals, plants, civilizations, languages, epochs, and buildings, but it places undue emphasis on negativity. Birth is more originary than death because the latter is conditioned by birth and receives (at least part of) its meaning from it. Statements such as "death conditions birth" or "the meaning of birth depends on death" are only true in a very convoluted sense that demands much more elaboration than "birth conditions death."

Ethics, and philosophy as such, should not begin with mortality. The widespread fascination with death has serious motivations, but if it leads to the neglect or the repression of birth, it shows that a culture has become overly worried or tired or desperate or hateful toward itself. Before indulging in this fascination, we should ponder the difference between the emergence of a universe in birth and the decay of this universe that accompanies the unfolding of its promises. Gratitude and hope seem to be more appropriate responses to the fact of existing than anxiety and despair. Birth cannot be demanded; my being-born is a gratuitous promise full of possible unfoldings. Mortality threatens these; it may put an end to further unfolding, but it cannot undo the unfoldings that have become history. Dying is a modulation of life, and death cannot be detested if life is less appreciated than nonexistence. Birth and death are not diametrically opposed: birth is lived as an absolute beginning without any necessity, whereas death is the farewell to a life that survives to some extent (for example, in the memory of others and in works or traces left in history). Against this asymmetry one might point to the parallel that exists between the retrospective memory of others in which a human life survives its death, and the expectations that precede a birth. This parallel is not convincing, however, because birth can only be expected after conception has been revealed, and, although conception itself can be hoped for but not expected, death is certain—once a life is given, nothing can efface the traces or anticipations of its realization.[11] Not being conceived is nothing special; no history is stirred. In contrast, dying is a drama. On the other hand, and at the same time, death is normal, whereas birth is amazing.

What happened at my birth was the emergence of my existence, which I later became conscious of as given to me. We expect death to be a loss of consciousness and self-consciousness, although we do not know for sure whether that will be the case. The experiences through which we anticipate our own death are not sufficient to predict whether we will return to nothingness or not. Hope cannot be entirely repressed, but doubts are appropriate. Was there any self of mine before I was born? Nothing in my experience proves this; but as a possible belief, such a conviction can hardly be refuted. If metempsychosis were a possibility, it would lessen the radicality of birth and death and establish a certain symmetry: both would be repeatable events within the ongoing process of an eternal self that emerges from the night of another dimension into the light of worldly history in order to disappear and reemerge again and again. Plato's Socrates seems to have found consolation in such a possibility, but he was wise enough to present it as a song of hope,[12] not as the guaranteed result of a phenomenological or deductive analysis.

Is Death a Possibility?

In his famous analysis of *Dasein's* "being toward death," Heidegger calls death the extreme or ultimate possibility (*die äußerste Möglichkeit*) of our "existence" (*Existenz*) as the ability to be (*Seinkönnen*).[13] But is death a possibility that we can be (and thus project and understand as a possible performance, a *Seinkönnen*)? Does not death entirely escape my "I can," my ability to be? Is Heidegger's description, notwithstanding its emphasis on our finitude, a last attempt to subsume death under the modern project of autarchy? In dying, I am still involved as an active participant, but can I choose my annihilation? I can accept that death will take me away, I can surrender or even welcome my no longer being there, but I cannot appropriate or own it. In this sense the rupture is not mine.

Against Heidegger, Levinas has argued that death is not the possibility of (*Dasein's*) impossibility, but rather the impossibility of any existential possibility.[14] Death comes to me in order to kill me. I cannot embrace this enemy, not only because it is nothing, but also and primarily because all the pride of my "I can" is crushed when it overpowers me. Death is the negative, destructive, hostile face of the positive, granting, gracious energy that produced my birth. Both attest to my utter, original, and ultimate inability to secure my existence; both refute the thesis that my being is first of all ability, performance, "I can."

A Note on Anxiety

If life by itself is an attempt to persevere,[15] death inspires anxiety. My existence will disappear; someone or something outside or within me will erase, undo me. Nothingness always already threatens me, because I might die at any moment.

Is this the most radical and extreme anxiety that disturbs human lives? A negative answer is revealed in the mood of those persons who exclaim that not to have been born is preferable to this miserable existence. Well known is Theognis' lament:

> For man the best thing is never to be born,
> Never to look upon the hot sun's rays,
> Next best, to speed at once through Hades' gates
> And lie beneath a piled-up heap of earth.[16]

That such a complaint is not the monopoly of an early "pagan" past is shown in Jeremiah's words:

> Cursed be the day I was born!
> May the day my mother bore me not be blessed!
> Cursed be the man who brought my father the news,

> Who made him very glad, saying,
> "A child is born to you—a son!"
>
> Why did I ever come out of the womb
> To see trouble and sorrow
> And to see my days in shame?

And listen to Job:

> May the day of my birth perish
> And the night it was said: "A boy is born!"
> That day   may it turn into darkness
> May God above not care about it;
> May no light shine upon it
>
> Why did I not perish at birth
> And die as I came from the womb?
>
> Why was I not hidden in the ground like a stillborn child
> Like an infant who never saw the light of day?[17]

Although the burden of certain lives and the suffering they entail might explain such lamentations, it seems hard to believe that they express the final outcome of the attempts to cope with them;[18] but even if that were the case, they do not testify against the fact that death inspires anxiety. However, the desire for "peace," silence, and nonexistence might be felt more strongly than the fear of destruction. The violence of death is then perceived (rightly or wrongly) as the last obstacle to be overcome before the night closes on a past existence.

Mortality as such cannot be the most terrifying phenomenon of life. Not even the greatest pain should make us curse a suffering life, because suffering, pain, and dying can be embraced if they are elements of meaningful events or deeds. Heroes die for great causes. A long life without meaning is not better than a meaningful but short and painful life. The desire for meaning reaches farther and is rooted more deeply than the desire for maintaining what we have. In former times, the worth of honor was so strong that only cowards could prefer to be living dogs rather than dead lions. *Kalokagathia*, justice, and love have motivated innumerable persons to prefer dying over fame, success, or wealth. Socrates taught that it is preferable to suffer injustice (for example, capital punishment) than to commit it,[19] and Jewish, Christian, and Muslim martyrs testified to the worth of religion by accepting death as the unjust punishment for their faith. An all too complacent culture might be scandalized by such examples of heroism; but not only heroes take seriously the fact that meaning is necessary for justifying human lives.

Which meaning or meanings are indispensable and superior has to be discovered by life itself—and it is a central task of ethics to thematize this discovery; but in a formal and abstract way, we can already state that a meaningless life is not worthwhile. The fear of death is certainly extreme if it concerns the final act of a life that is not only without worth, but even destructive of meaning. However, the reason for such anxiety does not lie in mortality but rather in the destruction of meaning. What we fear most of all is not to die, but to destroy what is valuable, worthy, worthwhile. To cause evil (to be a devil) is worse than risking disappearance. As the possibility for meaning, life is a match that can be won or lost. From an ethical perspective, the anxiety that our life will turn out to have been meaningless is more revealing than our fear of dying: through that anxiety, we discover that we are responsible for the meaning our life will have had when it is transformed into a corpse.

Some of the assertions in this section anticipate later chapters of this book, but it seemed fitting to state without delay that death is not the most relevant issue for an ethics of mortal spirits.[20]

Active Patience

Between birth and death, my life continues to be both given and threatened, making me the recipient and the actor at the same time. My nonnecessary existence amazes me. Why should I *exist*? Why should *I* exist? Why should I, who exist, be such as I am? Why did history bring my parents together, and why should I be born from their union? These questions seem unanswerable. But the fact is that I am given to myself. I am the dative of a gift that is my existence as this "I" that I am (including my being the dative of this gift). I am double: the one who has received, and the one who is received. This double "I" continues to be received and to receive itself. I am continually given to myself, and I continually receive myself as given.

I experience my existence as a nonnecessary, amazing, but inevitable fact. I cannot choose, or undo, or refuse the givenness of this fact. At the same time, however, it does not leave me totally inactive. I must accept it.

Even if I would like to refuse the gift of life—for example, because, like Ivan Karamazov, I would rather return my entrance ticket to this horror-filled world[21]—I would have to first accept the available means and skills to make myself disappear. Basic affirmation and acceptance are unavoidable. This acceptance is a fundamental activity, but it is the activity of someone who submits to all the forms of passivity that are involved in being part of this joyful and horrible world.

My affirmation—my confirmation—of my being given to myself is motivated by an agreement with the amazing factuality of my existence and that of the universe in which I am involved. I want this gift. But many things in the world and myself are not agreeable; I would like to change them because they are painful or ugly or cruel. My disagreement can grow and overwhelm my basic agreement, but it cannot take away my attachment to my own being and the world with which it is involved. Even anger or hatred toward myself, although expressing a desire to change my mode of existence, do not condemn my existence as such. At the bottom of all my actions lies a passion that aims at saving and maintaining myself, a *conatus essendi*, a will to persevere.

In the face of constant threats of death and pain, a human life strives for survival and unfolding. As given to myself, I am burdened with a task: the unfolding of my existence over the course of my life. As long as I exist, I cannot impede this development, but I am urged—that is, simultaneously forced and invited—to make something (good or decent or noble or fitting) out of it. I am not free to refuse life, but I am urged to freely participate in the way in which it will develop. The facts are not fixed once and for all; their configurations and their meanings change, and I play a part in these changes. As the recipient of this fundamental gift, my actions are always a combination of patience and activity. What I do is always my way of participating in what happens to me. Rather than the unrestrained choice between abstract possibilities, freedom is a personal response to the suggestions that are contained in the concrete situations of particular stories. Some situations do not allow for many variations, but even then I am free in my manner and style of enduring them—in peace or resentment, hatred or rebellion.

Patience is the basic virtue, because our initiatives are always preceded by the fait accompli of our being given as always already placed and historicized individual existences. All action is rooted in patience, but the quality of a life depends on the manner in which this or that individual appropriates the factuality that it must endure.

Should

Having situated the initial question in the course of an individual human life, we now need to focus on the "should," which seems to distinguish moral questions, as normative, from those questions that ask what, how, or why things and events are, but not how they ought to or have to be a certain way or at all. Several subquestions emerge when we try to determine the essence and varieties of "should" in relation to morality. We certainly must position ourselves with regard to the much debated question of the above-mentioned distinction between "is" and "ought." However, while reflecting on it, we will be struck by a great variety of meanings that can be indicated by "should" and "ought." The "analogy of 'good'" thus indicated can be analyzed in various ways: we must distinguish between the different qualities and dimensions that are implied when we call a thing or event (for example) "decent," "nice," "tasteful," "normal," "beautiful," "pure," "innocent," "obligatory," or "holy." Once we have determined which features characterize the strictly moral or ethical dimension as distinct from other dimensions of "good" and "should," we must, within this dimension, distinguish the different conceptions and evaluations of morality, as they have developed in different epochs and cultures, including our own, so that we become aware of the context that is presupposed by our interlocutors.

All these tasks—(1) the clarification of "should" in its relation to "is," (2) the specification of "good" and "should" from normalcy and good taste to the most sublime heroism of virtue, and (3) the description of the culturally (co)determined characters that morality presents in different societies or epochs—cannot be achieved before we enter in medias res. They coincide with the unfolding of the central question, as I hope to show. The remarks that follow in the remainder of this still-preparatory chapter are thus only anticipations of arguments that must be developed in later chapters.

Is and Ought

Many ethicists refer to Hume for claiming that there is a fundamental opposition between "is" and "ought" and for a parallel opposition between factual and normative language.[22] In doing so, they seem (1) to know what "ought" means, and (2) to think that the universe (of reality or thought or language) is divided into two parts: that which is and that which ought (to be, to be desired, to be accomplished). Obviously, the meaning of "is" in this presupposition cannot have a universal meaning because the meaning of "ought" falls outside of it. This is a strange implication, for is it not true, is it not a fact that, for example, duties are obligatory and ought to be fulfilled? Is ought not anything; is it nothing? Is a norm, even if its force depends exclusively on thoughts or feelings or commands or conventions or wills of human minds, not real? Are norms nonexistent? Or does "existence" not imply "being?" Apparently, Hume and the ethicists who appeal to him have restricted the meaning of being to the extent that all realities that should exist, fall outside of it. Besides beings, the universe must then contain other "realities" and "facts" that ought to (be? be done?) although they are not. But how can one then speak about norms and duties at all? If ought is not anything, it cannot cause problems; but to say that norms (or all that "ought" to be done) are other realities than beings that are, is obviously to contradict oneself. In doing so, one can no longer treat any "ought" as a fact. The problem has then evaporated because there must be a realm of "ought" outside of the realm of being, while, at the same time, there cannot be any realm of ought.

To save the opposition between "is" and "ought," it is necessary to limit the being of "is" to a specific kind of reality. But in doing so, one creates a new problem: how can we still name the universe in which "being" and things that "ought" (to occur or to be done) form two realms? From Parmenides to the end of the Middle Ages, this universe was conceived as the universe of beings (*ta onta, ta panta*), and "being" or "is" was understood as that to which all beings owed their essence and existence. If "being" is restricted to "thingness" or "scientific objectivity" or "valueless reality," the universe is divided into two parts; one must then invent an expression for the remaining part, to which all "norms" and "values" and all things that have an imperative or normative or obligatory or valuable character belong. The universe that is (and on which the theoretical parts of philosophy and science concentrate) is then utterly uninteresting and without worth. Some people are so impressed by modern science and its presumed objectivity that they deem all nonscientific facts or judgments "subjective" and doubtful. But even if this myopia became the rule in philosophy, they must still address the question of whether subjectivity is anything and whether any fact is interesting.

The opposition between "is" and "ought" cannot be thought; it is a meaningless *flatus vocis* as long as the universality of "is" and "being" is understood or employed in judgments about "ought" as not-nothing. The opposition of "is" and "ought" creates a fundamental contradiction in the language of ethics.

Many attempts have been made to deduce "ought" from "is" or to base it on some kind of "ought-free" being or factuality. These attempts are not based on the presupposition that "is" and "ought" are opposed, but instead on the hypothesis that the meaning of "is" or "being" is more universal or more fundamental than that of "ought," and that the latter can somehow emerge out of the former. Two ways are then open.

(1) We could try to defend the thesis that some meaning of "ought" (for example, some value, some kind of being required, being good, being obligatory), although implicit in and always accompanying the meaning of "being," must be discovered by thinking about "being" or some of its configurations. In this hypothesis, "ought" and "is" are simultaneously given—they belong together—but our awareness of this belonging would require an awakening.

(2) The other way would be to view being as primarily given and then show that "ought" is a qualification of certain kinds of beings. Some beings would be free from any ought-aspect; they could be perceived and evoked without any normative or evaluative connotation, whereas other beings would be characterized as beings that ought to be done, to be desired, to be appreciated, to be.

If it could be demonstrated that all beings have at least some moment of normativity—if, for example, all beings show that they ought to be appreciated, at least in some respect—the first way would be appropriate. The second way converges with Hume's position insofar as it separates two sorts of realities within the universe; it differs from his position, however, insofar as it maintains the universality of being.

This book argues for a radical revision of the contrast between "is" (in the sense of "is a fact") and "ought" (in the sense of "ought to be appreciated, desired, accepted, done, praised"). Its fundamental position implies the thesis that all that is, makes an appeal to us; what is awakens, provokes, challenges, invites, and demands; no being is without value; *being* and *being* (in some sense) *good* coincide. This thesis cannot be demonstrated if one believes that all philosophical arguments must start from disinterested descriptions of valueless things or kinds of being. If such arguments were possible, they must make the transition from beings without "normative" character to beings that have a normative character. But how is such a transition possible? If it is possible to "see" or "feel" or "intuit" that all beings are—in different ways—interesting, appealing, valuable, demanding, or obliging, the transition cannot consist in a bridge between two sorts of beings or in the transformation of valueless beings, but only in a sort of awakening. But if it is never possible to be sure of anything normative on the basis of immediate experiences, all ethical arguments remain hypothetical and problematic. This would destroy the possibility of any normative ethics.[23]

All attempts to deduce an "ought" from a completely unnormative "is" must fail. This thesis seems to be confirmed by the practice of those who propose such deductions. I do not know of any publication in which a norm is convincingly deduced from facts that have not yet shown any normative, valuable, or demanding aspect. As soon as we make an abstraction of the ought that accompanies all beings, we cannot rediscover it without presupposing it in our argumentation. All of the attempts that I have read fail because of this circularity. And this can be expected of all future attempts because the abstraction of a "being without ought" (value, normativity, "should") has, by its exclusion, already destroyed the required bridge. What remains of being after this abstraction is so uninteresting that it cannot even attract our attention.

"Ought" is as original and originary as "being" itself. This must be shown and "seen" (or felt or intuited), not deduced or construed. If "ought" is something basic and authentically original, it can only be given immediately. We must therefore look for authentic experiences in which all kinds of being manifest their being as (being) appreciable, praiseworthy, respectable, demanding, or in some other way valuable and interesting. Similar to the being of things and ideas and rules and duties, the fact that they should be appreciated, honored, realized, enhanced is given and shown or it is "only an idea" (that is, an illusion). We will see that the perception of this givenness demands an appropriate—open, well-disposed, purified—attitude. To understand the meaning, the difference, and the unity of "is" and "ought," a katharsis rather than a deduction is required.

Varieties of Should

Do we understand the meaning of "should" in "What should I do?" The "obligatory" or "normative" character that permeates the entire field of ethics must be characterized in order to comprehend the central issue. At the beginning, we cannot even be sure that "normative" and "obligatory" are the most appropriate terms for this character. In any case, these words already privilege a certain kind of "ought" and "should"—that of norms and obligations—as the framework for ethics.

Norms and obligations fit well into a modern conception of morality. Other elements of this conception are freedom, autonomy, choice, rights, equality, and democracy.[24] The free realization of reason in theory and practice, rational self-realization of all human individuals and universal respect for their inalienable rights are seen as the sources of the moral and legal order that ought to rule the world. Moral life is thematized in terms of normative judgments and the application of general rules in a way more or less parallel to the application of legal rules to cases of the public world. Although morality, as concerning personal interiority and motivation, is distinguished from public law, neither duties toward oneself nor duties with regard to God receive much attention. The center of ethics is occupied with the social complication of rights and duties. Although the modern classics emphasize the objective rationality of autonomous behavior, their heirs most often insist on individuals' freedom of choice, restricted only by the right of other individuals' equally arbitrary wishes and decisions.

This sketch of modern morality functions here only as a reminder that its general ethos and its ethical theories adhere to a particular conception of "should." In order to rethink the roots of ethics, we must be aware of the *doxa* and the ethos that rule our own time before we critically adopt, reject, or amend them, especially if we have good reasons to suspect that the ruling *doxa* is already losing its vitality.

Similar sketches of premodern times, however simplistic, can sharpen our awareness of the shifting meaning of "should" according to the prevailing standards of history. The ethical climate expressed in the philosophy of Plato and Aristotle, for example, is very different from the moral rigorism that rules Kant's philosophy. Instead of Kant's respect for "rigorous duty," (*die strenge Pflicht*), linked to the sacred character of reason and justice, Plato's and Aristotle's admiration is provoked by *kalokagathia*, whose irrepressible splendor links human beings to the gods. Good taste, the flourishing of a well-born *physis*, aristocracy of behavior, and a balanced character as the fruit of a good formation are here the central notions. To feel and behave as beautifully as a mortal god—that is what human beings should achieve, if they have the capacity for it. Thus they embellish the cosmos, whose splendid movements are divine.

Another "should" comes to the fore in the medieval vision according to which the universe is created out of love by the one and only God who participates in human history through incarnation, redemption, and resurrection. Everything in creation is moved by the divine attraction of a love that invites acceptance, obedience, and self-sacrificing devotion. The law is not alien to the essence of human and other beings. Reason discovers God's ordering in the created mirror of his thought and life. Nature, as the essence of all things, has no independence; insofar as it is uncontaminated by evil forces, it proclaims God's glory. By following nature's own suggestions and participating in a history whose actors include God, moral life becomes integral to religion. "Should" includes the work of reason and free will, but it also includes spiritual beauty and justice; all these elements are now moments of a religious drama, however. As such, their meaning is fundamentally different from similar elements in the Greek or Kantian frameworks.

A complete history of the various meanings of "should" and "ought" that rule the moral conceptions and practices of various groups and periods would leave us with the question of why even the basic qualification of morality as such does not seem uniformly shared by humankind. If our conception of morality is scattered into a fundamental plurality regarding its imperative or demanding or exhortative or inviting or tasteful character, will we then not be forced to abandon all hope of writing an ethics that transcends particular groups in particular times? A radical relativism seems inevitable.

Against this conclusion several defenses are possible. A first hypothesis would be that one of the particular conceptions of morality is the correct or best one and that the other conceptions must be evaluated according to their resemblance to the first. The others are seen as variations on the (most) true conception, but to different degrees. Contradictions among conceptions must be resolved through reference to the better ones. History can then be seen as an ongoing experimentation with the adequate meaning of "should" and the obligations contained in it. According to this perspective, one may argue that the fully correct conception has not yet been found. If so, we can only refer to the best of the conceptions revealed until now and try to develop its orientation.

Another hypothesis takes more distance from the plurality of particular moralities. It assumes that none of these can be the universal standard for judging all others. More or less similar to the plurality of languages, the various conceptions of the moral challenge would present a variety that cannot be reduced to one standard morality. This supposition allows for an interpretation according to which their multiplicity is the differentiation of a hidden unity. All conceptions of "should" or "ought" would then refer to a common source that remains obscure, although it reveals great depth and force by generating impressive variations.

A consequence of the second position is that no one can monopolize the meaning of "should" or "ought." Every ethics is particular because of the particular mode of "should" from which it originates. Its value or worth is determined by its proximity to the hidden standard. But how can we measure that worth if the standard escapes our endeavors to describe it in an ethics of our own? This objection presupposes that a standard cannot function as such unless it is possible to capture it in the clarity of representations and words. We will see that such a presupposition is false: many implicit standards guide us despite their obscurity. For example, the Good attracts, moves, and orients by being loved; but in order to love it, clear and perfect knowledge is neither required nor sufficient.

The only way to approach the radical meaning of "should" is by way of a method that begins with a determinate and familiar ethos in order to critically revise and purify it, thus making the initial acquaintance more authentic and adequate. Some degree of trust is a minimal requirement for this method. It is supported by a combination of two convictions: (1) I am already caught in and familiar with a particular web of perspectives, opinions, and interpretations; and (2) I am oriented toward the Good, and this orientation makes me capable of a critical revision of that particular web. This procedure transforms the necessity of our limitations into a virtue: the experience of a first, one-sided, contaminated position is the beginning of an experiment in which that experience is tested and, if we are successful, purified. Life, as it is lived by us, contains the criterion for truth and goodness in itself. The difference between the initial position, made up of the *doxa* and the ethos that are assimilated, on the one hand, and life's desired wisdom (which is the criterion or standard of "should"), on the other, indicates the work to be done. The experiment of life itself is a necessary component of ethics, for there is no criterion more fundamental than the "ought" (or the task) that lies within it.

The fine line between relativism (in whatever psychologistic, historicist, or finitist form) and absolutism (or dogmatism) is not appealing to philosophers who want to eliminate all references to obscure forces and attractions. Sometimes, however, such references are necessary in order to remain loyal to the truth. No one can guarantee a priori that good questions—and especially basic ones—can be answered clearly, but should this scandalize us? If human life is mysterious, should philosophy then be without mystery?

Genealogies

We no longer belong to modernity, but many of our opinions, evaluations, wishes, and ideas are still modern. What distinguishes us is our skepticism about many elements of the modern faith. For example, faith in Reason[25] has been undermined by Marxian, Nietzschean, Freudian, and other suspicions. Faith in science died long ago, although some philosophers still imitate scientific methods in their own thinking. Faith in progress has almost become laughable because our own century, the most murderous in history, has employed its ideologies and scientific conquests for the destruction of nature and the slaughtering of millions of men, women, and born and unborn children. Skepticism and relativism infuse the air we breathe; we know a lot, but we are unwise and rather lost. Experimenting, especially with situations, ways of life, feelings, relations, theories, and art forms, is "in," but where do we belong? Several traditions offer identification with a specific past, but most of them appear dated, and it is difficult to choose between them. Some new movements look attractive, but one should not become too serious.

In the meantime, it is impossible to live without attachment or identification. Most of us solve this problem by following the customs of the society in which we live and speak and work. The prevailing *doxa* and ethos mark our lives. True, there are noticeable differences between fundamentalist Christians, agnostic secularists, and all the others, but they share much of the same customs and rituals, language games, opinions, and fashions. In a way, each of us is everyone or anyone. Originality expresses itself in variations on the common themes and modes.

Identification in space goes together with identification in time. Part of the latter lies in the education one receives from parents and teachers. Another part, especially in the case of intellectuals, lies in the genealogies through which they think of themselves as heirs of a certain history. For some who regard western history as a battle between enlightenment and obscurantism, the Enlightenment was the breakthrough of an exemplary mode of thought that must extend to all areas of reality. Others see the Enlightenment as a period in which the natural sciences, despite their great importance for a more comfortable, healthy, democratic, and informed human life, have narrowed the human outlook and blocked the search for wisdom; their gratitude for modern enlightenment is tempered by the awareness of huge losses in spirituality. Some turn to the Jewish or Christian past, whose traditions deserve to be retrieved in postmodern ways. Others, who deny or ignore the greatness of that past, try to resuscitate elements of pre-Christian Greece. Still others try to integrate the best of Greece, Judeo-Christianity, and modernity in a postmodern form of Occidentality. Finally, there are those who think that the time is ripe to attempt a synthesis of eastern wisdom and western civilization.

The historical and cultural identity of artists, scientists, philosophers, theologians, and other professionals does not depend on their profession, but it plays a role in their growth and self-knowledge. The influence of their deepest convictions and orientations on the style of their profession is greater than the other way around. This is especially true for philosophy. Explicitly or implicitly, every philosophy shows the prephilosophical framework and genealogy within which it develops. When philosophers locate their thoughts in relation to the history of philosophy, their version of this history is a genealogy of the family or school to which they belong. Some see themselves as members of the philosophical nobility while looking down on other families; others are proud of their democratic and commonsensical tradition; still others are not ashamed to declare that three thousand years of Jewish and Christian identity inspire their philosophical search for wisdom about the really important questions.

The prevailing ethos of the contemporary western society privileges atheism and antireligiosity. Its preferred genealogy presents secularism as progressive, enlightened, and superior. Convinced Hindus, Buddhists, orthodox Jews, Christians, and Muslims consider such a genealogy poor, superficial, rather desperate and miserable, although they recognize the true conquests of secular modernity. One important distinction between the two types of genealogy lies in the difference between the dimensions in which they move. A person breathes differently within three thousand years of spirituality than within the scientific walls of enlightened modernity.

Philosophy has its own rules, which must be observed by all participants. A thinker's identity cannot be withheld from participation in the universal language of philosophical conversation. If philosophy is not only universal but also fundamental, it cannot be indifferent to faith. That is why Jewish, Christian, atheist, and Muslim traditions are recognizable, even in philosophy.[26]

A Nucleus

The experience from which the chapters of this book are developed can be summarized in the following way:

(1) Becoming aware of myself, I find myself involved in a particular world of people (parents, educators, others like me), places (houses, streets, countrysides), institutions (laws, customs, rituals), events (historical and private), and several communities with their own histories and traditions. These people, communities, and histories have formed me. I share their culture, including their beliefs and their customs. Much of my identity is a result of this engagement.

(2) I experience my involvement and the social, cultural, doxastic, and ethical identity ensuing from it as a fact, a situation, a form of life that, although mine, does not coincide with me as the one who has to live this form. I am aware of a difference between my having become such and myself as the subject that cannot but accept this suchness in order to live it, that is, to appropriate, develop, vary, transform, and accomplish it. The difference manifests itself in two central phenomena: Desire and Freedom.

(3) Desire emerges when the fact of my having become such-as-I-am-now disappoints me. In discovering what I am, I recognize myself as a mixture of desirable and undesirable elements. It strikes me thus because I am inhabited by a Desire that cannot stop evaluating what I am. Not only must I live the form of life that has become mine, I also must cope with the Desire that drives me, beyond all the mixtures of desirable and undesirable things and events outside and within me, to the truly Desirable.

(4) If I have to cope with my factuality and with an unchosen Desire that commands me, who is this "I" that must reconcile what it has become with what its Desire wants it to be? I must have a distance from both in order to be capable of recognizing and appropriating them as mine and working with them. On the one hand, I am their servant, forced to accept them as they are (a partly undesirable life and a dictatorial Desire); on the other hand, I am the leader, because in the end, it is I who am responsible for what I become. As soon as I am aware of the threefold structure indicated here, I no longer have an alibi with regard to the undesirable ele-

ments of my life. Although "made" by others and by circumstances, history, culture, and so on, it is I who have to answer for what I do and did and want and am becoming. Despite and thanks to all the influences without which I would be nothing at all, I am the author and actor of my life. Acceptance is the beginning of this authority, the condition of all initiatives. Freedom is the name for the difference between the subject and its determinations, including its Desire and its culture, character, talents, and history.

Let us see whether this nucleus can be unfolded into an ethics. Obsessed by Desire, I, who am this particular person, have to discover what Desire in me desires and how my life can be led toward greater concordance with its desideratum. The search confronts me with all the realities of a human life: persons, stories, events, plants, trees, animals, the sun, moon, and stars, houses, schools, states, history, the world, the universe. Each reality affects and challenges me: I must respond—but is my response appropriate? Responsivity is part of responsibility. I will never be autarchic or autonomous: reality suggests, invites, commands, and often forces me, but I am free and forced to respond in my way to those challenges.

The search is not without conversions; for as a mixture, I am not pure. From the outset, I am contaminated with undesirable elements. Discovery of true desiderata therefore goes hand in hand with a katharsis of my mixed wants, inclinations, tendencies, and wishes.

Neither the search for the Desirable nor the exercise of freedom are private enterprises. The preceding summary is full, too full, of I, I, I. . . . This entire chapter is centered around the striving and reflective ego, even though it contextualizes its concern for "my" own moral success. This egocentrism was triggered by our concentration on the sentence, "What should I do?" As if this could be the beginning! We have neglected the fact that this question, as a question about the "what," presupposes that I should (do something) in any case. But how do I know this? Before I can ask "What . . . ?", some voice must have summoned me: "You should . . . you ought to . . . you must. . . . " Certainly my parents have told me how to behave; my teachers, society, the church, and several communities have prescribed what I am to do; but how could their orders convince me and why do I no longer think of them when following the guidance of my conscience?

Whose voice has awakened me to morality? The Father, the Mother, Culture, God, Reason, Conscience? Whatever the answer is, before I can ask "what should I do?" or "how should I live?", I have already been addressed by a voice that positions me as a respondent. Its summons makes me a "you" before I can establish myself as an "I." As responsivity, morality follows an address. This is why ethics includes a good deal of social and religious philosophy. God, the human Other, and Conscience are omnipresent when I respond to their call.

CHAPTER 3

Affections

Affection

Being involved in the story of a surrounding world is to be affected without and within. People greet me and smile or shout at me, the death of a friend saddens me, light and warmth caress me, cold air thrills my lungs. While I pick roses, the thorns prick my finger; the outbreak of a war changes my career. All beings with whom I share the same space and time touch and partially determine me. I experience myself as constantly affected by what I am not. Affection envelops my commerce with the world.

Not only do many kinds of beings (stones, mosquitos, parents, friends, events) touch me, but I also feel affected by my own life with its contacts and adventures. I feel a pain in my stomach; I enjoy a restful feeling in my body and mind; I feel exhausted (that is, I myself feel that this same I is exhausted); I am amazed by my own existence including this very amazement; I am grateful for feeling grateful. I thus discover myself as "auto-affected": I am always already affected by my own existence (including my activities and passivities).

Affection by what I am not and self-affection cannot be separated; they imply one another. Even a stomachache involves the world of which my body is a part, although, as mine, it is not worldly in the same sense as things or tools or other persons. Even the most intimate experiences, such as remorse or inner peace, do not leave the world and its history unchanged; yet it is not always easy to describe how my "interiority" is interwoven with the "outer" world. Affection encompasses the self and its world; it is the immediate feeling of the involvement they share.

Various moments and levels can be distinguished in this human affectivity. We enjoy the solidity of the earth when we stand or walk on it; we feel free when we breathe the air or swim in the surrounding fluidity of water; fire warms and fascinates through its burning light; we delight in hearing sounds that caress the ear, whereas shrill noises cause us pain; the obstacles we must overcome are tiring for our bodies but they strengthen our courage. The places where we dwell and the situations we encounter suggest specific ways of habituation and adaptation.

Moods

At the bottom of our involvement lies a pervasive mode (or "tonality") of "having" our existence: a specific mood, a kind of tuning or attunement. Such a mood can be heard in all the expressions of a particular individual but perhaps most clearly in the intonation, the melody, and the rhythm of his or her singing or speaking. The difference between Brahms's and Mozart's basic moods can be heard in their works, and similar differences can be seen in painting. The "music" of Rembrandt's portraits, for example, is remarkably different from those of Frans Hals or Velazquez. A mood is a characteristic mode of modulating human existence, a fundamental and global response to its inescapable givenness, the background music of its being-there as being affected by the world and itself.

Like all other affections, but even more fundamentally and intimately, moods unite the world and me in one feeling. Involvement acquires a specific coloring and character in mood. The world forces me to accept its necessities and suggests possibilities for my reactions. I am the one who can respond to its challenge by graspingness, melancholy reticence, reproachful bitterness, enthusiastic gratitude, or some other sentiment. My mood tells me and others how I am receiving the basic gift. This reception is not the result of a clear choice or decision; it precedes all reflection, but something of my freedom is already engaged in it. Once I have accepted and furthered my existence in a mode and style of my own, I am engaged in the *way* I "happen" and "want" to be involved in the existent self that I always already am. My existence, together with its inevitable affections (by world and self), cannot be refused; it is necessarily mine because it precedes all responsiveness and responsibility. However, my *mode* of being-affected, *my* style of feeling, reveals how I "wish" to enact my being as originally given and already affected. If basic moods already involve an element of "wishing" or "wanting" or "willing," ethics must begin here. The affective mode—the mood—in which I accept my existence as mine permeates and colors the entire "work" of life.

Different people are supported by different moods, but similarities permit us to distinguish between joyful, melancholy, bitter, peaceful, warm, cold, passionate, or phlegmatic kinds of people. Is it then also possible to evaluate moods as "better" or "worse"? If ethics begins on this level, should we not be able to distinguish more appropriate moods from moods that are less appropriate responses to our contingently given, situated, affected, and self-affected existence?

Enjoyment and Anxiety

Heidegger's description of anxiety (*Angst*) has been praised by many intellectuals of the twentieth century.[1] It would be cheap to attribute its influence merely to the specific situation of a fin de siècle or the global horrors with which that century was filled. Heidegger himself presented anxiety as the mood that provides access to being as such, distinct from the collection or universe of all beings. The no-thing that characterizes being as not-a-being cannot be perceived when we are overwhelmed with joy about "the fruits of the earth" or satisfied by the "normal" course of everyday pleasures. *Angst* liberates us from all attachments by exposing us to the dimension of the "nothing" from which all beings, including our own existence, emerge.

It cannot be denied that the contingency of our own existence and that of all other beings, if fully experienced, awakens a feeling of deep insecurity and helplessness. Neither myself nor any earthly power can guarantee the continuation of my existence. It cannot be ensured; nothing holds me; I am floating on nothing, suspended in a void.

However, anxiety cannot constitute the primordial mood of my being, for it can arise only as a response to a fundamental threat. Existence as such is experienced as that which—although unnecessary and without ground—is given as being there. Before anxiety creeps in, the experience of my being as that and what I am—a human existence—takes the form of an original consent and agreement: I embrace it, try to persevere in it,[2] and protect it against the nothingness from which it has emerged. Anxiety accompanies this experience, but it rides on the back of a positive assent: the *Jasagen* through which I appropriate my contingent, fragile, unprotected, but nonetheless given, real, and cherished existence.[3] A profound kind of contentment and self-love, perhaps even some sort of (as yet unaddressed) gratitude, are more appropriate responses to the factuality of my existence than anxiety about its possible disappearance. Even amazement comes later, because it assumes a distance that permits me to ask why I exist rather than not. Indeed, the thought of my nonexistence refers to an unrealized possibility; to that extent, amazement has some affinity with the anxious thought of my nonexistence after death.

Acceptance of our existence, self-affirmation, self-love, endurance, perseverance, and concern for ourselves are conditions of life. All of these are positive responses to the givenness of our being; anxiety can only accompany them as a shadow, motivated by life's contingency and fragility. If so, the fundamental mood that permeates a human life expresses a profound kind of agreement. The appropriate response to the fact of one's own life is peaceful or even joyful (despite the threat), rather than anxious, depressed, bitter, or resentful. If the experience of our givenness referred to some kind of giver, the appropriate mood would be gratitude. In that case, thinking would originate in thanking.

Death, anxiety, and tragedy are popular, but their horror could not be felt without reference to affirmative experiences of existence and life as such. The basic enjoyment of life is independent of its mortality and other disasters that might occur. Under the pressure of extreme suffering, some people have exclaimed that it would be better not to have been born, but existence as such cannot be weighed against events that arise within it. Although the possibilities of human existence may remain unfulfilled, neither mortality nor pain can deny that they could be enjoyed as a possible future. In suffering we experience the destruction or repression of cherished possibilities, not of life as such. A finite life is better than nothingness, unless finitude is incongruous with living. If that were the case, human life would be a demand for infinity, but would that still be a human life?

Pleasures and Pains

Living is both enjoyment and pain. Both are undergone, but each is differently received. The passivity of enjoyment is a passion: life loves itself and enjoys everything that fosters it. Being in agreement with the gifts and promises of the world procures pleasure, joy, delight; but when I am pained, I resist. Something does not go; my passion for life is thwarted; hostile forces have entered into me. Reactions to pain and pleasure are spontaneous; it is hardly possible to refrain from seeking pleasure and fleeing pain. If pain persists, body and spirit mobilize all their energy to fight it. Life always desires pleasurable affections. Hedonism seems to dominate the entirety of our striving, but seldom are we altogether free from suffering.

Many strategies are developed to conquer suffering, but we are not able to grasp pleasure directly. Pleasure is not the result of some work or purchase. It accompanies desirable things and events; it befalls us but escapes our control. By realizing or acquiring pleasurable beings, we can cause them to affect us. Such a strategy is used by infants in seducing their parents to still, caress, or console them. The same strategy is operative when adults display their charm in order to be loved. Perhaps it is even possible to interpret entire cultures as the interplay of hedonistic strategies.

There are many levels of *hēdonē* and hedonism: from vulgar pleasures and everyday pains to the most sublime delights and the deepest anxieties of mysticism. The distinctions between various levels and the analysis of their structures must indicate whether we can gather all kinds of *hēdonē* under one name (pleasure, contentment, satisfaction, joy, and so on), or not. Utilitarian ethicists often presuppose that all pleasures are differentiations of one generic phenomenon and that they correspond to specifications of human *need*. Human actions, they think, can be explained as operations of an economy based on needs. Pleasure would essentially be the satisfaction of a need, whereas pain would be the feeling of frustration or deprivation. If these presuppositions are correct, the ethics of pleasure and pain can be reduced to the normative science of an economic system of hedonic negotiations, oriented toward the most pleasurable balance of pleasures and inevitable pains. If the qualitative differences between the various hedonic experiences (pleasure, satisfaction, joy, delight, ecstasy) are too great for an economy (which presupposes a certain homogeneity), the basis of such a utilitarianism (including all hedonism) falls away.

In the next chapter, we will see that the reduction of all tendencies, inclinations, wants, and wishes to "needs" neglects a host of phenomena. At this point in our reflection, however, it may suffice to observe that the factuality of our situation awakens in us a drive toward agreement and away from discordance with that which attracts us most. I will call this drive *desire* and argue that a phenomenology of desire is necessary to discover what motivates human action in its many modes.

In considering the relevance of "pleasures and pains" for ethics, and using a generic language, which later must be amended, it is paramount not to treat them as independent entities. They are no more than aspects or qualities of events, actions, moves, or encounters that affect and involve us. Pleasure is an occurrence that makes me feel "good" in a certain dimension or part of my existence. It crowns certain experiences, whereas pain is the experience of something that does not go well with me (again, in a certain dimension of my life). I cannot feel any pleasure or pain in isolation from that which, by affecting me, makes the affection pleasurable or painful. The evaluation of any pleasure thus cannot be separated from the specific affection and the specific phenomenon that affects me. We do not strive for "pleasures"; we strive for pleasurable phenomena and loathe phenomena that affect us painfully.

Pleasures and pains are not objective qualities of things and events, however; they are part of our affections, that is, of experiences in which a human individual is affected by some phenomenon. Because the hedonic or "pathic" quality of each affection depends on the particular character of the affecting phenomenon as well as the disposition of the affected subject, it is not possible to determine universal laws about the hedonic qualities of all affections. Some people find culinary pleasures important, whereas others, who might be addicted to good poetry, are indifferent to delicious patés and wines. Some people gladly suffer for sacred causes, whereas others despise the joys of contemplation and charity. If "pleasures and pains" are "subjective" in this sense, it is obvious that a universally valid ethics cannot be built on calculation of hedonic degrees and balances. Or is it possible to stipulate how one, in various encounters and affections, ought to feel? Are pleasures and pains themselves ruled by universally valid norms?

The Structure of Affection

Phenomena address—touch, confront, surprise, amaze, stir, trouble—us. Whatever they do to us, we are affected by them as soon as we pay attention to them. Things, events, persons, pains and pleasures, duties and tasks compete for our attention. They try to attract our awareness; in different degrees of insistence, they address us, call on us, appeal to us.

However, their ways of appearing and affecting are diverse: each phenomenon has its own manner of provoking us.

Once I pay attention to some appearance, I cannot refrain from being involved in a relationship with it. I can still dismiss or turn away from that which confronts me, but once I allow it to impress me, my life is affected. Affection is the way in which a phenomenon is received by the affected person. Perception is one element of reception, but this can be wholly affective, almost independent of any of our five senses. For example, a situation can be felt to be *unheimlich* or peaceful, although our feeling does not seem to be caused by any specific thing or person heard or seen or smelled or touched. Even some objects inspire awe or anxiety without displaying features that our senses can recognize as awful or terrifying. Unless we accept that our senses themselves are "affectible" and affective, we should make a distinction between the visible, audible, smellable, tastable, and touchable aspects of phenomena, on the one hand, and the affective dimension of their affecting us and of our being "touched," "moved," emotionally disturbed, delighted, or pained by them, on the other.

As soon as we allow something (or someone) to affect us, we are challenged: being affected (that is, feeling an affection) is feeling provoked and urged to react. In their address, phenomena suggest and request, or even demand, a response. As affecting us, they demand an affective reaction. Such a reaction, however spontaneous, cannot be completely arbitrary, because this would show madness; in our response, we must accept and "recognize" the proper character of the affecting phenomenon. Our response—even the most immediate and spontaneous one—must therefore involve a form of adjustment, at least to some extent.

If a certain phenomenon threatens our well-being, thus making us anxious or angry, we will react with hostility and attempt to remove it or transform it into a friendlier phenomenon. In such a case, adjustment involves us in a process of self-defense and destruction or radical transformation. Vis-à-vis favorable phenomena, we adjust to them in a more hospitable way: we welcome them and adjust ourselves to them by changing, if necessary, our disposition. Often the affective adjustment will be a sort of negotiation in which we adapt to a constellation of affecting phenomena, which, at the same time, we try to adjust to our own manner and course of life. We want to adapt to the available surroundings, but we also want to transform these surroundings into a situation in which we can feel at home.

If things and persons and events that touch and move us urge us to respond in an affectively adequate way, our adjustment is an elementary form of justice: our affection must "recognize" and "do justice" to that which—in a glorious tree, a human face, a trusting animal, but also in a horrible monster, a criminal threat, or disgusting behavior—displays its own nature in the confrontation. The challenge that lies in all affecting demands is therefore an affective response that negotiates a double "justice": we must adjust to the demands that belong to the proper being of the phenomena while urging them to adjust to our just demands. The ideal of such a negotiation is a harmonious attunement in which all involved can freely be and display what they are.

The structure of affection is wholly relational. Feeling is not the experience of an isolated, self-enclosed subject. When I feel good, healthy, excited, or sad, I am not totally absorbed by my self and certainly not by my mind or consciousness alone. There is always something else that affects me; I feel that something affects me, when I feel myself; I feel an affection *as* done to me and undergone/received by me; I feel myself (as) touched by something. The affecting thing (the "affectant") can be a nice surprise, a friend, the sun, a bouquet, my own body or one of its parts, a mental pain or idea, and so on; but within the unity of the affection, there is always a distinction and a relation between me as feeling affected by the affectant (X) and the latter (X) as affecting me. Simultaneously, there is—within the unity of being and feeling myself (as affected by X)—a distinction and a relation between me as feeler and me as felt. The complete structure of an affection is therefore the unity of a multirelational configuration: (1) *I* feel (2) *myself* as affected by (3) the *affectant*. Even when the third element of this configuration is something in me, such as my stomach or my own sadness, my feeling (myself) determined by it maintains this structure. Affections are "intentional" (in the phenomenological sense of this word), not isolating or solipsistic.

The relationality of feeling is also a fact on the level of our moods. It is not always clear what makes us melancholy or depressed or joyful; it can even be unclear what sort of mood we are in; but this does not mean that the way we feel is "without cause" and unmotivated (the motivation might be sub- or unconscious) or unrelated to any touching or tuning phenomenon. What makes us joyful or melancholy might be our personal situation, the epoch or world in which we have to live, or a combination of all of these, but no mood can dissolve our relations with impressive phenomena or abolish the distinction between me as affected or impressed and me as feeling that I am impressed.

In the next chapter, we will see that desire, as an affection that is always already oriented, cannot be understood without understanding its orientation toward a desideratum. This does not mean that the desired end is necessarily known before the desire is felt; the orientation can work before the desiring individual feels itself governed by it. The clarification of our most fundamental desire is itself part of the desired end, but it may take a long time, perhaps more than an entire life. Intentionality and constitutive relationality do not depend on explicit knowledge of all the terms involved. They rather invite us to discover what they hide.

Affectivity and Cognition

To respond affectively to phenomenal challenges would not be possible if the challenges were not "known," "perceived," or rather felt, by the respondent. Affection implies therefore some sort of cognition.

Some truths cannot be discovered otherwise than through, or rather by way of, affection—for example, the sadness or the trustworthiness of a person, the threatening or exhilarating character of a situation, the splendor of a perfect summer day, or the horror of evil.

Although some truths are essentially affective, we may also risk the thesis that all truths have an affective component. The argument for this thesis would have to show that human beings cannot affirm any truth without simultaneously being involved in it through their feelings. All affirmations and negations contain an interest, and this is felt to impact the mood, the affective disposition, the underlying tonality, and the tuning of the person who has that interest.

An illustration of the thesis can be found in the "feel" that accompanies the study of a philosophical system. In trying to reconstruct and "realize," for example, the philosophy of Bonaventure or Spinoza or Kant, one becomes aware of different climates of vision and thought. To grasp the full meaning of their thoughts, one must sympathize with them, at least in a methodic, although not necessarily committed, way. "The experience of thinking" is supported, often even oriented, by a characteristic pathos. It is even doubtful whether the meaning of a philosophy is still rendered faithfully when its conceptual and representational elements are separated from the affective stream of life in which it is rooted.

Affections are preconceptual, prerepresentational, and presensible modes of acquaintance with and response to the phenomena that we allow to draw our attention. Sympathy and antipathy, fear and sorrow, pain and suffering, pleasure, joy, and delight, love and anger, anxiety and hope are spontaneous responses. When phenomena impress us, they elicit an affective "cognition" from which recognition may emerge. To the extent to which all beings strike me as challenging and demanding, they also let me feel what and how they are. Therefore, all beings have, by the very address that is contained in their appearance, both a normative and a revealing character.

Affection, Perception, Theory

Being affected is being in contact with the affecting reality, which thereby reveals some aspects of it. It is an initial perception.

All sense perception is at the same time affective. Not only tasting and smelling, touching and feeling, but also hearing and seeing from a distance establish a contact with impressive, moving, surprising, amazing, and engaging phenomena. Seeing, for example, can make me anxious or joyful or gloomy. Hearing is even more clearly emotional: the melody and the timbre of a voice or birdsong can cause delight or make me aggressive. I feel the other being *as* affecting me and I feel myself *as* affected by that being. What touches me is inseparable from my feeling of being touched, but it is more than a moment that can be wholly integrated into my own development. The affecting "other" (thing or person) surprises me. Although the other and I, in affection and perception, are united, our union still leaves a space and time for me to welcome or to reject the surprising phenomenon.

The immediacy of my being affected modifies my ongoing self-affection, but it also reserves a nonintegrated element for the phenomenon, which, in this sense, remains other, "outside," independent, and able to surprise me again and again. Amazing things remain amazing; they cannot lose their surprising difference by repeated perceptions or by a conceptual grasp of their secrets.

A great danger of scientific and philosophical theory lies in the attempt to reduce all that is amazing (or shocking, exhilarating, saddening, shattering) to epiphenomena of the intellectual quintessence that can be discovered in it. Theoretical transparency can easily drive out the emotional clarity and precision that are characteristic of revealing affections. Poetry is better at doing justice to them, and this is one of the reasons why the quarrel between philosophy and poetry is as old as the birth of scientific theory. By losing the affective relevance of phenomena and feelings, one loses an essential part of the truth.

However, not all kinds of feeling and emotion are precise, adequate, luminous, and well attuned. The affective correspondence to which the phenomena invite us, demands correct adjustments to allow them to display their own splendor (or horror). Some or many of our affective responses to the facts of the universe are inadequate: they may be awkward or primitive, savage or sentimental, complacent or harsh, and so on. To do justice to everything that touches or moves us—and therewith to allow a more complete truth to be revealed—our affectivity must be educated, formed, and reformed. Although affections are essential for a well-attuned ethics, it is also true that they themselves ask for an ethics of affectivity.

Cultures of Affectivity

If each surprise confronts us with a challenge that demands a well-attuned response, how are we to meet this challenge?

The more or less adequate ways that we allow various kinds of beings to impress and challenge us and the kinds of responses by which we integrate them into our lives are rarely or never original; the culture in which we participate has taught us how to receive and react. Indeed, our education as initiation into the culture (or cultures) of a particular country and family has preshaped not only our opinions and behavior, but also our affective commerce with the phenomena of human existence. We have learned how to sense, feel, appreciate, welcome, savor, ignore, abhor, avoid, dismiss, embrace, enjoy. The result is a customary mode of sympathies and antipathies, a spontaneous evaluation and an already set pattern of emotional responsivity. Our culture has provided a pattern for the entire process of affective dealings with the reality. It tells us which reactions are normal and which are exaggerated, pathological, insensitive, heartless, or strange. Thus every culture constitutes models of emotionality that are propagated by tradition and education. Individuals vary in customizing the pattern in which they have been trained by their educators. The community to which one belongs radically influences not only the opinions and the mores that guide individual behavior, but also, and more fundamentally, the emotional climate attested in the "music" (tonality, melody, rhythm) of their lives. There is a good reason for Plato's extensive critique of the "musical" (that is, affective, musical, poetic, and dramatic) formation in *Politeia* III and IV: if intellectual and behavioral correctness is not supported by and permeated with a well-attuned affectivity, theory and praxis remain uncivilized. Inversely, if the most appreciated music is savage, the dominating ethos is wild and violent.

To illustrate the preceding, we could focus on a narcissistic culture, according to which the primary questions would be: "How do I feel?" "Am I O.K.?" Narcissism is inhospitable to the appearance of persons, phenomena, and events that do not easily fit into the emotional life of the self-obsessed person. To put off the suggestions and demands that another's emergence involves, the modern Narcissus no longer concentrates on his beauty, but rather on his individual rights. This self-enclosure begins in the dimension of self-feeling: all other feelings are appreciated only insofar as they liberate, enhance, satisfy, or intensify his self-affection, and those affections that do not answer this criterion are either rejected or distorted. Therewith a principle of inadequacy and falsification is borne: other beings are no longer allowed to display and be what and how they are unless they fit into my overall self-satisfaction.

The affectivity of well-educated individuals is not wholly determined by the culture of the communities to which they belong. Even in this most spontaneous dimension there is freedom: each individual is to some extent responsible for his or her affective disposition. This freedom is expressed in the experimentation that cannot be avoided when someone is confronted with situations to which an adequate response is not immediately obvious. To find out how—through which pathos or mood—I must react, in cases where normalcy is not clear or when I have begun to doubt the adequacy of the "normal" response, I must experiment with my own emotional possibilities, but I can be helped by models and heroes of other times or cultures. For example, I can try to correct my narcissistic style of life by trying to emulate what seems to have been the affective orientation of Saint Francis. Or I can try to escape from the workaholic avoidance of confrontation with myself by focusing on the many neglected facets of the cosmos that provoke "work-free" responses from aesthetic admiration to religious awe.

Emotional experimentation is particularly necessary in times of cultural crisis. When the polymorphism of available and acceptable but conflicting patterns has unsettled the normalcy of the traditional pathonomy, individuals are left to their own sensitivity. Most often they will find companions with whom they can form new traditions through new, experimental forms of criticism, poetry, and praxis. Perhaps the affective climate of the epoch will change under the pressure of an elite group or a majority that could emerge from their attempts. It is also possible, however, that their emotional economy will not convince others and they remain exceptions or even abnormal cases: more or less "mad" symptoms of a critical time in transition.

Affection and Virtue

Our affective spontaneity has been civilized through enculturation. We have learned how to interpret the variety of appearances as threatening, enjoyable, ugly, consoling, touching, and so on. Our culture has interpreted and responded to the suggestions of the phenomena in its own way, different from, for example, the Japanese or the Bantu way. However, no culture can ignore or arbitrarily distort the suggestions that come from the appearing things, persons, events, and constellations themselves. Any affective hermeneutics is bound up with beings as they show themselves to be. But it is difficult to decide whether one cultural hermeneutic is better than another in bringing out the properties of the various phenomena.

As educated persons, we know what the customary or "normal" ways of responding and reacting are. We have learned to conform to the affective patterns that are set by our surroundings. The prevailing modes of affective interpretation, reception, and responsiveness function as standards to which our emotional life should conform. Thanks to the ruling normalcy, the primitive and wild character of our passions and emotions is tamed, held in check, smoothed out, made more or less decent—in brief, civilized. If our culturalization is completely successful, in the end, we will agree with the criteria of our culture, preserving, as true traditionalists, its "norms and values," beginning at the level of emotional perception and evaluation, reception and integration, reaction and engagement.

However, even on this level, we are somehow responsible for our own moods and other modes of affection, and this responsibility, too, must be awakened and developed by an education that is more than mere repetition. Our affective disposition, the customary mode of our emotional life, may be preshaped by a particular culture, but it also differs from the average way insofar as it is the outcome of our personal reaction to that culture.

It is possible to simply conform to the normalcy of a culture, but even such conformism betrays a form of responsibility. It is me, who has given in to the force of a tradition, sparing myself the question of whether the prevailing hermeneutic is altogether appropriate. In any case, during my education, I will have developed a style of my own, even if I am now a conservative. A total separation from my culture seems impossible, but there are many degrees of difference between a conservative stylization and a rebellious farewell.

In the history of art, we can study how prevailing modes and codes of affectivity are constantly challenged and superseded by different manners of feeling and reacting with regard to the universe of surprising phenomena (which, in some sense, remains the same). The history of music is certainly the best illustration of this thesis, but drama, poetry, and painting are likewise revealing. Compare a landscape of Van Eyk with the landscapes of Rembrandt or Corot. Or listen to the emotional charge of Donne's poetry and that of cummings.

Each person has his or her own emotional disposition and "economy." The "music" that accompanies a life as a hidden but felt *cantus firmus* "colors" and "modulates" all its other dimensions; it cannot be neglected in any attempt to describe how a person "has" or "holds" herself in relation to the universe.

Excellence in feeling has been thematized since Plato's critique of *paideia* in *Politeia* III–IV and Aristotle's descriptions of well-tempered *pathē* in his *Ethics*. Virtue begins with well-adjusted emotional responses to events that affect us. Habitual ways of coping with emotions are virtuous if they are well proportioned to the phenomena that elicit them. A multitude of passions disturbs our equilibrium, unless we have learned—through *paideia* and *askēsis*—how to harmonize and temper them. A good and beautiful economy of passions and emotions demands good taste and style. The characteristic "music" of each human life creates the general climate in which all its theoretical and practical activities can thrive or fail. Just as Mozart and Brahms are immediately recognizable in their symphonies, so the emotional tonality of each person reveals a characteristic stance and style. No behavior can entirely hide the affective soil from which it emerges.

Values

Affection implies evaluation. This important principle can be illustrated on all levels of affectivity; for instance, with regard to the hedonic aspects of affections. To be affected is pleasant or unpleasant or a mixture of pleasure and displeasure. Can any affection be entirely neutral in this respect? Can we be affected without being pleased or pained at all? How could such an affection be interesting to us? It can if there are interests other than hedonic ones—for example, if "good" does not per se imply any kind of pleasure or pain.

Affections are spontaneous evaluations of the affecting phenomena insofar as they impress us as good (appropriate, useful, favorable, worthwhile) or bad (evil, meaningless, dangerous, destructive, inappropriate) or a mixture of both. Can a phenomenon be neither good nor bad? Can anything be entirely without value? Without interest? If it were, would we pay attention to it? Even if there were phenomena that strike us as neither good nor bad (and neither pleasant nor unpleasant), this would not necessarily contradict the thesis that affection implies evaluation. If it is true that all phenomenality is met with an all-encompassing and primordial desire that is responsible for our interests (see Chapter 4), the outcome of our evaluation could still be that some phenomena do not present any positive or negative interest. As unavoidably interested beings, we evaluate all that touches us. Because a thing is interesting (as good or bad or mixed), it moves us toward or away from it. The spontaneous reaction implied in our affection is an initial, more or less appropriate and revisable, discovery of its (positive or negative or mixed) "value."

"Values and norms" is a phrase frequently used in social sciences. What it means is not easily explainable, however. As for the philosophy of "values," a voluminous literature has been produced, especially in Germany and France, in the first half of the twentieth century, but the topic has almost disappeared from actual discussion, although the word is still used as if it were commonly understood in some obvious sense. If we want to use the word *value* in ethics, at least some distinctions are necessary.

First of all, it is paramount to clarify that values are not things, substances, or entities about which one can talk as if they were separable from the valuable beings that "have" them.[4] Some, perhaps all, phenomena are valuable because of their positive, negative, or mixed value, but "a value" is a dangerous expression. "Having value" or "being valuable" (for example, interesting, tasteful, good, ugly, uncanny, disgusting, admirable, funny, ridiculous) indicates that the value-having or valuable phenomenon not only is, but ought to be, appreciated (or depreciated) because of certain of its aspects.

Is value a quality? Certainly, but (1) what sort of quality is it, and (2) what is a quality? Perhaps these questions cannot be answered in their generality. In any case, there are many kinds of quality and value: superficial, profound, fundamental, marginal, essential, and so on. If all beings are valuable, at least in some respect, a full theory of value is part of a complete ontology, which would study the many meanings of "good" as a transcendental characteristic of being. Such a theory would contain or even coincide with a fundamental ethics, if ethics can be taken in the very broad sense of a theory that shows the universal ought-character of all that is. In this broad sense, the ethical relevance of "values" lies primarily in the different claims the various beings (persons, things, events) impose on our evaluation as far as this informs our behavior. If we take the adjective *ethical* to mean something more restricted, closer to the everyday meaning of "moral" and obligatory, we must delineate this meaning from other, for example, aesthetic, religious, sportive, hygienic, epistemological, scientific, technical, and gastronomic "values." In all cases, however, we must not allow the substantive "values" to seduce us into treating them as substances, entities, things, bills, or shares. For if we fall into that trap, we will lose sight of the constellation of valuable "things," persons, events, and situations with which we have to deal. The hypostatization of "values," which, as valuable entities, would rule our appreciation, motivation, and action, would put a veil between the real world and our appreciative involvement in it.

A second temptation to reification lies in the "objective" character of values that is suggested by the current use of the phrase "norms and values." Nothing has any value unless there are (real or possible) persons who can and must appreciate or depreciate and thus recognize its being or not being valuable (that is, useful, beautiful, healthy, holy). The term *valuable* means that something ought to be recognized as such, but if the earth were emptied of all persons, that claim could neither be perceived nor voiced; it would be a "claim" for and by nobody, a potential claim that could not become real again unless there were a chance that the earth would be repopulated by beings who have a sense for appreciable occurrences.

The value of X consists of that which makes X interesting, impressive, valuable *for* someone. X demands recognition of its value and is "proud" of being good, useful, nice. In order to recognize its value as the reason for its "pride," one must establish a relationship of appreciation and recognition; one must "do justice" to it by adequately responding to its claim.

As we will see in the following chapters, different kinds of being demand different kinds of appreciation and recognition. A complete theory of "values" and evaluation must therefore combine (1) a phenomenology of the different modes in which various kinds of being claim our recognition of their value with (2) a differentiated treatment of appropriate ways of responding to these claims.

CHAPTER 4

Desire

I am aware of my life as a characteristic movement: I sit and go; act as most people around me; share in the opinions and manners of my community; try out my own variations of behavior, speech, and style; experiment with my talents; and contribute in some way to the story of my country and culture. I move along in my commerce with others, but sometimes I amaze myself: Why do I live this way? How is it that I follow this course? Diverse reasons may cause such a moment of reflection. I might, for example, feel dissatisfied by a lack of recognition or by my own clumsiness and failures. Or I might be struck by a feeling of utter meaninglessness. Even if I am, on the whole, content with this life of mine, there are nonetheless qualities or customs in it that disappoint me. I like myself, but not entirely. It is very difficult to accept all I have and am without any misgiving, irritation, remorse, or repulsion. I am especially worried by my infidelities to others and myself and by the silly things I say or do in agreement with "everyone" else. I can even loathe the basic mood that permeates all of my thoughts and actions. The mixture of liking and disliking, in which I experience my going along, is a complicated and shifting mode of affectivity. I feel that I am not simple. How can I reach total agreement with myself?

Most discordance in life seems to be caused by Desire. Under many names, it has dominated the moral and religious cultures of East and West. All of literature is full of Desire, and many classics of philosophy present it as the origin of our search for goodness and wisdom.

Felt discordance reveals in me an orientation beyond the state of being that I have reached. I am aware of a stubborn tendency toward a more desirable course of life. Desire puts me at odds with much of what I am and feel and do; awareness of this desire is *conscience*.

What Desire desires is not immediately clear to me. If it coincides with "me" (in the sense of my deep, originary self), it is also true that I do not initially—and perhaps never quite will—know what "I" (*au fond*, originarily) desire. What I ultimately desire, my Desideratum, is a secret. It fascinates and obsesses the human "soul" without being known. It is vaguely felt, obscurely suspected and surmised, yearningly presumed.

All cultures can be interpreted as erotic experiments: religion, poetry, the rituals of daily life, the codes of law, and so on proclaim the omnipresence of a desire that restlessly tries out all sorts of contacts and unions. Can it be satisfied at all? Does it seek an illusion, rather than a secret? Is it greater, deeper, more demanding than life itself? Are we condemned to be its slave without any chance of finding peace?

The emotional modulations, poetic interpretations, practical ritualizations, and theoretical explanations through which the various cultures have attempted to shape and clarify Eros offer guidance, but they have also burdened us with a heritage whose illuminating suggestions are mixed with spurious contaminations. It would be extremely arrogant to ignore this heritage, but the authenticity of all its parts cannot be assumed. They should be tested. A phenomenology of desire is therefore required. We must appeal to the most authentic experiences of desire; but how can we discern which of our experiences are authentic, more pure than others, more illuminating for a discovery of the originary? This question is central for an epistemology of authenticity, but a treatment of it must be delayed. In this chapter, I will restrict myself to a few hints.

Since philosophical investigations are always preceded by concrete, possibly contaminated experiences, we must begin by testing the quality of these experiences. With respect to our experiences of desire, we must confront them with Desire's own demand that we recognize and experience it as it (really, authentically) is. The possibility of such a confrontation presupposes that we must take our factual experiences to be only attempts at correctly and authentically experiencing what and how Desire itself is (moves, pushes, obsesses) and "wants" us to be. We do not entirely coincide with our experiences but rather always have a certain distance, a sort of margin from which we can test, criticize, revise, and reform them. As we will see, we have a criterion for testing our feelings in ourselves. Desire governs us, urging us to adjust to it.

To begin with, we must experience exactly what Desire feels like. Testing affections can be compared to testing perceptions. If we are not sure whether our perception of a thing or event is correct, there is no other way to ascertain or deny its truth than through a new, more attentive and concentrated perception (seeing, hearing, tasting, or touching) of the same. Another person's perception might be needed to contest my description of the thing that both of us are looking at, but in the end, I myself must discover how that thing shows and "gives" itself. Phenomenology depends on the possibility of becoming more and more precise in feeling, perceiving, and experiencing—until we reach the stage of the absolutely pure. Further on, I will consider some conditions of the ascent to that stage, but let us first concentrate on some formal properties of Desire and follow its development In a more intuitive, rather than epistemologically ascertained, way.

Desiderata Involve Me

We desire a good meal, beautiful music, friendship, being loved. The desideratum is not a thing, but an encounter, a commerce, a contact, a form of sharing, a kind of union, a gratifying relationship. Very often it is not a static relation or a "state," but a shared activity, a union in movement, a change or action that would be impossible without contact with the longed-for reality. Desire moves toward realities distinct from the subject, insofar as it desires them, in order to enjoy them. This thesis remains true even if a subject desires a change or the conservation of its own being. In desiring enjoyment, desire celebrates a specific union of the subject and its desideratum. Thus the subject desires an enjoyable manner of commerce with the desideratum; or rather, the desideratum includes the desired kind of union and therefore a specific involvement of the desiring subject itself. When I desire a specific change in myself, that which I desire is I myself as specifically transformed through union with a thing, a person, or an event that takes part in the desired transformation. What I desire is a specific future of my present life.

Am I then imprisoned in my own life? No, my life is not a prison, because it is as wide as the universe—it is even wider, as we will see. It is silly to view my life as a box or prison or closed interiority in opposition to everything else. As Aristotle knew, "the *psychē* is somehow all things (*panta*)."[1] Whether this dictum is true of "the mind" is debatable, but life is surely open enough to welcome all meaningful realities. If desire is always desire for a manner of my own living, this does not exclude my simultaneously doing full justice to other things or persons. I am involved with many realities, whose future is as much theirs as it is mine.

If I myself am involved in the desideratum of the desire that drives me, its realization depends on the manner in which I will participate in it. My desire then cannot be fulfilled unless I myself, at the time of its fulfillment, behave in an appropriate way. Part of what I desire is a specific mode of my own communication with those elements. I desire to be, feel, welcome, embrace, and behave in a way that makes the encounter desirable. I have a part to play; total passivity will not lead to the desired constellation. Desire does not coincide with expectation; it demands appropriate action on my part. Its fulfillment depends as much on my own adjustment in attitude and behavior as on the fortuitous approach of other beings or events.

Desire and Desires

The fundamental eros that drives me is overwhelming and mysterious. It possesses me, but I do not have a clear concept of it. It is, however, always operative and concrete in the form of wishes, wants, inclinations, tendencies, passions, and decisions, which are better known to me. The particular desires that motivate my behavior are powerful, but they allow for a critical distance. Often this distance seems abolished by overwhelming passions, but several experiences remind us that passions are not omnipotent. First, they are multiple and often conflict with one another. We are thus forced to function as their arbiter. Second, their fulfillment normally contains a shade of dissatisfaction. Once we achieve or receive what we desire, it loses some of its luster. A degree of melancholy follows, or even accompanies, all arrivals.

The general statements uttered here should be checked by detailed analyses of various kinds and levels of desire. If it is true that our most originary Desire points beyond all the ends of the concrete desires that motivate the course of a human life, as the introduction to this chapter implies, the great Desideratum surpasses the world and its history. We are then condemned (or blessed) to desire some union beyond the possibilities of worldly lives. But is something that transcends life and history not a fiction?

The difference between Desire and desires has puzzled the spiritual masters of eastern and western civilizations. The ultimate horizon of Desire belongs to the essence of all desires; it accentuates at the same time the inherence of an erotic transcendence, the finitude of their possibilities, and the impossibility of idolizing their goals. A phenomenology of concrete desires must disclose how they pursue their own specific fulfillment while animated by a deeper Desire that points beyond. Desire reveals itself in the multitude of mixed and unmixed, pure and impure, deep and superficial desires that orient and disorient our lives. It does not coincide with any of them, but they are Desire's ways of participating in the story of the human world.

Constellations of Desire

A person's concrete desires form a characteristic constellation: the erotic ways of a romantic poet are different from those of a stoic philosopher or an ascetic monk. Since "the soul is somehow all things," the dynamic system of an individual's desires portrays the entire universe as a characteristic constellation of desirable and undesirable beings and events. The world of a stoic is different from the world of the romantics. Lives, with their worlds and histories, are differentiated by their erotic style. The truth of Desire must be discovered through a plurality of configurations. Hegel's "figures (*Gestalten*) of the Spirit" are not only figures of knowledge but also and foremost figures of Desire. A phenomenology of Desire should not simply stare at it, but rather describe the various ways of life and the worlds in which it is tried out. Aristotle's comparison between the ethical values of the dominant *bioi* of his time is such a phenomenology.[2] The second part of Hegel's *Phenomenology of Spirit* and Kierkegaard's *Stages on Life's Way* offer descriptions of other lives and life-worlds, but let us not either forget the refined analyses of the erotic adventure in Gregory of Nyssa's *Life of Moses*, Bonaventure's *Itinerary of the Mind Toward God*, Teresa of Avila's *Castle of the Soul*, John of the Cross's *Ascent of Mount Carmel*, and so many other works of spirituality.[3] Although the latter concentrate on direct descriptions of self-lived experiences, the former emphasize reflection; but both combine experience and reflection, which makes them indispensable sources for a complete phenomenology of Desire.

The comparison of different versions of desire and desirability is a synchronic parallel of the diachronic study of the movement through which different erotic constellations follow one another as stages in history or on the path of an individual life. The transitions between the stages of a well-developing life are motivated by Desire itself. Originary Desire tests the desiring subject's own attempts at concretization; it criticizes them in affective, practical, and reflective ways; it prompts the transformation of the concrete desires and tests the erotic worlds in which these are unfolded. The discernment needed for erotic testing does not come from a commanding person, society, or god outside the desiring subject. The latter cannot obey such orders if it does not recognize them as desired by the very Desire that from within motivates the testing. How other persons, societies, and God cooperate with the subject to convert it from deficient to better stages should be shown when we analyze the proliferation of its adventures.

Conscience

The search for the primordial and ultimate Desideratum is guided by an elementary, vague, and undefinable awareness of the Desire that motivates this very search. We seem to be closer to Desire itself than to what it ultimately and primarily desires, but neither is clear to us. Desire is too close, the heart of our hearts, the motor of our dynamism, the origin of conscience and all motivated consciousness. What conscience "knows" is not much, but it has a direction. Its awareness is oriented. When it discovers the desirability of various beings and events, it appreciates but also relativizes their worth; all those that are desirable are fine, good, great, but they are not *the* (real, ultimately and originally desired) Desirable itself. And all those that are undesirable or repulsive are bad, but they are not (the ultimate and fundamental) Evil itself. Conscience is Desire insofar as Desire is aware of itself. This awareness can deepen and grow, and such growth is necessary for it to become knowledgeable. Wisdom is the goal, but this cannot be the fruit of reflection alone. If Desire itself does not become wiser, no ethical insights will emerge.

Desire is not a certain quantum of energy; its quality, intensity, and direction change under the influence of encounters and adventures. Through such changes, it gains a deeper self-awareness. Conscience acquires more light. Growing knowledge of our drivenness requires a maturing life; experience, critical self-evaluation, purification, and simplification lead us toward sagacity. Philosophy must follow life: supported by growing wisdom, it tests its own translations of experience into concepts. Indifference toward the adventures of good and wise persons produce empty ethics—as empty as the hollow sermons of hypocritical moralists.

The Project

The thesis (or hypothesis) that governs this book states that human beings are driven by a radical Desire that cannot be identified with any of the many limited wishes, wants, or tendencies that arise over the course of a life. It is a thesis expressed by many philosophers from Empedocles and Plato to Nietzsche, Blondel, and Sartre. "All humans strive for *eudaimonia*" (Aristotle); "Eros moves the universe toward the Good" (Plotinus); human beings are moved by a "*desiderium naturale fruendi Deum*" (Augustine, Bonaventure, Thomas, Scotus); human life is driven by a desire for the synthesis of the good (*das Gute*) and well-being (*das Wohl*) (Kant); "all pleasure wills eternity" (Nietzsche); and so on.[4]

Do such expressions belong to philosophy? Can their truth be demonstrated through scientific, mathematical, logical, or linguistic methods? If they could, they would not be originary, as, for example, Plato and Aristotle knew very well. If philosophy is a radical enterprise, its most relevant statements cannot be proved, but their truth can be experienced, lived, practiced, embraced, trusted, monstrated, displayed, and analyzed. Their coherence can be shown and their meaning can be clarified in the hope that readers or listeners will recognize or "remember" their fundamental truth.[5] In this respect, philosophical texts are similar to works of art: the basis and core of their meaning is not provable; it cannot even be captured in sentences; but discourses can dispose readers to a form of fundamental recognition and acquiescence. Have we not ever had the *Aha-Erlebnis* of "Yes, this is what I have always been searching for"? Let us hope that, even for readers who reject the propositions of this book, the testing of its suggestions will not have been a waste of time.

Plan

The plan of the following analyses is simple. As a provisional tool, I will use the traditional distinction between form and content. In this chapter I will concentrate on the formal properties of Desire, whereas the following chapters will be devoted to a consideration of the "contents" that are desired on the human journey to *eudaimonia, beatitudo*, happiness, *felicidad, bonheur*, success. The latter task involves (1) the description of experiences that promise to still our desire or desires); (2) an exploration of the various levels on which something like happiness seems to be obtainable; (3) an analysis of the time of desire (as progress and regress, arrival, presence, loss, absence); (4) a meditation on the absolute or relative desirability of desirable things, persons, states, and events; and (5) the turns and conversions necessary for certain discoveries of the Desirable.

Formal Analysis of Desire

Praenotanda

The traditional distinction between form and content is here a strategic simplification: it makes a beginning possible but must be given up as the work progresses. Form cannot be thought without content, and different contents ask for different forms. Therefore, we cannot treat forms without continually referring to specific contents. "Form in general" would have a clear meaning only if all possible contents had something in common that would fit into that form. Would this not presuppose that being, at least to some extent or in some aspect, is univocal? A content cannot be thought without form, either. The distinction presents the content as something that "fits" into the form; but must it not have a form already in order to fit (or not)? In any case, forms and contents cannot be treated as separable entities. All talk of one or the other is therefore abstract and provisional only. It must be followed or accompanied by synthetic corrections.

A second caveat is required. Many poems, novels, dramas, and phenomenologies have expressed how Desire rules human disasters and delights, but all of them have done this in specific languages from particular perspectives and with particular intents. Are all attempts to write a valid phenomenology of Desire condemned to produce only particular, or even individual and private, versions of Desire?

The project of a definitive description, rendering all further attempts superfluous, is arrogant. It ignores the perspectivism inseparable from human finitude. However, a relativistic interpretation of this perspectivism fails to understand that particular angles or aspects can coincide with universal, although incomplete, truth. If someone can sympathize with the perspective from which a particular but exact description is given, that person will indeed have a similar perception as the author of that description. A mistake that is often made lies in the absolutization of a perspective. By stating that a specific angle—a particular cultural or personal interest or language, for example—is the only true mode of perceiving or treating reality, one not only narrows, but also distorts, the truth.

This answer to relativism risks suggesting that the totality of all perspectives would together make possible a complete description. However, Desire seems to escape every attempt at complete translation into words, even as a summation of all particular and perspectival approaches. Yet it is possible—as good literature proves—to effectively focus the readers' minds on experiences that they share with the writer. Through and beyond a description, we communicate preverbal meanings that are given in common experiences.

Conscious of the incompleteness and inadequacy of the following descriptions, I can only (1) try to reach the highest possible universality and precision allowed by a particular language, culture, form of life, and personal perspective; (2) present the result to the critical reactions of my readers; and (3) critically reflect on the result of my attempt and the reactions it elicits.

Analysis

1. We are driven. Vitality plays a role; youth, especially adolescence, is the period in which Desire manifests itself as ambition and conquest, but it is not confined to any age. The epics of Ulysses, the story of Abraham, the quest for the Grail, the blue flower of romantic literature, Kafka's Castle, and many other texts celebrate the dynamism behind the stories of human life.

2. Toward which end or goal or dimension are we driven? This question accompanies the entire course of a human life, but a definitive answer is delayed time and again. Obscurity, or rather an enigmatic kind of secrecy, belongs to our Desire and its desideratum. This is part of Desire's fascination and intensity. We would be disappointed by any clear answer. Mephistopheles's declaration that "the secret is revealed"[6] can only forebode devilish boredom. We are on the move toward an unknown but deeply felt or prefelt horizon. This horizon is called by many names: happiness, well-being, *eudaimonia, beatitudo, makariotēs, bonheur, felicidad, geluk, Glückseligkeit*, and so on; but all of these terms are vague, waiting for

further precision that might provide us with a clue. Rather than being an answer, they invite us to participate in a quest.

3. We desire meaning; the greatest fear we have is not fear of death, but fear of meaninglessness, the fear of being useless, not worthwhile, "*bon à rien.*"[7] *Meaning* is one of the most difficult, vague, deep, and obscure words—again a word that invites rather than gives an answer. Its vagueness and obscurity do not justify rejection, however; on the contrary, they prevent us from narrowing the horizon of our quest. Similar to truth, being, thinking, and all basic notions of philosophy, meaning orients our life and thought by indicating a horizon that is at least wide enough to coincide with the universe insofar as this is relevant for human lives.

4. The direction in which Desire points must be discovered by being awakened to it through encounters with desirable persons, things, and adventures. Desire becomes conscious of itself by enjoying or abhorring being touched, surprised, shocked, delighted, or hurt. Without such encounters, Desire would remain indeterminate. Anticipating what must be said about the desired "content," we can already state that different kinds of phenomena have different ways of surprising Desire. They suggest that and how Desire can and must respond to their appearance, thereby offering Desire a chance to discover what it wants.

5. Desire tends toward striving, quest, and conquest because it is the experience of a lack. It does not possess what it desires. Possession can be accompanied by a desire for continuation or future repossession, but a fulfilled desire does not tend toward anything; rather, it enjoys what it has. Lacking what we desire causes displeasure, a sort of pain; fulfillment, on the other hand, is experienced as pleasure, joy, or delight. Often, however, pain and pleasure are indeterminate: I feel "good" or "bad" without being able to say why. Have I acquired what I desired or despised? Often, desire obsesses me without letting me know toward what end I should move. Since I am not in possession of that end—I do not even know it—I suffer without being capable of escaping this pain. Would we feel better if there was no pain or lack at all? We would then not only be content, but we would also be without a quest—playing around like animals, not bothered by the ambition to overcome what we are lacking. Desire keeps us alert and on the move: we are not yet what we want to be. The negation stretches our life toward a better future.

6. Desire is not a need. Hunger and thirst are needs: their satiation is felt as the filling of a void. Other cravings, too, such as greed and the lust for power, can be filled, at least to a certain extent. Many social scientists

and utilitarian philosophers think that all human behavior is motivated by needs. They see a person as a cluster of needs with different ends. Not only money and power, but likewise music, sex, insight, and religion would satisfy specific needs. The motivational system of human action can then be studied as an economy of quantitatively and qualitatively different, but generically homogeneous, impulses. For a scientific study of this economy, a reduction of the qualitative differences to specific quantities would be ideal, if it were possible. The specific urgency of each need and the value of its satisfaction could then be measured by mathematical methods and expressed in terms of money, the great equalizer of all human ends. If you find this picture of human action too vulgar, replace "money" with "value" and talk about the "value system" of the human economy.

Both need and desire lack what they strive for, but the lack of desire cannot be filled as a void. It is not a hunger that can be stilled. As it approaches its desideratum, its intensity and pain grows. Examples can be found easily—not only in the most intimate experiences of the mystics, but also in the desire for love, for justice in the world, for living a meaningful life, and for making other people happy. Such desires do not tend toward consumption, absorption, or assimilation; rather than being a sort of hunger, they are outgoing, ecstatic. Or, as Levinas wrote, "they nourish themselves on their own hunger."[8]

7. The famous thesis that all people strive for *eudaimonia*[9] is not so much a description of the variety of human pursuits as it is a characterization of the human *physis* or "nature" or dynamic "essence." The word *orexis* used in *On the Soul*[10] places the accent on the outreaching character of this essence: it stretches forth beyond the multitude of needs, wants, wishes, and desires toward—what? Desire never and nowhere reaches the end of the future that is opened up by it. Restlessness is the consequence. The unremitting lack of a Desire makes human life a painful task. The temptation is great to flee or repress this pain by attachment to those needs and wants that can be filled and stilled, but Desire will call us back to its unlimited exigency. The voice of conscience cannot be completely muted.

8. Human substance is a particular kind of movement. Desire does not let us stop; once in a while, it might allow us to rest, but its urging does not fade away. Pauses are periods of recollection and preparation for new discovery. As desiring, I am always ahead of myself, somewhere in an unattainable future, which I cannot even imagine. I am caught, painfully withheld from the great Desideratum while at the same time tied to it.

9. The most essential issue of my life, the heart of my heart, lies in a

desired but never attained future. The time of Desire is a delay without end. I am longing for it but cannot grasp it. I extend further than I am, stretched out beyond the measures of all my conquests.

Desire opens up a time of anticipation and frustration. The future given by Desire is not a particular moment or period, but rather the always delayed future beyond the time of a mortal life. What I desire is more indeterminate than death. Although I do not know when I will die, it is certain that I will—but will I reach the most desired end of my life?

10. The time of Desire is threatened. My time might run out before "the thing itself" comes or before I am ready to welcome it. Anxiety thus belongs to our erotic pursuits. Even despair may tempt me. Loss of all hope would block Desire's future, but I am not able to stop the erotic movement, and this is always accompanied by at least some hope. Depression follows blockages; the disappearance of hope causes disgust, *taedium vitae*[11]; even needs and wants and all "values" lose their color and music. Night falls. But how, then, can I go on living?

11. Hope is more essential for Desire than certainty. It looks forward in trust while knowing that success is not guaranteed. Something other than my talents must favor my course. Doing what I can, I look up to Fortune. Certainty changes Desire into expectation. In counting on an event, I do not lose my desire for it, but I am no longer plagued by doubts or ignorance. Certainty can be selective, however. For example, I know that someone comes at a particular time, but I have never seen her face. The secrecy of her face remains as long as I have not met with her. Even if we knew for certain that the Desideratum would overwhelm us at the moment of death, its mystery would remain; but we could nonetheless prepare ourselves for that moment. Some of the indeterminacy would disappear, but how much time is still left before the day of death? By causing us the pain of a continual delay, Desire might seduce us to hasten its fulfillment. Here and now I demand what disturbs me without end. Is this impatience the reason for our idolizations? Endurance is needed for us not to fall prey to the illusory aggrandizement of beauty, knowledge, love, wealth, honor, and so on.

12. Hope trusts that Desire somehow, somewhere, will reach what it desires; but this trust wants signs and signposts along the way. Many persons, things, and events charm our hearts while always pointing simultaneously beyond the horizon of the attainable. Their charm claims our attachment, and this can overwhelm our sense for the beyond. A struggle

ensues to maintain the double signification of all desirabilities. The enjoyment of love, beauty, honor, and peace clarifies the attraction that comes from behind the horizon; every good wants to be enjoyed as it is in and for itself, but this "itself" includes its signifying. In its self-givenness, the enjoyment urges us to follow the suggestions of its pointing. Its own delight is recognized as a hint through which the secret reveals some of its charms while withholding the modeless mode of its own.

13. Is the Desideratum a longed-for event, a final goal that can be realized or acquired in some moment of a human life? If it is, it should last from that moment until death. The preceding periods should then be arranged as approximations or preparations. Several utopias have been imagined as the most desirable goals: justice, peace, happiness, pleasure, beauty. But are we really able to imagine a period of human life that is completely fulfilled? Desire and movement would then be confined to the continuation of that mode of life. Some people claim that they are "perfectly happy." Do they know themselves? Are they lying? Is their happiness what Desire desires?

It seems that we are in a bind: on the one hand, we cannot enjoy life if it does not fulfill at least some of our concrete wants and desires; on the other hand, Desire does not stop at any such fulfillment. Each acquisition is accompanied by the experience of a not-yet: this here and now is not yet what we are longing for. Is the entire course of life an endless repetition of "not-yets"? Must we conclude that Desire renders a fully meaningful life impossible? Or is Desire, as it is described here, a fiction? Is it a romantic supposition, the divinization of some craving that mature adults should have overcome? Romantic artists are not the only ones to have testified to the infinity of human Desire, however; mystics are perhaps more authentic interpreters and their extreme realism has more credibility. If Desire is infinite, whereas life sustains itself with finite conquests, the core question is the following: how can Desire, in its pointing beyond the finite, motivate the ongoing enjoyment of our lives?

14. The movement issuing from Desire changes me. It does not leave my past behind, but conserves it in an ongoing transformation of my existence. Some adventures remain vivid in my memory, but others fade away, although they might have greater impact. Eros is the great transformer; it produces new manners of standing and moving, binding them together as moments of one search. Through desire, I become what I am, but transformed. I cannot escape this law.

15. Is Desire a command, or rather a fate? If I cannot escape this drive, how can it then be an imperative? Desiring itself is not given as a task; it constitutes me, without allowing me to dismiss or abandon it. The only way to stop it is to destroy my very being. Desire does, however, command me in at least three ways. First, it orders me to discover and practice manners of concretization and fulfillment. Second, it demands that I take it up as mine. I must consent to the inexorable fact of my drivenness and accept the responsibility for what it makes me do. Desire hands me over to myself; betrayal is not allowed; I am the one who must live it in a meaningful way. Third, Desire includes a tendency toward purification and authentication.[12] It is itself the criterion for the evaluation of all its concretizations in wishes, wants, appetites, and inclinations. As an erotic being, I am my own standard and highest law, but this "autonomy" precedes the differentiation of reason and emotions. Desire uses reason to help human lives to succeed. It is the source of praxis and theory. Its first command is "Strive for meaning!" From this, all other commands follow: "Prevent or convert all kitsch!" "Purify the impure!" "Overcome the inauthentic through growing authenticity!"

16. As the tendency that transforms the subject, Desire generates a movement of return into the subject itself. Does its exodus coincide with an *odyssea*?[13] Perhaps, but first we must see whether the erotic adventure does not lead to encounters so radically transforming that the returning subject is no longer the departing self. The concretization of Desire reshapes the person who obeys its commands.

17. A project is accomplished when the projected product or skill is produced or acquired. A human life is Desire's project, but when is it complete? Death interrupts completion; rarely does a life seem to be complete before it is replaced with a corpse. Do the dead warn us that life's achievements hardly ever coincide with the desired end?

"I have not yet realized what my Desire urges me to realize." "I already am and am not yet what I have to be." Such sentences are perfectly understandable. Regardless of what certain logicians might say, everyone can recognize these sentences as descriptions of a basic human experience. The delay that belongs to our dynamism is caused by the difference between our factual existence and the demands of our own Desire. If death is an interruption, however, "delay" seems to be a euphemism: will we ever coincide with the end of Desire? Is the contradiction between the desiring ego and the living ego constitutive of the human essence?

18. Having stated that *eudaimonia* lies in the perfect accomplishment of human life according to its typically human possibilities, Aristotle immediately refers to Solon's rather grim and gloomy "*telos horan*!"[14] The orientation of a mortal being toward *eudaimonia* creates an aporia, a dead end: as long as we live, nobody can call us *eudaimōn* (accomplished, happy), because horrible things can still happen to us or be done by us. But how can we call someone happy who is dead? In hindsight, certain heroes and saints might appear to have been *eudaimōn,* but what we say about their lives could be neither said nor experienced by them. "I am happy" thus seems an impossible expression or the hurried expression of a fleeting moment whose continuation cannot be guaranteed. If death is the radicalization of an essential delay, who then could ever say "It is accomplished"?

Is death the end of a human life, its final horizon? If so, do we then live for a final disappearance into nonexistence? We are converted into humus, ashes, earth. Is this what Eros becomes in the end? Can consolation be found in the life of others, the community, the tradition, the history that survives me? This would presuppose that Desire makes me will and wish for what is good for others. Can Desire, although it seems to begin in egoism, manifest itself as profoundly altruistic? Can I—can any individual—ever be entirely reduced to an existence-for-others?

19. Is death indeed the ultimate horizon of a human life? Does the movement of life, generated by Desire, run into nothingness? Is Nothing then the horizon? Or does Life—via generation and corruption—use individuals as temporary instances of its ongoing history? Does the meaning of an individual life lie in its service to a historical community?

If human individuality has a dignity (*Würde*) that cannot be reduced to an interchangeable "value" (*Wert*) within some economy,[15] death is a real problem for any serious thought. The individual's dignity cannot be absorbed by a community, a history, or other individuals; it must be respected and retained as pertaining to this unique person. The temptation is great to interpret the perduring delay (the not-yet) of Desire as a reference to a future beyond death where Desire could be fulfilled. We do not have a representation of such a future, however. Death conquers us by breaking off the line of life.

If fulfillment beyond death is possible, its character must differ radically from the temporal possibilities offered by a mortal life. The expectation of such a fulfillment would change the entire frame of mortality. Desire itself, all of its satisfactions, and the fundamental mood of a hopeful life would refer to a dimension beyond the time of mortality. Can this reference be interpreted as transcendence toward eternity? Infinity? Plato's *Phaedo* is an attempt to exorcise our anxiety through the hope that new mortal existences will be available for us, but the *Phaedrus* argues that the purest souls will be able to escape the endless repetition of one metempsychosis after another in order to enter the dimension of the divine.

20. Reflection on human mortality should not seduce us into thinking of a perennially continuing or repeated existence similar to a mortal human life. Death confronts us with the radical difference between human life as we know it, and the—at least thinkable—possibility of another, nonmortal, nontemporal, nondisappointed life, in which Desire can reach its referent. If this possibility is not a pure fiction, Desire is deeper and reaches further than any mortal life and any temporal experience of the universe. If "being" is identified as that which is manifested in "the world," Desire refers indeed to what is "beyond being"; if "being" encompasses all desirability, however, Desire does not surpass it, because both Desire and being would then transcend time.

The beyond is called the Good, the One, the God, the Absolute, *esse subsistens*, Father, Logos, Fire, Spirit. In following Desire's reference, we may suggest that it points neither at a phenomenon nor at the being or phenomenality of the "world" and its phenomena. The negation involved in the reference, together with the affirmation that lies in Desire itself, allows us to speak about the beyond through a kind of broken analogy. Before we do this, however, we must cope with the aporias indicated above: how do we respond to the limitations and disappointments of our mortal satisfactions, gathered and symbolized in our being condemned to death? Does Desire teach us that humans are impossible beings? Do we want too much, thereby creating our own tragedy? Should we try to limit our desires by practicing heroic asceticism and modesty as antidotes against the *hybris* of an innate or inherited arrogance? Are we victims of Greek, Jewish, Christian, and Muslim mysticism when interpreting our drive as a desire for the Infinite? Should we take a cure against romanticism?

With these questions, we are at a crossroads. The range of the fundamental reference or transcendence is at stake. What is the horizon of a human life? Is it the Infinite, God, the world, humanity, history, finitude, death . . . ? The most important question cannot be answered through formal or structural analyses; it demands a reflective retrieval of real experiences.

Erotic Diversity

Goods and the Good

Diotima taught Socrates that Eros cannot find rest in the beloved, whose beauty is real but limited. Desire pushes us from one desirability to another, from superficial to deeper, from lower to higher forms of beauty. If the ascent succeeds, it leads to a sudden revelation: beauty itself is none of the desirable phenomena that meet us on our journey; it is the secret toward which the entire diversity of beautiful people, things, works, institutions, and stories point as their granting origin.[16]

Beauty—or the Good[17]—itself cannot be the summit of the entire range of good and beautiful phenomena whose qualities and degrees of splendor can be compared. It is not the highest of all, but the incomparable "giving" to which all of them owe their goodness and beauty. It is therefore "beyond" and "before" as well as "in" and "with" all splendid persons, things, and events.[18] However, we would not even have an inkling of beauty itself if we were not touched and moved and delighted by the variety of finite wonders that surround us. There is no way of reaching the Good itself directly, no possibility of bypassing the empirically given diversity of limited goods. If the Good somehow exists, it can be contacted only through and in the desiderata of the many desires that rule our practical, theoretical, and emotional involvement in the empirical world where we live. All of them attract and tempt us; they elicit our activities and promise us some sort of rest, but none of them can completely pacify our yearning. And yet, this world and its attractions are all we have to experience and cultivate. To be possible at all, the experience of the Good itself must therefore be an "aspect" or "moment" or a hidden secret of our dealings with its finite manifestations.

The way in which the Good itself appears desirable, promises fulfillment, and *is*, differs radically from any other appearance and being. To evoke it, we need a series of negations: Desire is not a hunger, not a kind of greed or thirst; the ultimate Desideratum is not beautiful or good, it cannot even be said to be as an entity (not even as the highest one); although absolutely overwhelming, it cannot fulfill; it neither stills nor ends our longing because it is beyond all these, beyond being, and thus most urgent and absolute.

The discovery of this absolute difference does not dissuade us from any attempt at reaching out to it. On the contrary, it intensifies our long-ing. It does not silence the voices of the finite desiderabilia that populate our universe, but rather refers us to them and their call for an appropriate response. Conspiring with our desires, they must give us a taste for a well-ordered "economy" of desirability (a "system" of "values"?), which might reveal to us what it means to be in touch with the Good itself. It is then necessary to explore the world and ourselves insofar as they form an erotic "economy" in which, perhaps, the *erotikon* par excellence will grant us a glimpse of its inescapable absoluteness.

Eclosion and Cultivation

Our desires are ours, but they are awakened by desirabilia that, if we taste them, become desiderata. Awareness of our desires thus emerges from existential experimentation. Even if they are provoked by instruction or imitation, budding desires must go through a phase of personal experience; otherwise, even our motivations would be artificial, improper, or inau-thentic and not really felt.

Sometimes we must learn from others that certain things that seem repulsive are in fact desirable; most often, however, or perhaps always, we must learn how to desire in a proportionate, tasteful, well-attuned, decent way. The ruling culture and our educators have provided us with models, norms, and practices that bring our desires into shape. We are civilized, not savages. The existing culture has even given us a code for preferring certain desiderata over others, a sense of proportion, and guidelines for adequate evaluations. If we obey our culture, we can know—at least with regard to the most common or popular desires and desiderata—what we should de-sire, how we should desire and strive for it, which desiderata we should prefer, and how we should combine the various desiderata and desires that occupy the human soul and scene.

Indeed, desires overlap and conflict with one another. An overall as-sessment therefore seems necessary, but which criterion helps us in estab-lishing a hierarchy that determines the proper claim of every desirability? A particular culture has its own characteristic "spirit" or mentality, which implies one or more criteria for its code of appreciation. But how does your culture justify its criteria? And if you, for some reason, cannot agree with the code of your culture, how will you proceed to establish a hierarchy of your own?

Any hierarchy of desires is a complicated dynamism: not only does the diversity of our desires cause frequent conflicts, it also moves us from one compromise to another. As soon as we seem to have found a kind of erotic balance, we are already on the way to another constellation of combined desires. We are not only driven by a manifold of particular desires, but there is also a desire in us for a good, or rather the best possible, combination of all desiderata. A human life is a journey from constellation to constellation. What is the ideal "economy" of desirability? Or: what is happiness?

Happiness

So long as we see human life as the attempt to obtain the most successful fulfillment of our desires, happiness can be conceived only as the enjoyment of a satisfactory combination of desiderata. This presupposes a successful cooperation of the many drives awakened in us by many attractions. How can I deal with them? Since they compete and often conflict, I must negotiate with them and propose compromises. The more or less peaceful household that results can be characterized by its particular pattern or style; if it is unified, it reveals a dominant "spirit" and will in any case have its own emphases, a characteristic hierarchy, and a specific dynamic structure.

A caricature of happiness can be found in an economic theory of "values" (for example, hedonic values or pleasures) according to which human beings strive for the highest quantity of value. As we have already seen,[19] happiness could be defined through the calculation of the highest volume and intensity of value (or combination of values) if we were able to press the decisive value or values into a quantitative formula. Money is here the great example—and greed is paradigmatic of such a desire for happiness.

Can happiness be reached by accumulation or multiplication? Kant remarks that happiness, although naturally and necessarily desired by all, cannot be grasped by a clear concept.[20] We imagine it as the sum total of utmost satisfaction. This includes the successful harmonization of the many desires that would dissipate us if we were not able to hold them together in an overall unity. However, such a totality cannot be defined or calculated a priori; the most successful unification of our erotic chaos depends on many empirical and contingent features of the circumstances, things, and individuals involved in our actions and passions. The image of complete happiness is thus a rather indeterminate and tentative representation, a kind of guess, rather than a concept whose precise contours could be defined. And yet this vague representation seems to motivate all human ideals and endeavors. Do we not want to acquire happiness for ourselves and others? Disappointment after disappointment cannot convince us to abandon this desire. Moments of bliss seem to point toward an all-encompassing blissfulness in some indeterminate future. Even without proof, hope seems justified. Or must we learn that all these spontaneous reactions to the thought or the word of happiness are surreal, narcissistic, infantile illusions? But even then we should be able to understand the force and structure of that thought.

A conceptually justified definition of eudemonic unity seems impossible unless certain conditions are fulfilled. If one of our many desires could submit all others to itself, either as subordinate means or as integrated elements of its own design, a form of unified happiness would result from the successful achievement of such design. Addiction (for example, to sex, work, alcohol, music, or television) is an example of such a dominant desire, but there are less degrading forms. An artist, for instance, can subordinate all her other desires to full artistic dedication, or a saint could do and think and feel everything only for the sake of its religious significance. When unification depends on one desire that emancipates itself from "the many" to the position of ruler, the desiderata of the other desires are no longer desirable for the sake of themselves. The entire dynamism of life is then restricted to its artistic, religious, alcoholic, or workaholic meaning, unless the dominant desire is not one among many, but rather a metalevel or second-order desire that gathers and encompasses the entire economy of competing desires with their desiderata as components of its own totality. Such a metadesire coincides with the aforementioned desire of an erotic harmony. Several candidates for this formation have been proposed: Are we driven by an overall desire for pleasure? For perfection? For reasonability? For goodness? For being godlike and beautiful?[21]

It is not a priori certain that such an encompassing desire by itself would be able to end the war between the many drives that besiege a human individual. If it itself is a finite desire, its work of unification must limit the desires gathered in it, but how can it do this without some kind of repression or "violence"? A finite metadesire cannot refrain from adding its own limitations to the finitude of its subordinate elements. Perhaps an infinite desire, or rather—since we are human—a desire for and open to the infinite, could offer space and full freedom to all finite desires.

If the question of ethics concerns the success of life as a whole, we must find a way of unifying the dynamic elements that otherwise would disperse and scatter us. Despite all the obscurities that surround the "idea" of happiness, we are obsessed by it; but is it a good candidate for the ultimate beloved reality or rather an idol and illusion? Perhaps we must consider the possibility that happiness becomes less problematic only when it is no longer imagined and desired as the ultimate, but rather as a complement or supplement, conditioned by something less finite. Perhaps the ultimate and absolute Desideratum is not happiness, but something better. The Good itself? That which "makes" us and all things good? If so, how then does happiness relate to the Good and vice versa? Can both be captured by one Desire? If not, how can we be or become one and undivided in ourselves?

Utilitarianism

Utilitarianism assumes that all human desiderata can be seen, evaluated, striven for, and enjoyed as particular kinds of a generic good. Our ability to compare them in order to establish our preferences and choices presupposes that they represent variations on a common theme, differentiations of a generic quality that constitutes their desirability. Once this quality is sufficiently grasped, it functions as the criterion for designating things or experiences as good, whereas the principle of preferences lies in the degree to which that quality is present in a desired good. For example, if the overall quality that constitutes desirability is pleasure (or, more precisely, pleasurability), the principle of preference lies in the higher quantity (volume, duration, and/or intensity) of that quality. If we are able to formalize this quantity (for example, the duration and intensity of pleasure) in mathematical terms, we can invent a calculus to create a scientific ethics (for example, in the form of a mathematically supported hedonism).

But how can we agree on the generic quality that makes certain ends desirable? And how can we prove that it can be translated into quantitative terms? The latter question is sometimes answered by pointing out that we continually demonstrate our preferences for certain ends by paying a higher price for them. Money or some equivalent is the element by which our comparisons of more or less desirable things are expressed. It would be sufficient to ask how much someone is willing to pay for different kinds of goods to discover the evaluative hierarchy of this person.

That this quasi-economic theory is inadequate becomes apparent when we try to insure personal manuscripts or family pictures and other souvenirs. The theory becomes scandalous, however, when someone asks how much it costs to rape a person or buy somebody's convictions.

The first question is even more difficult to settle in economic terms. Some would argue that even on the generic (meta)level, the choice of a certain quality that could serve as the criterion for evaluation can be discovered by observing how much people are willing to pay (or to give or to endure) for each of the various (generic) goods that present themselves, such as pleasure, joy, a peaceful conscience, the well-being of many people, self-interest, human perfection, a great culture, the church, or the glory of God. The mistake of this proposal is twofold. (1) Although it is interesting for sociology, psychology, and history to know what and how most people desire, it does not answer the question of what is (in truth) desirable, because the latter entails what people should (or ought to) desire, even if they don't. (2) A theory that proposes one of the above-mentioned generic "goods" as the one that ought to be pursued in all more specific and concrete strivings, cannot present it as competing with other generic goods, because that would imply that it is not the overall genus, but again only one kind of good among others, although the theory claims it as *the* criterion. Why does it deserve a higher place? If this question makes sense, we have to move to a higher level: What is the generic quality that is represented as quantitatively preferable by the proposed desideratum?

Are we then to give up the idea that all desiderabilia are species of one genus? Are we perhaps even abandoning our hope that our many drives can be bound together in one satisfactory unity? If we are condemned to erotic dissipation, if harmony and happiness are delusions, human life is a story of negotiation and war, interrupted by periods of truce and partial satisfaction. Polytheism is then the norm, although the competition among the gods may lead to various hegemonies according to the victory of, for example, Wealth (*Ploutos*), Power (*Zeus*), or "Love" (*Aphrodite*).

Desires and Desiderata

When Plato contrasts the philosophical life with a life that is obsessed by *epithumiai*, his examples are most often taken from gastronomic and sexual hedonism. As expressions of our similarity to animals, eating, drinking, and sex represent those desires that must either be civilized in order to become human or else be left to their own devices, which then will lead to inner division and self-enslaving tyranny. *Askēsis* and sublimation are needed to purify these desires from their ugly, antiphilosophical, unethical savagery. Plato's polemics against hedonistic theories insist on the contrast between these "lower" desires and higher ones, whereas the *Symposium* and the *Phaedrus* show how erotic desires can be transformed into love for spiritual beauty and fecundity in oneself and others.[22]

Although the sublimation of eros has been a popular topic in western thought and literature, I have not found much on the radical difference between the animal mode of eating and drinking, on the one side, and their human, civilized mode, on the other. There are plenty of treatises on culinary and enological arts and table manners, but a true phenomenology of eating as a typically human activity is lacking. And yet, such a phenomenology is needed to refute all theories that conceive of human beings as composed of a spiritual and an animal (or merely corporeal) part. There is nothing properly animal in human lives: all their parts and elements are always already different from parallel elements in animals; they are entirely human, although there are many human modes. Only humans can be bestial, for example, or neat or refined or becoming and so on. If dogs or cats behave "neatly," they are either interpreted through our metaphors or humanized to some extent by daily participation in human ways of life.

Civilization and sublimation of quasi-animal desires would not be possible (1) unless these desires are transformable, and (2) unless humans also have other, "higher," more "sublime" desires that can assume and reshape the former.

The desire for eating is a need, but it can be cultivated for its own sake, for example, as an urge to overeat. It also can be refined, but then one has to have good taste. Civilization involves more than neediness; the stylization of our needs betrays a specific taste. But taste must be learned and developed through interaction with an already existing culture. The latter would not be possible if we were not bound to certain communities by the desire for being at home in some social constellation. We have desires for friendship, love, belonging to a family or a nation, but also desires for being useful, just, beautiful, good, the "best"; we have aesthetic, moral, cognitive, spiritual, and religious desires. Are we then a legion of different drives or is there rather one Desire that encompasses all of them as the details of its own self-differentiation?

A classification and phenomenology of our erotic multiplicity is possible only through successive concentration on particular desiderata, but the question of their unity must be kept in mind. Does this unity lie in a specific constellation of particular desires, rather than in one ultimate Desire that is their origin and end?

Several constellations are possible and real. According to their different emphases, we can distinguish hedonistic, aesthetic, ethical, moralistic, religious, and other styles of life and then further distinguish them in more precise categories. If one ultimate Desire binds them together, this will permeate and inspire all of them.

If "good" is equivalent to "desirable," all other desiderata will owe their final goodness to the ultimate Desideratum, but this relationship does not preclude any characteristic goodness that differentiates them from one another. Neither does it preclude the possibility that one particular (and therefore limited) style of life—for example, an aesthetic and artistic one—might be *the* way in which certain individuals realize their allegiance to the ultimate end or "good." However, if one Desideratum is the ultimate and encompassing one—that is, if we must reject polytheism as the ultimate truth—it necessarily conditions and codefines the meaning and the worth of all desiderata and desires. Without it, there would then be no final meaning for a human life.

The search for authentic desirability can be led only by our already active desires, most of which have been civilized by education and adaptation. But can we trust them? How do we know that our desires and the hierarchy that until now has prevailed among them, are authentic? Are we able to distinguish (more) authentic and pure desires in us from inauthentic and perverted attractions? Where do we find a criterion?

Since Plato and Aristotle, the western tradition has located the criterion in human nature (*physis, natura*) or essence (*ousia, eidos, idea, essentia*). But do we (who might be corrupted) have access to the purity of our "nature" beneath or hidden in the factual mixture of our erotic existences? The culture to which we owe our formation is no safe guide, because it might be as corrupted as we are or even more. How then can we trust the wisdom of its customs, proverbs, sermons, poetry, and philosophy?

Just as a blurred perception can only be corrected by a better perception, a corrupt desire cannot be purified unless new contacts with the desideratum convince us of a better appreciation (or depreciation). The criterion lies in a better, purer, more exact orientation and evaluation. And only such an evaluation can reveal what was wrong with corrupted estimations.

Spontaneous desires must be treated as initial indications of a certain phenomenon's goodness. However, suspicion is justified until we have fulfilled the conditions of an appropriate katharsis. The question of Desire therefore presupposes not only a study of all the desiderata as they present themselves with the demand that we respond to them in an appropriate way, but also an analysis of the kathartic process that eros must undergo to know what it should desire.

CHAPTER 5

Correspondence

Following the formal description of Desire and desires, we began focusing on the desirable "objects" or "ends" to which they orient us. A systematic phenomenology of human desiderata would demand a reconnaissance of the entire universe, its various dimensions, levels, entities, qualities, and so on. Since we are already involved in these dimensions, we do have experience with the desirable and undesirable aspects of the things, plants, animals, persons, stars, events, communities, and stories that populate the universe. On the basis of our experiences, we can now treat more systematically a question that we have already answered in a rather immediate way: to what extent do the various entities or events correspond to our desires, or vice versa? We like a good Bourgogne and find pleasure in a sunny day; we desire good company and long for love; Mozart's last concertos for piano and orchestra touch us deeply; and we have always wanted to enjoy visiting the Alhambra again. However, we abhor violence and cruelty, injustice and hardship, extreme heat and cold, and all other pains and evils that the world contains. They do not correspond to our desires. But we are also aware that our reactions to them are not always appropriate; we are not always patient or hospitable enough to give them a chance. We are bound to our universe in a variety of mutual responses, but correspondence can be a problem.

By asking whether certain occurrences correspond to my desire, I make myself the standard by which they must be measured. When this standard is seen as the criterion for distinguishing good and bad, I myself, as a desirous subject, am the judge: good is what I feel or consider to be desirable, whereas the contrary is bad. Some of my desires will conflict with one another if I cannot combine them according to the patterns of combination and subordination that are available to me. How can these patterns be justified? Shall I just appeal to myself as the judge? Surely, I myself want to manage the erotic economy of my motivations.

Certain modes of questioning privilege the subject by conceiving of the universe as being for the sake of it. One expression of such questioning is utilitarian: the overriding interest concerns the use or utility of all things, events, and persons. Are they useful for me? Do they satisfy me, give me pleasure, make me "happy"? If these questions become obsessions—or if they have become so "normal" that other interests and questions no longer come to mind—the subject's universe will coincide with the totality of useful things and relations. All other beings become insignificant, or they are not even perceived. A utilitarian outlook reduces the universe, humanity, and history to a small world—as small as the subject who creates it. Other forms of subjectivism are also possible: some artists despise utilitarianism because they are fascinated by the aesthetic side of the reality, whereas moralists are blind to all that remains outside of their struggle between the morally good and bad.

By making the subject's desire the supreme criterion for correspondence, the universe is viewed, shaped, interrogated, and evaluated according to the demands of that desire. However, should we not first investigate and evaluate the quality of this desire and the subject who appeals to it? By taking for granted that the actual desire of any subject can function as the measure for evaluation, contingent subjects and contingent desires are idolized. Such idolization constitutes the fundamental mistake of all subjectivisms.

A long-standing tradition, attested to in the work of philosophers such as Parmenides, Empedocles, and Plato, has insisted on the necessity of initiation, conversion, purification (katharsis), and illumination. Not only philosophical inquiry, but also our most basic perceptions presuppose that the subject be open, well oriented and well attuned, willing, and unimpeded to receive and perceive the given as it is given. Many obstacles—public opinion and the customs of the ruling culture, the dogmas of the learned, and especially the habits of the perceiver—are interposed between "the soul" and the phenomena of the world with which it is engaged. Actual desires are not necessarily pure; most often, they are contaminated, overrated, idolized, or linked to wrong desires and things. The question of what really is desirable differs greatly from the question of what many or most people deem desirable. The array of factual wants, wishes, desires, and inclinations cannot provide the answer to the first question. Voting procedures and statistics are powerless; only true and pure desires—not "the facts"—provide the answer. Appeals to the subject are therefore justified only when there is at least some guarantee that the subject's desire is pure or that the subject itself, although not yet entirely pure, somehow knows or senses what pure desires desire.

A pure desire desires what is truly desirable. This sentence implies that the desiring subjects themselves must be evaluated before they can be recognized as judges possessing a criterion in themselves. The standard by which they must themselves be judged lies in a perfect subject, who, in this context, is the subject of pure desires. How the factual subjects and their desires relate to this standard must be investigated, but the first task of an ethics is to discover what pure desires are and how they relate us to the truly desirable "objects" of the universe.

Perceptivity

A perception is good when it perceives what is really there. A desire is pure when it moves us toward something truly desirable. Striving for a certain desideratum requires that we prepare ourselves for a successful encounter with it, for example, in the form of acquisition or union. Such a preparation implies adjustment to the particular features of the desired entity. In the encounter, I must open, adjust, attune, and adapt myself to the reality of what I want to be united with. The desired union is not possible if I do not adequately respond to the specific nature of the desideratum. The same is true of perception: to perceive well, I must be open to the object without forcing it to fit into any preconceived pattern; I must make myself as receptive as possible and adjust to the conditions of its presentation. There are many ways of distorting the givenness of the given. I have already mentioned the utilitarian, the aesthetic, and the moralistic ways. However, there is also the scientific way, and this is perhaps the most stubborn and dangerous. By reducing all phenomena to objects for an "objective," nonengaged, calculating, and manipulating relation, it excludes many others, among which are the most interesting features of the world. The "objective" outlook is excellent for a particular kind of study, which has proven its worth in the scientific explanation and technological use of nature, but it is blind to many typically human features of speech, sight, touch, thought, art, and religion. To give or manifest themselves as they are, such phenomena need other modes of reception. By forcing them into the patterns of scientific observation, we cannot see or hear or feel what and how they are. We could even use moral and juridical metaphors: good, exact, appropriate perception "respects" the phenomena and "does them justice" by allowing them to show what and how they really are.

We began by asking what in the universe corresponds to the desires of a human subject and discovered that desires themselves must be purified. We now have seen that the phenomena in the universe "want" and "demand" us to correspond to the manifestation of what and how they are. *Correspondence* is thus also a name for our capacity to respond appropriately to all that is given. Even on the most elementary level of epistemology, there are radical differences between appropriate and inappropriate, open and closed, receptive and obsessive attitudes. Not everyone is able to give an adequate description of how things are. A truly empirical study demands from us many virtues: we must be free of unsuitable patterns and distorting prejudices and have a refined sense for distinguishing the proper character of the various phenomena that surprise us. If we realize the difficulty of describing, for example, a flower or a face, we might discover that our perception is often sloppy and imprecise, and that we betray the phenomena by replacing them with images or "ideas" that are in our mind.

Each kind of being and each individual entity demands a distinctively appropriate approach to be perceived as that which it shows itself to be. The perceiver must learn how to approach it, but this can only be done in the encounter itself. The paradox implied here refers us to a problem that is thematized in Aristotle's *Nichomachean Ethics*: how can a nonvirtuous person become (that is, learn to be) virtuous? The answer is: to be courageous, one must repeatedly act courageously until it becomes a habit. But how can we begin to act courageously?[1] The habit of perceiving well is one of the epistemological virtues required by philosophy in order to do justice to the reality of all there is. To acquire this virtue, we must turn away from the falsifying habits that we have developed under the influence of popular manners of representation, public opinion, science, the media, or other delusions. Conversion and refinement of the senses are necessary for authentic observation and faithful description. Phenomenology requires purification.

Katharsis

To take things and persons for what they really are, one must have a clear eye, a sensitive touch, a sharp nose, a fine ear, a refined sense, and a good feel. How can we acquire these? By looking at, listening to, touching, or feeling aspects of beings that are out there and in here. Our senses do not become better by turning inward or outward, but only by coming in contact with the proper modes of being and occurring through which "inner" and "outer" phenomena make themselves known.

The point of opposition between exteriority and interiority is debatable; the threshold that is supposed to separate them is certainly not a clear boundary. We can even defend the thesis that we *are* the world or that "the *psyche* somehow is all things."[2] But for our purpose, it suffices to use this contrast in an average, nonanalyzed sense. The only awareness we need in this context is the insight that each affection of the mind by some phenomenon is simultaneously an affection of the mind by itself. When touched by something, I feel myself touched by it; when surprised by a melody, I am aware of my being charmed; in looking at a tree, I am sensing my own admiration for its glorious crown. The apperception that accompanies all perceptions is an experience of the experience in which I am involved when affected by something else.

If our experience of something is always also the experience of this experience as mine, all experience is double: it encompasses my being affected by something *and* my being affected by this, my own, experience. This makes it possible, even inevitable, that I am involved with something other and at the same time remain related to, and thus in some sense distinct from, that involvement.

As we saw earlier, experience is never a "value free," merely factual event; it also always has a normative moment. In looking at a flower, I cannot refrain from seeing to what extent it is beautiful; in feeling the sun on my skin, I unavoidably feel whether its warmth is pleasant or not. This law of experience governs not only our response to the phenomena, but also our experience of that response. Self-experience as apperception and "meta-experience" of our phenomenal experiences include evaluation. In experiencing how I am affected by and am responding to some phenomenon, I evaluate the quality of this response. For example, I hear myself answer someone in an angry tone and at the same time feel that this response is not appropriate. Or I have the impression that some person I know is standing there, far away, in the horizon—but do I see her clearly? Let me look more carefully. Field glasses may help, but in any case, only some kind of second look can resolve my doubt. Or, again, I am enjoying a piece of music, but is my taste good? Should I enjoy this music? Is this music good enough to be enjoyed?

If an experience always coincides with a critical evaluation of it, we can understand that the style of our experiences can change. If I feel that my way of responding to a colleague is not appropriate, I might try to change it. The same is possible with regard to landscapes, institutions, dogs, birds, trees, the air, the night, and so on. The evaluation of our habitual ways of responding to phenomena implies the possibility—and often the actuality—of self-criticism: I do not (yet) correspond adequately to the things, animals, persons, and events that surprise me; I do not give them the opportunity they need to display what and how they are; I should be more open, more hospitable, less suspicious.

If all experiences and habits of responding are evaluated by the very subject of those experiences, where then does this subject find the criterion for its evaluation? It cannot be found in the evaluated experience or habits because these are under investigation. Does the criterion lie in the accompanying "metaexperience" of the evaluated experience? This can only be the case if this metaexperience either somehow knows or senses which mode of responding to the experienced phenomenon is the correct one, or if it possesses a general rule for correct responses in general. In the first hypothesis, the metaexperience itself anticipates the right form of the first-order experience; in the second, it knows what correspondence as such is and we should try to make that knowledge explicit.

However, even a metaexperience can be criticized, for example, by someone who holds a different standard for correctly responding to the phenomena, or by myself in retrospect. It is possible, for instance, that I look back on the history of my musical taste and find my former self-evaluations too sentimental. In such cases, the criterion of my critical metaexperience has changed.

If we take "conscience" in a very broad sense, it is equivalent to the kind of (implicit or explicit, conscious or preconscious) "knowledge" that enables human beings to evaluate their own responses to the phenomena. There are considerable differences between individual consciences, however. Some consciences are "lax," others "strict," "rigorous," or "demanding." Apparently, consciences, too, can and must be evaluated. But what then is the criterion for this evaluation? Where can we find the conscience of all consciences? It must somehow "have" or "know" or "contain" the supreme standard that permits us to evaluate the very criteria of all factual consciences, metaexperiential evaluations, and straightforward experiences. At least three levels are involved in the constitution of the perceptive, affective, and practical reception of the phenomena. All three are bound to one another and to the phenomena by the imperative of correspondence. To be recognized as they truly are, appearing beings require a completely uninhibited mind. Since most minds are contaminated, however, most perceptions are blurred approximations. To adequately evaluate the responses involved in each experience, the metaexperiential criterion must accord with the supreme criterion, which is nothing else than the imperative of perfect correspondence. But how does our consciousness recognize the concretization of that criterion? How do we know whether we do or do not allow beings to be what and how they are and how they "want" to be seen, heard, or felt?

The only way to answer this question is by getting in touch with those very beings while maintaining a healthy suspicion about our ability to do them full justice and checking whether our spontaneous impressions and descriptions really correspond to their appearance. We are steeped in standard modes of perception that have become ours through education in a typically modern culture. Even on the most basic level of our contact with places, periods, things, plants, animals, and persons, we are children of modernity, incapable of seeing and hearing in ways characteristic of other times.[3] When we become aware of the perceptual differences among various epochs, several responses are possible. Modern arrogance will regard its own ways of sensing, thinking, and acting as superior and will judge those of other epochs as false, primitive, or subordinate; it prefers scientific observation over an open mind. Another, more humble response opens our selves to the possibility that other modes of perception and other styles of response might show aspects of being that we have ignored or "forgotten" as a result of our fascination with standard manners of access.

It is a great mistake to think that all human beings are equally perceptive. This illusion might seem to be true to those who restrict themselves to simplified cases of perception, for example, seeing glasses on a table or cats on mats; but even in these cases, minimal analysis shows how difficult it is to perceive exactly what is going on.[4] It is clear as day that the timbre of Jesse Norman's voice, the harmonies of Brahms's symphonies, the aesthetic qualities of Van Eyk's paintings, or the religiosity of Teresa's writings require appropriate aptitudes to be perceived and appreciated at all. Blindness, deafness, and insensitivity are more widespread than a "democratic" empiricism is willing to concede. Perceptivity demands education; to be civilized means in the first place that one has acquired sensitive senses and a refined taste.

The learning process required for openness and precision can be helped by contrasting the mode of perception characteristic of our epoch with those of other epochs, but also by following the indications through which masters of perception and correspondence in our own culture point at unnoticed, hitherto "invisible," phenomenality and experiences. Such indications are given by certain poets, musicians, painters, architects, heroes of morality, saints, and mystics, but also by less cultured persons insofar as they are not contaminated by science and standard philosophies. Some poetic descriptions, for example, might at first appear strange, from another time, "primitive," uninformed, and so on, but when we look at the described phenomenon a second time, we might discover that they have indeed captured something we had neglected or repressed.

Others whose "soul" is more accurate than mine show me how our senses can be refined. Can I achieve such refinement on my own? This seems possible, for instance, when my responses to a certain phenomenon, for example, a human face, indicate a perceptive mode that causes me trouble or makes me suspicious, motivating me to try a radically new approach. The success of such an attempt is not guaranteed, however. Perhaps most of us will fall back into the old habits that initially created the problem, unless we are helped by others who have the genius of seeing, hearing, and feeling anew.

At this point, we have reached the intersection of phenomenology and hermeneutics. The ideal of phenomenology includes a fresh, unprejudiced description of what the phenomena themselves show of themselves to a completely open mind. However, the development of phenomenology has led to the conviction that no unprejudiced mind exists, because all minds are already shaped by the various cultural patterns and modes of representation, thanks to which they have become civilized. Some authors conclude from this discovery that the initial ideal of phenomenology should be given up. According to them, it is impossible to separate the various cultural elaborations from a precultural dimension that would present us with a hermeneutical kind of relativism. This result is neither necessary nor appropriate, however. It neglects the undeniable truth that some descriptions—or interpretations, as they prefer to say—are better, more perceptive, and more accurate than others. Only if some criterion is operative are we capable of recognizing certain descriptions as more revealing than others, and such a recognition is necessary if we want texts and other interpretations to help us perceive and understand the phenomenal reality. Hermeneutics, as the critical interpretation of interpretations, does a service to the phenomenological project by analyzing and comparing various interpretations of the phenomenal reality and offering some of them as more appropriate than others. Whether, indeed, some of these interpretations are adequate depends on the possibility of discovering through them the reality as it is. In other words, hermeneutics makes progress in correspondence possible.

Present and past descriptions of the world and its components constitute the "text," or rather the library, from which we learn how to receive and respond to the reality in which we are involved. However, we do not have the capacity to fathom all books and cultures competing for our attention. The ideal of an "*uomo universale*" is an illusion. In fact, we live within the confines of a limited conglomerate of cultures, subcultures, and traditions. We belong to specific families with their own genealogies,[5] out of which we compose our own variations. Hermeneutics links us to several family histories, but each of us remains responsible for the way in which we appropriate and renew them. Without belonging to a family history, I would hardly perceive anything interesting in the world; but without the variety of its interpreters, a heritage would die.

The word *tradition* indicates the continuity of an always already given, always retrieved and renewed history, in which a cultural or spiritual community generates a loyal but transformative posterity, thanks to which the past becomes a future. Without tradition, a human being would be an anthropoid, the mere possibility of civilization and culture. Good manners of eating and drinking, cooking, building, praying, and thinking would not exist if their authors had not been formed within the traditions that they maintain by selectively transforming them. This is as true of Hobbes, Descartes, Spinoza, and Kant as it is of religious innovators. Self-made persons do not exist; all skills and works are produced by a combination of tradition and retrieval, even on the level of affection and perception.

For example, to see that another person's face, as such, forbids me to kill that person is an authentic experience described in the work of Emmanuel Levinas.[6] Many critics have attacked this work, claiming that it is unphilosophical because, they argue, Levinas replaces the phenomenological description he owes us with quotes from the sacred scriptures of his religious faith. Several answers to this objection are possible. To begin with, religious scriptures are not necessarily less perspicacious in perception, affection, and thought than the profane writings of Descartes, Kant, or Quine. However, the point that should be made within the context of a confrontation between phenomenology and hermeneutics is the following. Many people do not see that "Do not kill me!" is written on the face of all human beings, nor do many see that all persons have basic human rights, even though they believe that this is the case. But why do they not see this, while Levinas and others claim to see both truths and try to make them visible to others? Could it be that one must first have learned from an existent tradition, via parents or educators, that the other is inviolable, a truth that later on can be perceived as shining forth from the very presence of the other's face? If this were the case, the retrieval of a traditional conviction precedes an awakening of the senses to the truth of what really and phenomenally is there to be seen. Although it is really visible, we would not see it without the guidance of that tradition. Once our eyes are opened, however, an appeal to the tradition is no longer needed; instead of believing what it says, we have seen that it is true. The actual awakening to a new view or insight might most often be a combination of one's own efforts and guidance by others; to oppose these factors as different in time is probably too schematic, but in any case, we must recognize that even sensation and perception have a historical dimension.

Similar arguments can be given with regard to the mystical experiences of John of the Cross, Teresa of Avila, and many other extraordinary as well as ordinary persons. What they perceive cannot be declared inauthentic on the grounds that most people are not aware of having such experiences. This fact—if it is one—is not an objection if we presume that mystical experiences are conditioned by a high degree of purity and love. The average dispositions of average people are not authentic enough, although they may vaguely recognize in themselves some echoes of what the mystics wrote about.

The difference between better and worse perceptions is accepted by all psychologists and philosophers when they restrict themselves to less interesting levels of observation. The reason for this is that these levels permit more "democratic" checking procedures than the levels of art, morality, religion, taste, and refinement. However, authenticity and democracy make poor bedfellows. Refined senses belong to the best in each domain, and the levels that everyone can check are the most trivial.

Again, the conclusion must be that katharsis is a necessary condition for all ethics. Before we ask which "objects," ends, or rules must govern the distinction between a good and a bad life, we must ask who might be considered to be exemplary in the art of experience and how we can acquire excellence in that art. Apprenticeship in experiencing is certainly helped by good examples and traditions, but the final answer to the question of whether an experience is accurate can be given only in the very attempt to correctly respond and adjust to the phenomena as they "want" to be received. Even the selection of examples and traditions depends on that answer. We seem to move in a circle, but somewhere in the encounter itself, there is the beginning and the end.

Questions

If correspondence is understood as the appropriate response, coming from the heart, to the realities that occur to us, to me, it is certainly an important principle of ethics, perhaps even *the* principle. However, the schematic picture suggested above is much too simple. Many questions must be asked and answered before we can determine the extent of its relevance.

A first question arises from the suggestion that the human task would lie primarily in an appropriate response to each and every phenomenon encountered. Not only human faces and words, but also animals, trees, landscapes, and skies, would have their characteristic claims. What, however, about the human subject itself? Can the rule of correspondence be extended to myself, insofar as I am also confronted with my own being as a phenomenon that claims recognition, justice, respect? If so, is self-recognition, as demanded from me, similar to my recognition of other phenomena? Should we not rather presume that I myself and all other phenomena are so different that it is hardly possible to subsume them under one and the same categorical language?

A special problem emerges in this context when we focus on the phenomenological differences between the claim that is revealed in the appearance of other humans and the one that is revealed in my own existence. Self-respect is not merely an instance of the general respect we owe to all human individuals.

A second complex of questions emerges from the fact that we never deal with isolated phenomena, but always with phenomenal constellations in which not only the studied phenomena but also we ourselves are involved. Even the most intense concentration on a singular object or event is engaged in a context and coperceives a universe within which the perceiver as well as the object is situated. An obvious instance of this can be found in our moods. In boredom or melancholy we are aware of the specific way in which our life-as-a-whole is attuned to our world-as-a-whole. When we feel heavy or light, somber or sunny, peaceful, grateful, or content, we feel how we are in touch with the universe. As part of a referential world, I deal with shifting constellations rather than with singular phenomena.

A third question regards the role that the principle of correspondence seems to attribute to the human subject. If it is our primary task to adapt ourselves to claims that come from elsewhere and precede our initiatives, are we then not condemned to the secondary role of reactors instead of being recognized as free—that is, original and creative—actors? Is "correspondence," as it is proposed here, a mask for an anti-Nietzschean reactivity or a reactionary anti-Marxism?

The fourth question that must be answered concerns a suggestion that might be read into an incomplete description of the phenomena that challenge us. If the universe is nothing else than a totality of phenomena whose claims order us to act in an appropriate way, does this assumption not entail that all phenomena are good, insofar as they tell us how to (re)act in order to be good? Does an ethics of correspondence presuppose the innocence of the cosmos as it is or as it was before human interference? Are we, in our freedom, the sole culprits, while all other beings are standards of goodness? Even if that were true, does "the real world," spoiled as it is by millennia of human corruption, allow us to distinguish the pure voices and commands of animals, events, faces, words, and so on from the tainted responses for which we humans are responsible?

In the following pages, I will begin to answer these questions, although I will change the order in which they have been listed here.[7] Obviously, a fully satisfactory answer presupposes the resolution of many epistemological and ontological arguments. We may therefore expect that the beginning will never end.

Situations

A treatise on ethics cannot be developed from the mere rule of correspondence if the latter is understood as timely and appropriately responding to individual phenomena (that is, appearances, objects, persons, occurrences, events). No phenomenon is isolated, and we cannot sever any thing or event from the situation in which we deal with it. "Circumstances" cannot be negated as if they provided only accidental surroundings; they are a constitutive part of all phenomena and of our dealings with them. Both they and we are situated.

A situation is, to begin with, a particular space and time defined and delimited by a characteristic constellation of phenomenal elements, a specific climate and rhythm, its own relationships to other situations, and a place of its own in the universe in which we move. Providing a complete description of each situation is a highly complicated task, because all of its experientially relevant components and aspects must be taken into account. Its relations to many other situations and to the existential universe in which it is situated cannot be left out. It seems, then, that we cannot discover the true reality of one single phenomenon without a full reconnaissance of the totality from which it emerges. Does the correct identification of one phenomenon presuppose a complete phenomenology of the universe? The answer could be that its description indeed demands a phenomenology of the encompassing constellation within which we, together with that phenomenon, are situated, but that all our descriptions remain incomplete and to a certain extent conjectural because we can never fully describe the totality. At the same time, we can still refer to the predescriptive, perceptive awareness of an individualized world. We feel and sense, in an often vague but perceptive way, how we ourselves and the other phenomena fit or do not fit into our and their surroundings. More than an explicit phenomenology, this "pathic" awareness orients our responses to the surprises that we encounter. Appropriate responses primarily depend on predescriptive attunement and sensitivity, rather than on explicit insight or theory.

If a concrete ethics of correspondence cannot be based on the generalities that have been formulated up to this point, and if the situations in which we must act are too particular and distinct from one another to be neglected or generalized, how then can we be more specific? In order to concretize our principle, we must at least distinguish the types of situated phenomena and the types of possible responses-to-phenomena-in-particu-lar-situations. Even then we would not be able to prescribe exactly how in-dividuals in individual circumstances should act; but we could at least set more specific standards for our behavior. The following chapters are at-tempts to sketch some ethically relevant features of different kinds of phe-nomena in particular situations. If we succeed, we will have clarified the sug-gestions and demands that are contained in their appeal to our benevolence.

However, will we not discover that the considerations of the present chapter are based on assumptions that fit only certain phenomena and sit-uations? Does not the very idea of a general theory about phenomenality, claims, appropriateness, and so on presume, without justification, that all "kinds of" phenomena, beings, claims, responses fit the general character-istics given here? Such a supposition cannot be taken for granted, however. Is a person, for instance, situated in the same sense as a stone or a cloud? Is your looking at me the same sort of activity as your looking at a flower? (Does the verb *look* have the same meaning in these two cases?) Perhaps the "analogy of being" (and thus of phenomenality, suggestion, ought, and appropriateness) will force us to amend the general statements asserted here. Or will we have to conclude that such statements can be justified only as a provisional access to more fundamental questions?

Nature

As we have seen, ethical thought cannot begin unless it accepts an ex-isting ethos as its—albeit provisional—point of departure. But every ethos must be tested, because its mere existence is not a sufficient reason for ad-hering to it as a perfect code and criterion for judging what is good or bad. Moral criteria can be chosen neither arbitrarily nor in the name of a par-ticular education or tradition; neither can they be derived from valueless facts. If the criteria are not self-evident, they must be derived from other criteria that impose their truth immediately.

"Correspondence" is here proposed as a general, still rather indeter-minate, criterion. Can it be developed into an outline of a normative, eth-ical code that would be valid in all cultures? Is such a proposal, or even the attempt to discover such a criterion, too ambitious? Is it too naive, too pre-postmodern to be taken seriously? The latter suspicion could arise in the minds of those who hear in "correspondence" a thinly veiled rehashing of a long-standing tradition according to which the "nature" (*physis*) or "essence" (*essentia*) of human and other beings plays a central role in ethics. Do we want to continue or to amend, without rejecting, the Greek, medieval, and early modern philosophy of "nature" as the principle of moral, juridical, and political evaluation? Would it be possible to define good behavior as acting "according to nature" (*secundum naturam*) or "in consonance with nature" (*homologoumenōs tēi physēi*)?

In order to understand the role of *physis* and *natura* in the Greek, Roman, and medieval literature, it is, of course, necessary to thoroughly forget the modern, scientific, and philosophical theories of nature; instead, we should try to reevoke the premodern *kosmos* as it was experienced in the religious contexts that were taken for granted before the modern "master and possessor of nature"[8] began ignoring them.

Here is not the place to give a summary of the fascinating story of *physis* from the pre-Socratics to our times[9]; but a few reminders can be offered to indicate the ethical relevance that has been attached to it for more than two thousand years.

"To live in consonance with *physis*" was the central commandment of stoicism; although its roots lie in the pre-Socratic literature, philosophy, and medical theory, Plato and Aristotle were its most rigorous analysts. Not only etymologically, but also with respect to their impact on the imagination of the philosophers who referred to them, the words *physis* and *natura* evoked living beings, especially plants, trees, and animals. Birth, growth, flourishing, degeneration, and death were key concepts and privileged metaphors in the elaboration of the role of nature. *Zōia* (living beings) were paradigmatic when "nature" was opposed to a variety of nonnatural things such as human choice, positing (*thesis*), art (*technē*), learning (*paideia*), and imitation (*mimēsis*). Nature had its own mode of appearance, shape (*eidos, morphē*), and being (*ousia*), its own way of emerging, moving, and dying (*genesis, kinēsis, phthora*), its own telos and law (*nomos*), and its own pattern of unfolding, including several processes of compensation for deficiencies, defense against harmful influences, self-restoration after damage, and overcoming of any excess. The various expressions of nature's independence and self-governance show its autonomy and autarky—notwithstanding divine as well as human powers of dissent with regard to the natural course of things.

Humans and even gods were not seen as opponents of nature; they belonged within the all-encompassing cosmos, which was entirely dominated by its "physical" character and laws. *Physis* ruled all beings, granting them their particular forms and movements. Humans themselves were oriented, driven, guided, and cared for by their own human nature, which was a part of all-encompassing Nature.

Jewish and Christian thinkers transformed this cosmic vision into another worldview while preserving many of its Greek and Hellenistic elements. In their universe, all gods lost their power to the one Creator of heaven and earth who did not submit to Nature, Fate, or any other might. In light of creation, all things had their own "nature" and "natural laws," but these, as gathered in one overall code (*lex naturalis*), were now interpreted as the finite expression of God's own will as unfolded in the divine and "eternal law" (*lex aeterna*).[10] The "natural inclinations" (*inclinationes naturales*), by which the various beings were oriented and driven, expressed what God wanted them to become and accomplish. Obedience to the rules that were implied in their innate orientation was understood as conformity to God's master plan. The proper nature of things provided them with the program for their activities—it was the inborn guidance granted them by God's providence.

In an atheistic culture, Creation and Providence have disappeared from the mental horizon. "Nature" can still speak for itself, but unless it has absorbed all the divinity of the God who has died, its claims have lost much of their force. Nature no longer impresses us as a power that should be obeyed, but rather as material that we should fashion or manipulate.

Objections to the premodern view of nature arise as soon as humans pay attention to the fact that their freedom permits them to resist, change, reshape, and restructure the "natural" course or development of materials, things, plants, landscapes, mountains, rivers, animals, and even other human beings. Not only can we choose a course other than the natural one, often we must resist and change a natural development. Our needs require us to change wilderness into farmland; to make fires and build houses, we must change trees into useful wood; to travel through the air, we seem to defy the law of gravity; to make our life easier, we transmute natural elements into chemicals that do not even look natural. Are all of these transformations demanded by "natural" orientations of an opposite or higher order? If so, which criterion rules our preference for certain natural tendencies? Do we not then need a supranatural criterion to evaluate the laws that are suggested by natural inclinations?

Our technological culture finds it hard to see nature as offering, or even imposing, itself as a guide for affective, imaginative, and rational behavior. We are too familiar with the scientific and technological outlook, according to which nature is there for our use and enjoyment, curiosity and observation, calculation, scientific exploration, and technological exploitation. The voice of nature is relegated to fables, myths, poetry, and painting, whereas serious and useful consideration remains "objective." We can do with nature what we want. Arbitrariness is not a sin. Our autonomy has replaced all other, divine or natural, forms of sovereignty. Only the law of our will counts; we own the world, and everything should obey our command.

Fortunately, there are still poets in the western world who hear the voices that are silenced by the technological marketplace. Listening—with ears, eyes, mind, and hands—is not an art in which our culture excels; in the form of poetry, however, it is tolerated, but we agree that all of this is "subjective" and marginal.

A critique of our culture should take into account many of its positive aspects while at the same time revealing its unnatural and insensitive characteristics. Provisionally, I will note here only four points.

1. Nature is not always a good guide for human behavior. It must be followed with discernment; we therefore need criteria to discern which natural suggestion we should trust and which not. For example, the fact that eagles devour lambs cannot be hailed as a paradigm for "natural and therefore ethically good behavior."[11] Many natural phenomena are monstrous, cruel, destructive, and—at least prima facie—evil. Appropriate responses to such phenomena include resistance, protection, fighting, and sometimes destruction. Such responses can be greatly helped by technological insights and possibilities. Are they then "natural"? If so, what is the nature to which we pay homage?

2. Nature or parts of it should not be idolized. The return of a certain (half-believing, half-playful) polytheism might be understood as an inevitable countermovement against the overwhelming objectivism that dominates our culture. However, neither the human will nor technology itself can save us from demony.

3. The emphasis on nature instead of freedom has led some ethicists to place animals on the same level as human beings and, under certain circumstances, to give priority to the care of animals over that of the handicapped or of unborn children. Such aberrations are perhaps inevitable when the concept of nature is narrowed down to an object of the sciences (which lack any organ for recognizing freedom).

4. All objections against the premodern idea that nature offers us ethical guidance cannot abolish the conviction that we ought to strive for some sort of attunement, consonance, and harmony. Does it not belong to the human task that we celebrate the splendor of nature and heed the promises of "mother earth"? Should we not respond with justice to its hostilities?

Art is the great symbol of an alliance with nature that reinforces its appearances and voices. We fail when we try to construct a rabbit, but the meaning and glory of human art are obvious when it unveils the splendor and horror of reality. True art is not antinatural, even when it deforms or simplifies nature. The most abstract art still refers to the given world, either as decoration or as insistence on some of its meaningful aspects.

The following chapters will raise many questions with respect to the four points stated here. Before we proceed to the next chapter, however another urgent question must be answered, again provisionally. Does not the description of correspondence offered above imply that human beings should merely react to phenomena without taking initiative?

Active–Passive–Reactive

The suspicion that an ethics of correspondence amounts to a reactionary plea for passivity can be argued from several perspectives.

Nietzsche's gospel of overflowing generosity and his condemnation of a merely reactive style of life can be developed into a refutation of all theories that stress the necessity of acceptance, although Nietzsche's own evocation of the eternal return implies a good deal of *amor fati* and acquiescence.

The Marxian concentration on the *homo faber* and the explicit or implicit ideologies of nineteenth- and twentieth-century technology, along with the modern eschatology prophetically announced in Descartes' "master and possessor" of the earth,[12] protest against any subordination of human freedom to facts and forces that leave us only with reception and obedience. In contrast to the premodern tradition, modern philosophers have defined intelligence and the will as active modes of being while locating the source of passivity in nonrational, material elements of the universe. Although Aristotle had identified pure being with *energeia, actus, actuositas*, activity, he also emphasized the difference between the pure activity of the infinite and the human mixture of activity and *dynamis* (which includes possibility, incompleteness, imperfection, and the passivity that is characteristic of finite intellects and wills). Did we moderns forget or repress the radical passivity and inherent receptivity of all created beings, including those who think and act? Or did we finally discover that, once liberated from the Infinite, we could rightly appropriate its privileges?

It is hardly credible that modern thinkers could deny or ignore the receptivity that characterizes all finite entities. Who can honestly state that any finite being is a "cause of itself," while recognizing that even our free existence is born, situated, educated, historically involved and motivated? There are, however, various possibilities of recognizing our unavoidable finitude and reacting to it.

In contrast to a proud attitude that sees all receptivity and obedience as humiliating or alienating, the recognition of fundamental and incidental forms of passivity indicates more realism and modesty. Although modest people may be in danger of letting things go without taking the initiative where appropriate, those who overestimate their powers must cope with disappointments for which there is no remedy. The dream of complete autarchy easily results in powerless rebellion, audacious but failed adventures, anger and contempt with regard to the existing universe, and the conviction that human existence is fundamentally tragic or ridiculous or both.[13] Acceptance of our finitude without blurring the lines between impossibility and cowardice leads to greater peace with reality; such an attitude does not approve of all that is experienced or done or suffered, but its initiatives take the measure of the concretely possible and integrate it into the projects of a peaceful, if painful, humility. Instead of a "tragic sentiment of life,"[14] acceptance implies a sort of hopeful obedience regarding the power that has arranged things as they are. Whether this power lies in "Nature," "the facts," Being, the gods, God, or anything else, remains to be seen. The character of a humble attitude and the mood by which it is accompanied differs according to the qualification of that power, but for this moment, the general statements uttered here may suffice.

To answer the objection that an ethics of correspondence is too reactive, we need a phenomenology of responsivity that shows its difference from both mere passivity and full activity. Chapter 2 contained some remarks to this effect, but a supplementary analysis is necessary.

That acceptance and obedience to the calls by which the phenomena provoke us do not constitute purely passive events is easily shown. An appropriate response is not an automatic reaction, such as that found in a laboratory, a mechanical device, or vegetative growth, because the attention, reception, and acceptance presupposed by a sensitive response is entirely dominated by the effort of inventing and realizing an appropriate (re)action. This process cannot be triggered if the respondent ignores or refuses to focus on it (although it remains true that the respondent cannot initiate the process without having been provoked). Reception and acceptance are not passive, as if the receiving subject were a tabula rasa; instead, they present a mode of hospitality through which the respondent welcomes but also filters what is allowed to enter and places conditions on its integration. (The latter point is important for the question of our openness to evil, corruption, or threats, which will be discussed below.)

The desire to respond appropriately, which is challenged by any phenomenon that attracts our attention, prompts us to a (re)action that is right on target—like the shot of an archer, as Aristotle says.[15] The activity displayed in the trial and error that prepares such accuracy is more active and more intense than the curiosity of one who flits from one object to another without concentrating on any of the phenomena that vie for attention. An ethics of perception cannot bless the superficial gaze of fundamental indifference.

If it is true that none of our actions begins from scratch—and is in that sense initial or "arche-ic"—all activity is, in some way, reactive: an action that responds (by imitating, retrieving, integrating, continuing, modifying) to some occurrence that provokes us to a reaction. Just as our thinking is always a rethinking born from seeing, hearing, or reading, so action is our way of participating in a history that conditions our originality.

Paradise Lost

Does an ethics of correspondence imply that the phenomenal reality is inherently good? Every answer depends on the meaning of "reality" and "is."

If it is our task to respond in an appropriate—well-attuned, sensitive, reasonable, and coherent—way to all the phenomena that we encounter (including our own phenomenal being), does this not presuppose that their claims are justified and that their ways of being must be respected, however they may happen to be?

Respect, as recognition of a respectable phenomenon's dignity or value, is not due to all phenomena, if many of them are detestable. The challenge with which the latter phenomena confront us does not provoke respect but horror, abomination. In such cases, appropriateness lies in the right mode and intensity of our disrespect or contempt or hatred or other appropriate aggressiveness. Correspondence encompasses both positive and negative reactions; it neither denies nor obscures the fact that the whole array of phenomena displays both the horror and the splendor of the universe and that most often, or even always, we must deal with mixtures of good and bad aspects of nature and history.

Is nature, insofar as it is untouched by history, good and innocent, worthy of admiration and love? Are we—or our culture and history—the only culprits while nature—or Nature—is innocent? Is the cosmos holy while sin is human?

It is not clear that we are capable of figuring out what and how nature is and shows on its own. Can we abstract nature from all human (including all observational and theoretical) interference? When we contrast nature and culture or nature and history, do we not inevitably evoke a nature that is already seen, imagined, and appreciated from a human perspective, a nature already relevant to our interests? What does it mean when we call floods, tornadoes, volcanic eruptions, and destroyed harvests terrible and lamb-eating eagles cruel? We perceive certain animals as monstrous and use their image to symbolize evil itself, but is their monstrosity more than metaphorical? Whatever the answer is, natural events and regularities are not sufficient to set the standards for human behavior. However, the question we are trying to answer is whether the natural phenomena that we perceive as monstrous are compatible with the idea that we must respond to them in a way equally appropriate as that of our responses to the jubilant song of birds or the warming beams of a splendid sun. The answer is yes: depending on the aspects of the phenomena in question and the circumstances in which we find ourselves, fight or flight can be as appropriate as the welcoming that is "deserved" by friendlier phenomena. When neither flight nor a successful fight are possible, the only correct response might be a well-calculated "passive" resistance in the form of patience. Although this truth is unwelcome to modern ears, the intense (re)activity implied in well-oriented and courageous patience is one of our highest and healthiest possibilities in our confrontation with the all-too-powerful forces of evil.

The presence of evil is obvious in human history. Wars, mass murders, worldwide injustices and lies—one must be blind to think of history as a benevolent sort of providence. The utopian illusions of the last three centuries have lost all of their cogency (if they ever had any); cynicism and overall condemnation are now the greatest dangers.

History has been interpreted as a second, more or less humanized, nature because of its supraindividual and public character. It is therefore not difficult to adapt the above consideration of nature to those forms of historical good and evil that determine our situation. With regard to historical powers of evil, a conquest is not always possible—especially for singular individuals. A lower degree of resistance or exile, if possible, might then be the right answer. Patience without cowardice or death with honor are sometimes necessary.

However mixed or corrupted our situation is, the rule of correspondence remains valid if we maintain that evil phenomena provoke us to appropriate reactions. Because they are concretizations of evil, they "naturally" demand negative reactions.

Correspondence presupposes discernment; we cannot simply take for granted that all the challenges that seem to issue from things-as-they-are contain justified claims. Corrupt situations must be redressed through the thorough eradication of the evil that, as a malicious weed, threatens to suffocate the good that is still present in it.

However, at this point, our proposal seems to get into trouble. If correspondence presupposes that we are able to distinguish good from bad phenomena, how then can correspondence itself be the principle that constitutes the good? Or, to put it another way, if correspondence is the criterion for a good mode of appreciation and (re)acting, to which kind of correspondence do good phenomena owe their goodness?

The paradox disappears if we understand that the goodness or badness of phenomena indeed results from their correspondence or discrepancy with regard to the inherent claims of those phenomena we accept as respectable. To illustrate this statement with an example, let us hypothetically agree that capitalism, despite certain advantages, is an essentially unjust phenomenon because it creates, maintains, and fosters disproportionate differences between the wealthy and the poor. The reason we evaluate it as bad or evil lies in its discrepancy with regard to the justified claims implied in the fundamental equality of all human individuals and the rights that follow from it. Correspondence and noncorrespondence, as well as goodness and badness, are here qualifications of an anonymous and "objective," although humanly motivated, institution rather than characteristics of a person or a group of persons; however, the criterion for moral evaluation remains the principle of correspondence. Even "purely natural" evils, if they exist, can be recognized as such only because of their discrepancy with respect to our idea of an "objective" reality that would be fair and friendly to the justified claims of the human race.[16]

For now, these indications must suffice. If "good" can be translated as "appropriately responding to phenomenal provocation," we should not only restrict it to personal encounters, but also thematize the supraindividual powers of nature, culture, and history. For greater clarity, we need more concrete descriptions of the characteristic challenges with which the various kinds of reality confront us.

Conclusion

For the last three of the four questions formulated above, I have indicated the beginning of an answer. The first question, however, cannot be analyzed until we have investigated more thoroughly several questions regarding the self and recognition of other humans.[17]

CHAPTER 6

The Analogy of Should

As we said before, the words *ought*, *should*, and *good* cover a wide range of analogical meanings according to the phenomena and the responses to which we apply them. The phenomena are valuable, desirable, good, insofar as they challenge—invite, urge, demand, command—us to respond in appropriate ways; we must "do justice" to them; but their challenges, their "rights," and the "justice" they demand are characterized by different qualities and urgencies. A mosquito does not forbid us to kill it with the same voice and force as a child, and a child demands another justice than that of the government. If it is a task of ethics to specify the various kinds, levels, dimensions, urgencies, and tonalities of "should" and "good," we need a phenomenology of all types of being insofar as they are challenging. If "doing justice" is an analogical concept, the entire universe must be described from the perspective of the many grades and shades of its "right" to decent treatment. That is, we need to write a complete phenomenology from the ethical perspective.

This task cannot be accomplished in one chapter or even in one book, but we can sketch an outline of its project with some hints about its execution. In doing so, I will provisionally rely on a few assumptions that must later on be questioned and perhaps revised. One of these assumptions is that we can speak meaningfully about a universe of challenging beings and not only about a scattered multitude of fragments without unity. The second assumption is that this universe is composed of several levels or dimensions, each of which has its own kind of being and its own form of demanding. The third assumption is that human existence, in its openness and responsivity to the universe, likewise composes a unity whose levels and dimensions, despite and thanks to their differences, form one whole. Since the purpose of an ethical phenomenology lies in providing an overview of all the different types of "justice" and "obligation" urged on us, the completion of our task would answer the question of how we can practice universal justice, that is, the question of living a life that is wholly good. The ambition of this book does not go farther than the sketch of some elements for such an answer.

In addition to the assumptions just formulated, this chapter presupposes a critique of an approach that has been practiced frequently in the traditions of western philosophy. Most overviews of the universe, as presented in explicit or implicit ontologies, approach it as "reality," that is, as an ensemble of *res* or things. Modern philosophy has narrowed reality further by treating it as a large Object composed of smaller objects and subjects that are parts or elements of it. Natural and cultural occurrences are not forgotten in this approach, but the framework and the paradigms that are used to understand the phenomena are "real" in the emphatic sense of "thingly" and objective structures. When talking about being, most philosophers focus on lifeless objects while presupposing that only some additions to their general ontology are needed to include lions, snakes, persons, events, stories, thoughts, artworks, communities, religions, and so on. The Husserlian and Heideggerian critiques of this objectivism are sufficiently known to relieve us of the burden of repeating them. But did Husserl or Heidegger replace it with a true ontology, one in which, for instance, speaking, giving, and being gracious are fully recognized in their difference from other types of being?

In *Being and Time*, Heidegger has shown that the objective (*vorhandene*) mode of being is not the basic mode of showing up, and that the human mode of being is an involvement in the world of shared work, equipment, utilitarian and communicative networks, social relations, shared interests, national solidarity, historical filiation. But did he, in that work, do justice to art, nature, face-to-face relations, and religion? Perhaps the purpose of *Being and Time* did not require a complete ontology—and in fact, the later works do take up the issue of nature, art, and religion. His neglect of the face to face, however, is a gap with crucial consequences for ethics, as I hope to show in the following pages.

Where and how should an ethically motivated ontology begin? Many philosophers began with nature or even with the least interesting and most primitive element of nature, matter, although sometimes they focused on organic matter or animality. Others focused on the human person, presenting the universe as being-for, being-given-to, or being-spoken-about-by persons. We can hardly focus on persons, however, without first situating them among nonpersonal entities, events, and relations within space and time. It is even obvious that no part of the universe can be completely isolated if we wish to understand its nature, especially when it abounds in relations to other parts or even—as is the case of a person—to *all* other parts of the universe. Beginning with matter need not be disastrous if it refrains from assuming that the full nature of matter can be found before we study the human mode of materiality. Indeed, corporeality differs essentially from the materiality found in atoms, molecules, minerals, stones, rivers, landscapes, machines, plants, and animals, but many philosophers have suggested that the truth about matter is found on the level of spiritless or lifeless beings, such that a philosophy of vegetal, animal, and human life needs only to add features to the material ones. They have forgotten that, as Aristotle clearly taught, human, animal, and vegetal corporeality represent three *essentially* different forms of materiality and that all life is essentially different from inorganic corporeality.[1] On the one hand, we cannot describe or analyze what and how a person is without acquaintance with materiality in its various forms; on the other hand, a philosophy of materiality must remain open to revision from the perspective of plants, animals, and humans. Beginning with a philosophy of nature can thus only be a provisional sketch, which must be redrawn when we move to a "higher" dimension (that is, a dimension in which nature is integrated into another mode of being). To emphasize the central role of personality in our investigation, the following sketch of an ethical phenomenology will begin with persons.

What, who, and how a person *is* must be examined from several perspectives, and this examination must be guided by several questions. Following a long tradition, one can focus on the question "Who am I?", which may be asked in a more "personal" or private or a more universal and anonymous way. As I will try to show, this question should be preceded by the question "Who are you?" because "you" is the first manifestation of being-a-person for me, the phenomenologist. I meet you and am affected, touched, challenged, and provoked by you who look at me, address me with your gestures, speak to me. Who am I when I see you looking at me, hear you speaking to me—and what is expected from me?

What the face to face reveals is of the highest importance for ethics because it is in this relationship that a phenomenon challenges me through a rigorous and unconditional command and demand: an obligation that I cannot escape, a duty.[2] Desire and obligation coincide in my being addressed by the appearance of another person: you.[3] Once this obligation has become manifest, I can discover other forms and degrees of being challenged and compelled, and therewith other forms of correspondence. The outline of such a discovery must be unfolded in the following parts of this chapter: once we have looked at the facing face (first section of this chapter), we must ask how nature and culture (second section), and more specifically art (third section), demand to be dealt with, and how the historical communities in which we participate bind and oblige us by their demands of justice (fourth section). Following these partial discoveries, we must ask how all the modes of phenomenality form a universe (first section of Chapter 7) and how I, who am affected by them, can maintain my unity in obeying their orders (second section of Chapter 7). In reflecting about the two totalities of the universe and the one who is engaged in it, the question of transcendence and religion cannot be avoided (third section of Chapter 7). If the universe is not closed, ethics cannot be isolated from religion, although religion cannot be confined to ethics.

Facing

We are involved in satisfactory, rewarding, irritating, frustrating, repulsive, and appealing relationships. We discover what we desire through the pains and pleasures, joys and disappointments affecting us in all our relationships. Perhaps our Desire reaches further than the satisfactions we have known until now, but that "further" can be discovered only through the experience of what has been given to us in the course of our involvement. To begin with, a survey of our desirable and undesirable experiences will be useful. Which kinds of encounters have been worthwhile? Which desiderata have provided us with joy? What were the conditions for our rewarding encounters? How should we behave in order to respond well to our desiderata? What do we desire in meeting with dogs or facing other persons, and how do such encounters suggest a specific form of correspondence? Let us begin by focusing on relationships of intersubjectivity.[4]

Philosophy and Intersubjectivity

Since the time of the sophists, social philosophy has been an integral part of western philosophy, especially in the form of "politics," including philosophy of the polis, empire, or state, philosophy of the family, and philosophy of the economic structures of the society. Friendship and love between two persons have also been thematized, especially by Greek and Roman authors, but they have rarely played a central role in the constitution of a philosophical system.[5] The Greeks were fascinated by the divine cosmos and the wonder of life; Christians concentrated on the relations between the human soul and God; modern philosophers were more interested in the rationality of the natural and social universe and the psychology of individual minds than in an ethics of face-to-face relations. Social philosophy from Hobbes to Marx, still prevalent in handbooks, treats interpersonal relations from an outside perspective, seeing them as constitutive elements of associations or communities. Nowhere in modern prephenomenological philosophy do we find a treatise on the face to face written from the inside—that is, from the perspective of someone who is involved in it. Even within phenomenology, the human other has most often been reduced to an element of universal or "intersubjective" validity. However, Husserl, Scheler, Heidegger, Marcel, Buber, Sartre, Merleau-Ponty, and some others have at least *tried* to describe how another person appears before me, the paradigmatic subject that speaks and writes in the name of all subjects. Yet Emmanuel Levinas is the first philosopher who has presented us with an extensive analysis of another person's "epiphany" as different from my awareness of myself. Instead of presupposing that the other is an alter ego, similar to and primarily equal to me (as other philosophers have done), his phenomenology has emphasized the other's facing me (*le visage*, "the face") and speaking to me (*la parole, le dire*, "the saying"), and the other's *visitation*. The following description of someone who faces me is heavily influenced by his oeuvre, although it differs from his descriptions in some noticeable respects.[6]

You and I

A face can be seen from different perspectives. For instance, a comparative study of physiognomies can measure the noses, eyes, mouths, and ears and study the proportions between them; a painter can focus on the form and the character of an individual face; I can look at the color of your eyes; before you leave the house, you can check the color of your mouth and cheeks. However, all of these forms of observation miss the one thing that is the most proper to a face: it faces. Your eyes look at me; your mouth speaks to me; standing there, you address me; you avoid me or you greet me. Your turning toward me in addressing me cannot be seen by any physiological, aesthetic, mathematical, or scientific observation; it demands an attitude that turns me toward you in order to receive and perceive your address. This reception can be puzzled, fearful, timid, welcoming, or hospitable; it can be hostile or grateful, loving or indifferent. The character of both your address and my response often depends on what you and I have already perceived of one another. If your approach spells hostility, I may be paralyzed by anxiety or become angry and aggressive; confronted with kindly eyes, I may feel welcomed or react with suspicion. But behind, or rather *in*, all differences of facial expression, there is the face as such. All expressions are variations on one message that is announced in the surprise of another's approaching me. What does the other, as human other, tell me, even if he or she never utters a word?

If I am obsessed by voracity, everything edible that appears before me will be eaten, even human beings. If science has monopolized my perceptivity, I can discover only objects for study. In both cases, I am incapable of seeing that someone looks at me and addresses me. Science and cannibalism ignore the face insofar as it faces me. They are blind to a basic structure of ordinary life in society. To perceive the other's facing me, I need a specific form of receptivity: I must allow the other to look at me, my vulnerably displayed body and character as they are involved in a particular situation. The other's gaze is itself naked and thus vulnerable, but it also contains an element of threat insofar as it disrupts my privacy and might dominate my world from a distance. If we try to understand the intersubjective structure of our encounter genealogically—in the way Hobbes, Locke, Rousseau, and Hegel did—we must presuppose that I initially am a monopolist, since no other person as yet has appeared in my world, which then is there entirely for me (alone). The first appearance of another human being is then a radical contestation: the other's emergence disrupts my monopoly by claiming a place of his own in the world. Shall I defend my sovereignty against this rival? Shall I attack the intruder, submit to his claims, or eliminate them by fighting or—if necessary—killing him?[7]

If I do not allow another to share the world with me, I am motivated by a desire to maintain my monopoly, but the face that looks at me, unprotected as it is, forbids me to do what such a desire suggests. The other's face reveals two truths at the same time: (1) I am a murderer if I let my life be ruled by the desire to monopolize the world, and (2) I shall not kill. The second truth is a prohibition and a command. The message in all faces, even the most threatening, tells me: "Do not kill me! Let me live! Grant me a space and time in your world, which is not yours alone!"

The amazing event of a face facing me can neither be described nor perceived in a "value-free," purely nonnormative manner; its visibility *is* a command, the basic command of intersubjective and social ethics. As I have already said but want to emphasize, this command cannot be heard unless I am turned toward the one who addresses me, and this presupposes at least some openness in me. If there is not any outgoing desire in me, the other's rivalry and my monopolistic will develop into a Hegelian dialectic of fight, conquest, submission, mastership, and slavery. Such a dialectic is ruled by desires for possession (that is, appropriation, use, and consumption) and domination that leave me alone.[8] Access to another dialectic, the moral dialectic of responding to the face, presupposes freedom from obsession by such desires—not freedom from such desires, but freedom from their absolutism. Since we cannot extirpate the desire to maintain and develop our own existence—a desire that demands a certain quality and degree of power and property—we are necessarily involved in a competition, and thus in struggles and compromises, even if we intend to make room for the other as a result of his insistence on having a place in this world. The moral order revealed in the other's face governs the rules of that competition, however. Dia-logic is the law to which the dialectic of masters and servants must be submitted.

Asymmetry

In looking at you who look at me, our contact is characterized by a special form of dissymmetry. My experience of the person you are and my experience of myself are different. Whereas I see you in front of me and look at the expression of your eyes, I perceive my own being-here kinesthetically. What I see in looking at you is neither similar to my own appearance in a mirror, nor to my figure as I feel it. I cannot see my face at all. That you and I are similar in many respects cannot be denied, but it is not easy to explain how we know it, and in any case, it is not given by an immediate perception. The basis of an argument about the existence of other (equal or similar) minds is thus not immediately given.

When I speak to you, while you are speaking to me, I hear the similarity of two voices, but the voice that speaks to me is radically different from my own voice; not only its timbre and melody, but its origin and direction are different as well. In addressing me, your voice is you as reaching out to me, whereas my speaking coincides with me,[9] the perceiver of both voices. Your voice and mine are not heard as two instances of one kind of "voice"; on the contrary, the two voices voice irreducible universes: yours and mine.

From the (abstract and hypothetical) perspective of a monopolistic ego, your apparition in "my" world awakens me to the awareness that I am not allowed to block your entrance into this world or to eliminate you from it. Insofar as I am driven by a desire to own the entire universe, I learn from your presence that I cannot kill you: I must set bounds to my unbounded desire for being "master and possessor."[10] Your being there demands more, however: I must welcome you to the world, and this demands hospitality. Your presence commands me to offer you the world as (also) yours. I must make room for your life and adjust myself to your nestling in the world we should share.

The experience of your presence does not, as such, require that you experience my presence likewise as obligating you. Your command, which obligates me with respect to you, does not reveal me immediately as equally commanding you. My experience of your right to exist—and thus to have the world as yours—entails that I must respect and even serve your existence such that it should be worthwhile to be lived, but it does not ipso facto reveal to me that you are equally commanded and obligated by me. The difference between your "height" and my obligation to you impedes a "symmetric" relation between your experience of me and my experience of you. If you experience me as likewise "high" while I experience you as "high," we are related by two relations of inequality that cross one another, thus constituting what we perhaps might call a "chiastic asymmetry."[11]

In order to become aware of our equality in rights and obligations vis-à-vis one another, a new experience is needed: the experience of a fundamental equality between your worth or dignity and mine, followed by the insight that I, too, must be recognized as having inviolable rights. The latter insight is contemporaneous with the discovery that I also have obligations with respect to myself.

I–They–We

Most modern social philosophies took it for granted that all human beings are similar instances of one species, paradigmatically exemplified in the one person that can be designated as "ego" or "I." They thereby neglect the difference between you and me. Treating our relation as an instance of "intersubjectivity," one neutralizes the experience of your commanding me by seeing it from the outside as a variation on generalities like "human relations," "association," or "sociality." That you and I belong to one humanity cannot be denied, but how we discover our equality in this respect is a difficult question. In any case, your being *you* and my being *I* cannot be reduced to instances of "being human." Our shared humanity does not as such imply the possibility of being you or me and addressing others or being addressed by them. You and I "have" the same human essence, but we are not just instantiations of it. On the contrary, we turn our humanity toward one another and decide about its meaning by realizing some of its possibilities as different ways of life for you and me. Your existence urges me to recognize my responsibility for a world in which you can enjoy life. By consenting to this obligation, I discover that I am different from Narcissus: I am able to restrict my unlimited (and consequently violent) desires; that is, I am free. Freedom is thus experienced as self-restraint in view of a socialized universe. This experience reveals my own dignity: I can act, feel, and will as a moral being; I can obey commands; and I hear the voice of obligation. I have a conscience.[12]

You, the Others, and I

When I say "you," I experience myself as addressing someone who actually addresses me or whose attention I want to attract. Before your eyes, I am someone who makes room and grants time for you and lets you dispose of materials that, without your intrusion, would be mine. I am obedient to the claim that is inherent in your existence (not simply your whim); I am—in this respect—"your servant."

But how do I perceive your facing someone else, a third person, him or her? Both you and the third are persons who could, even if they do not actually, pay attention to me; you and she (or he) address one another, and I observe how you and the third reciprocally command and respond to these commands. Do I indeed see or hear that you and the third command one another? Is this ethical moment of the face perceptible from the outside? Must I have discovered beforehand that each is a "you" for the other and an "I" for him- or herself? Can the ethical claim be perceived from other perspectives than that of an "I"? Does the statement that all individuals owe one another respect and service presuppose that its author, through sympathy or empathy, has identified each of them as equal to the author's own "I" in confrontation with "your facing me"? Does all ethics refer to "my" conscience, insofar as this is thought as the conscience of any ego? Is conscience essentially a first person phenomenon? If that is the case, we can understand why no ethics can be founded on the "objective" consideration of "an uninvolved observer" from the outside. The ethicist must have experienced personally what it means to be obligated by an appeal that is directly addressed to him or her.

The observation that all human beings put obligation on one another implies the reciprocity of a double inequality. Insofar as one's existence commands the other's, the first is "higher" than the other (not as better or more authoritative, but as claimant), whereas the second must obey; but the second is also a claimant who obligates the first. Reciprocity or mutuality does not conflict with this moral inequality, as it would in a Kojèvian dialectic based on fear of death and greed for consumption and power.[13] All intersubjective relations are ruled by the chiastic asymmetry of mutual obligation and obedience. If the persons involved correspond appropriately to this structure, their lifestyle expresses at the same time the humility of conscientious service and the honor of self-conscious dignity.

Lord and Servant

The words *lord* and *servant* have at least two radically different meanings. They can indicate the purely moral inequality described above, but they also can point at the domination and submission that belong to an economy of power. The distinction between these orders is a criterion for detecting whether individuals understand the difference between morality and violence.

A spontaneous response to violence is flight, self-protection, or combat. Combat ends in murder, a truce, or overpowering and submission. The power of masters over slaves is one form of violence. Subordination, service, and lordship belong to an economy of more or less civilized force. Since Hegel's, Marx's, and Kojeve's analyses of power and conflict are well known, it is not necessary to dwell on them in order to indicate the dimension to which the "economic" structures of power, lordship, and bondage belong.

Some "postmodernists" believe that all forms of service, obligation, law, and authority, including the entire realm of morality, are mere metamorphoses of violence. Some of them emphasize the "undecidable" ambiguities of the most elevated ideas and ideals of western civilization; others claim that all moral rules and restrictions are disguised attempts at domination or repression.

Although it is true that another's existence can appear as a possible threat, which then inclines me to fight or to avoid communication, it is always naked and unprotected, without force or power in its claims, abandoned to my benevolence, supported only by my sense of obligation.[14] Many theories, fantasies, and more or less plausible genealogies can be invented to argue for the hypothesis that my conscience is "nothing else than" an effect or relic of a violent past, but even if such theories or fantasies could be proven, they would miss the point. The question isn't whether morality has emerged from a wild and barbarous past, but rather whether it is anything at all in its own right, apart from the masks and perversions that most often go with it. The assumption that morality is reducible to a power play is as much a judgment about the conscience of those who embrace that assumption as it is about the meaning of their demystification. It is, however, remarkable that many of these authors seem animated by a desire to set things straight and to liberate humanity from demeaning practices and conceptions. Apparently, they do have a conscience and feel responsible for liberating others from their suffering under inauthentic constraints.

The moral inequality of reciprocal "highness" and *diakonia* is distinct but not separate from the economic and political dialectics that relate lords and servants through the consumptive and social needs that create scarcity, competition, rivalry, struggles for power and influence, property, and survival. Both orders of inequality, radically different as they are, are integral parts of the human condition, although they have different sources: self-centered needs and pure desire for goodness. The latter should inform and guide the fulfillment of our needs and wishes. Such guidance lends measure, and therewith limitations, to the outbursts of wild desires, thus proportioning our feelings and behavior. Those who consider all limitations and rules to be unjustified constraints revere arbitrary decisions, but how can they decide if the very criterion for choice must be chosen? Do they deny that all human beings discover themselves as always already oriented?

I and Myself

The double orientation of a person whose economy of needs (with its service and governance) is devoted to the moral service of others, creates a double allegiance within that very person. The reciprocity of our moral inequality reveals me to myself as being, at the same time, a lord to be revered and served by others and a servant called to serve the others' "height" or dignity. That I obligate others to serve me, without having chosen to obligate them, reveals my dignity. This not only precedes their choices, but also mine. My dignity imposes its demands on all human choices, including my own. I am therefore also in debt with regard to myself. I am double: the lord and servant of myself.

The moral doubleness of me and myself does not have anything to do with self-oppression, self-repression, self-slavery, or any other form of being hostile to myself. It is the most normal, natural, and essential structure of all human individuals. It constitutes them as moral. I am responsible for realizing my own unchosen, that is, given, worth. I must take care of myself, "be concerned about my soul,"[15] follow the orientations of what I always already am, obey the authority of that in me—my "essence"— which precedes my capacities of decision.

Self-concern, taking care of my own "well-being," is not necessarily narcissistic; it can be the purest form of dedication to the Good, insofar as this must be concretized (not only in others, but also) in me. The Good is impartial, but it "loves" all individuals as possible witnesses to its splendor and benevolence. Individuals are dedicated to the Good if they allow this dedication to guide all of their interests. Needs and wishes are not repressed but "formed" and fashioned when a "disinterested" interest in being-good creates order and proportion out of their turmoil. Disinterested self-love is the rule of decent self-interest.

Correspondence

I correspond to the face by responding appropriately to its vulnerable claim on me and my share of the world. Before your eyes, I become humble, without losing the respect I owe to my own dignity. I hope that you will respect this dignity, I even desire that you will love me (whether I am likable or not); however, I cannot count on your loving or respecting me because I know all too well how certain self-interests—in me as in you—resist the generosity of being-good.

The preceding analysis has focused on one fundamental and essential element of human behavior: the face-to-face relation constitutive for friendship in its broadest sense of a personal link between you and me. Lest we forget that this relationship remains abstract if it is not understood as intertwined with the care for my own destiny and the social—economic, political, and historical—relations that constitute communal forms of life, I add, by way of anticipation, the following remarks.[16]

While challenging and responding to each other, you and I participate in the communities of several "we"s. Together, with innumerable others, we share common destinies. Responding to this fact, we try to practice solidarity, including approval and confirmation as well as critique, conversion, and reform. Correspondence is here working toward better forms of "us," that is, toward amelioration of the customs and institutions that structure and characterize our "being-with."

Intersubjective and social correspondence is fundamental to an ethics of being-for and being-with. Friendship and solidarity, devotion to you and us and them must be unfolded in concrete situations and activities in order to become perceptible as principles of ethical life. The same is true of care for my own "soul." My first and all-encompassing burden is my life itself. Being good is realized by heeding what you, I, she, he, we, and they appear to be for those who are involved in our variously belonging together.

Facing as Revelation of Duties

What can ethics learn from the face that speaks to me? What does its addressing me signify? It reveals to me an absolute (or, as Kant would say, an unconditional) obligation, and I must condemn myself as morally bad when I ignore it. In looking at me, a particular being shows me the impossibility of reducing it to an object, an element, a tool, a structure, a form, an essence, a part of the world, or a moment of the universe. The speaker differs radically from all beings that can be spoken about or thematized in a reflective context. Not only the response to which you provoke me but your very provocation is missed when I take you up as a topic of my philosophy; your address can only be perceived when I welcome it as addressing me. What you tell me, the content of your proposals and propositions, is transcended by your proposing them to me. Speaking about them, you speak to me—rightly expecting that I will speak to you. Even if your addressing me is only a barely perceptible wink, you are right in feeling offended if I do not react to it. Your wink and my response to it cannot be treated as objects; they are not perceptible outside your and my turning to one another. If speaking about and speaking to (or looking at an object/question/topic and looking at you) can be distinguished as an objectifying or (in the grammatical sense) "accusative" speaking and a speaking that puts you in the dative, the "dativity" is the most remarkable structure that your appearance reveals. Once I have experienced someone's looking, smiling, gesturing, or speaking to me—that is, since my first days—I know that being can never be identified with objectivity. Since that time, it has also been revealed that certain beings affect me ethically by urging me to respond in a dative way to their provocation.

"You shall" (not kill me—but welcome me, help me to live and to live well) accompanies all manifestations of any person to other persons. The universe is not merely the totality of possible objects, themes, or topics, because then it would leave out the most important "thing": the fact that all things, objects, themes, thoughts, words, propositions, and stories are nothing unless they are presented (offered, delivered, pointed out, given, granted) by someone to someone. No phenomenon can "speak" unless it has been taken up in a speech or text by someone who, enabled by previous speakers, wrapped it in a certain interpretation before handing it on to another. The giving that mobilizes and transforms all possible objects and thoughts is a *paradosis* (a handing over) and a living tradition. It is well known that a tradition would die if there were no living (both conserving and prophetic) voices to take care of its transmission, but it is not always recognized that the very presentation of old and new insights is first of all an act of address and affection: someone touches someone in speaking to someone about something (or someone). This affection is the core of all interpersonal ethics: by affecting me, the speaker makes me aware of my obligation toward her. This obligation emerges not primarily because of the heritage that the speaker shares with me, but because of her addressing me. Even the face of a torturer forbids me to kill him, although, in exceptional circumstances, perhaps, there might be political reasons to override even that absolute prohibition. In the face of an educator, on the other hand, my initiation to the basic commandment is doubled by gratitude for the quality of her gifts, but the fundamental gratitude concerns the ethical initiation itself.

In facing me, you are the revelation of an absolute command, that is, a command that should not be disobeyed at any cost. It can indeed be disobeyed, but this has a disastrous consequence: by killing you, I destroy my own dignity, not yours. It is better to lose my life than to take yours; the worst thing that can happen to me is to live on without moral worth.

The absoluteness of the order that is revealed in your address disturbs the totality of all circumstances, contexts, networks, and processes in which you and I are caught. You (and I, insofar as I am also a you for others) show that the universe is either not a totality or, if it is, it cannot integrate the personal relationships that develop from the face to face. Our existence cannot be absorbed or "sublated" by anonymous constellations; we are not simply "in (or of) the world," but mainly different from anything worldly.

Since Plato, philosophers have attempted to distinguish personal existence from impersonal modes of being by focusing on morality; but most attempts have identified the difference as one between body and spirit, forgetting thereby that a human body entails the spirit to which it owes its specifically human character.[17] "The human phenomenon" is a monument of phenomenal absoluteness: no cost or profit or value can justify its subjection to any natural or cultural power, beauty, or meaning. Escaping all economies, it is the great exception to the law of networks and exchange. Although we may, in our reconnaissance of other modes of being, discover phenomena that seem to demand a similar obedience, such demands cannot have the same (moral) force. Should I prefer to die rather than to slaughter a cow? May I save a work of art if it costs a human life? The obligation that a human face imposes on me can serve as a guiding thread and paradigm (or *analogatum principale*) for my journey through the universe of things, tools, machines, stars, plants, trees, animals, landscapes, poems, paintings, music, dances, angels, gods, and so on. Respect for your absoluteness is the light that enlightens the earth; wherever we encounter analogous injunctions, we meet with beings who cooperate in making the entire universe meaningful from a moral point of view.

You Are Incomparable

That you—and I as a you for everyone else—escape the world (if "world" stands for the natural, cultural, and historical processes in which everything can be replaced or exchanged) is a cornerstone of ethics. Kant expressed its truth by making a distinction between value (*Wert*) and worth or dignity (*Würde*). A valuable thing can be exchanged for another valuable entity, but *Würde* has no price.[18] Persons cannot be reduced to elements in a system of exchange, and this is also true of those features and acts that are essentially personal (that is, in which a person's personality is involved). There is no economy of persons; here the economic paradigm does not apply.

This insight has profound consequences for the philosophical method as such. It excludes the imposition of economic or quasi-economic schemas on all phenomena that are strictly personal. Such schemas are found not only in all forms of structuralism and naturalism, but also in Hegelian and Marxian versions of dialectics. When persons are reduced to parts or components of a synthesis, their personality disappears. Extending this insight to personal phenomena, such as words, gifts, or gestures, we must state that these entail a presence of the giving or speaking person and therefore, they likewise escape any totality to which they may be reduced by an onlooker who denies their exceptionality in the name of principles such as quid pro quo or *do ut des*. All things *can* be seen and thought of as parts of an economic system, but such a view represses the genuine appearance of persons, which resists the laws of comparison, calculation, and fair exchange.

That persons are exceptional implies that they cannot be replaced. A market for persons is therefore immoral. However, this sentence must be qualified. It is not only possible, but it corresponds to certain aspects of persons, that their skills, talents, skin colors, IQs, characters, and the like, are compared; and there is nothing evil about choosing the best qualified person for an open position in an enterprise. What is morally bad is the reduction of a person to such qualities. But what then is the incomparable and unexchangeable core of the person's personality? At this moment of our investigation, we do not have any other answer than that which was expressed in the word *dignity* and the statement that the challenge through which a person obligates me is absolute.

However, sadly enough, there are situations in which someone is forced to choose among several persons: "Whom shall we kill? Your daughter or your wife?" The cruelty of such situations lies precisely in the violent attempt to reduce a moral situation that requires me to be responsible for both my daughter and my wife, to a merely economic situation where either choice is immoral. The economizing of morality is its suppression. A somewhat analogous choice must be made with regard to aesthetic phenomena when you are summoned to choose between a Velazquez and a Rembrandt or between two books. Such choices are made all the time— for example, when we put a book into our suitcase before a journey; but moral dilemmas are dramatic and tragic because the evil that results cannot be mitigated by a good alternative.

By way of anticipation, we can already say that a culture where such dilemmas have become customary is decadent because it is a fundamental task of any organized community to reduce the number of its moral impossibilities. If chaos or civil war (or Hobbes' "state of nature") symbolize all immoral situations, it is obvious that we must begin by abolishing such a state of affairs (*exeundum ex statu naturae*) in order to make moral action possible at all.

Respect, Justice, Compassion

What sort of duty is imposed on us by a person's appearance? What kind of attitude corresponds to this absolute command? If "respect" (*Achtung*) is the answer, as Kant said,[19] we must amend his explanation by remarking that respect forbids us not only to reduce a person to being a means, but also to consider or treat persons as mere objects. Putting someone into the accusative cannot be the last word on that person. It must always be combined with and be subordinate to the dative of a speaking-to. This truth can be illustrated by the following experience: when someone enters the room while I am talking to you, you feel offended if I begin a discourse about you in the third person to the newcomer. My changing you from a "you" to a "him" or "her" degrades you by reducing you to a theme or object. Objectification, even of persons, is not necessarily wrong—it happens all the time in medical or psychological consultation, for example—but it cannot be the ultimate and encompassing perspective. When I talk *about* you, this should be a subordinate element of some talking *to* you. As soon as the "about" dominates the scene, you have disappeared.

Is the respect to which your existence calls me an issue of human rights? The answer depends on the meaning of "rights." As human, rights should specify the absolute claim that is constitutive of the human dignity in you. As such, they diversify the fundamental right that characterizes you as radically—not gradually—different from animals, monuments, texts, works of art, structures, and powers. Recognition of this universal right respects your humanness (Kant's *Menschheit*) as fundamentally different from all other genera and species.[20] This difference cannot be reduced to a generic or specific or individual difference. You are neither a mere case of one genus or species, nor a mere member of one worldwide community. To consider you such would be to overlook that which makes you a you: your unicity. Or—to use the thematizing language of traditional philosophy—as unique, an individual person is a separate genus and species by itself. True, each person shares its humanity and many specific features with all others; but all these commonalities are only components, qualities, or structures of and within unique individuals.

So far, doing justice to you has been defined as responding in the dative to you as the unique subject of an absolute right to recognition of your radical difference. What distinguishes you reveals your difference. In your humanness you differ from all other genera and species, but as "you," you disrupt even the homogeneity of rights.

However, these generalities do not sufficiently determine the commandment through which your existence summons me to justice. What should I do for you, offer you, say to you? How should I help, serve, encourage you?

Perceiving you is not only being touched by your right; you are more than a self-subsistent and self-moving individual, more than a unique self that withstands thematization and generalization. You are also a being of desires and needs. But needs and wants by themselves do not constitute rights—not even those needs that must be fulfilled lest the needy person die. For is not mortality a most common and natural property of all humans? If survival were an absolute right, existence would be a scandal. There is, however, one "need" that must be satisfied, because otherwise the person who has it would live "for nothing," senselessly, without meaning. This "need" is as radically different from all "other" needs, wants, wishes, inclinations, drives, and impulses, as Desire is from desires or as a human life is from all other kinds of life. Your most fundamental claim or "right" lies in my recognition of your ultimate difference: your radical Desire for a unique and ultimate meaning (and the possibility of realizing such a meaning if existence is not to be absurd).

In perceiving you in light of your (and my) Desire (see Chapter 4), I am touched by your neediness, vulnerability, poverty, fundamental helplessness, and mortality. The combination of this misery with the dignity of your being-there affects me in the form of a basic concern that can easily become compassion when you suffer, or shared enjoyment when you thrive. The appropriate response to your appearance is more than respect for your right; you elicit care. "To care for your soul" is another name for the commandment that through you affects my Desire.[21]

Concern and Desire

Our journey through the various dimensions of being as being good is motivated by Desire. The face shows that being can manifest itself as an absolute command and that being good is realized in obedience. When, in continuing our reconnaissance, we ponder the claims and responses that are appropriate to other phenomena, other modes and intensities of "ought" will appear; but with respect to all the dimensions of being and goodness, we must ask how they relate to the Desire that propels us forward. Do we really desire to be challenged, claimed, and commanded? Do we want to obey?

That we desire to have a clear conscience is manifest in the experience of remorse. The pain of having maltreated someone is worse than many other pains. I feel divided within myself, or even torn apart; how can I heal this split? How can I find peace? Forgetting, rationalization, dissipation, and other strategies might repress my shame, but they do not destroy it. The psychology of conscience should help us to understand what happens when people try to still "the voice" of conscience: how, for instance, human hearts can soften but also harden through the awareness of their crimes, or how attempts at repression force a conscience to take refuge in a sort of subconscious underground, from which it produces strange effects, more painful than the pains of straightforward remorse.

However, a clear conscience, too, must count on certain dissatisfactions. If I want to be just, I cannot adopt my own contentment as the one and only criterion of all my actions. If I desire to be faithful, I cannot constantly give in to the desires of a pleasurable life. Are we then just a battlefield of competing desires?

Duty or obligation is not a desire, nor is it conditioned by one or more desires (except perhaps by the desire to be good; but can the latter be put on a par with other desires?). An obligation emerges from a phenomenal demand, whether or not I am inclined to welcome it. But could I accept and realize its demand, could it become a purpose for me, if it did not somehow appeal to some desire in me? Some circumstances confront me with the most radical choice—for example, when I am tortured if I refuse to betray my son. If I prefer to be killed rather than commit an ignoble action, I am a witness to the overriding worth of the person or cause to which I am devoted. Such a witness or "martyr" is willing to sacrifice all the desires that motivate an ongoing life. But how can a martyr be motivated to such heroism, if not by some greater desire? Is it possible to contrast the ensemble of all mortal desires with a Desire that is not afraid of losing the entirety of a life and all the possible satisfactions of its mortal desires? Could the originary Desire analyzed in Chapter 4 be (among other things) a desire for innocence, purity of conscience, and being good until the end, even if this costs us our own life? In that case, moral goodness would realize a meaning that belongs to the ultimate Desideratum. The worth of being good in a moral sense would transcend the contentment of an entire life. If happiness, as Kant and the hedonists thought, were the summation of possible satisfaction, goodness would be different from, and sometimes hostile to, happiness. If, however, Desire, in its originary and ultimate difference from all finite desires, differentiates itself *in* those desires, moral goodness could be the ultimate but secret desideratum in all other desiderata and ends. The good itself would then not be some entity or relation beside, above, or beneath the ends of our desires and their more or less successful realizations in "happiness"; it would be the ultimate "form" that renders all desiderata good insofar as these allow Desire itself to guide and organize their realization.[22]

Although Desire initially may be experienced as a craving for fulfillment—the nostalgia for a lost paradise or a romantic quest for "the blue flower"—the encounter with someone who speaks to me interrupts the ellipse of our reaching out in order to return in wealth. The face demands a conversion of our movement: instead of letting me turn around and back to my desire of private happiness, the other shatters my egocentrism, if I am willing to be addressed. Giving in to the other's insistence reverses the orientation of my Desire. It does not abolish its longing but redirects it. A new kind of desirability reveals itself when it dawns on me that the other's existence is worthwhile in itself and irreducible to my enjoyment of conversation or friendship. The shocking experience of not being alone is the greatest event in my life if it converts me to the insight that I can act and desire, and even live, for another. Why can such a life be desired? Because being addressed by a face reveals the possibility of an irreducible meaning: devotion to the other makes sense for me. If such a meaning is absolutely desirable and if it is not only more than, but radically other than, the desirable multiplicity of all that I can enjoy by having, consuming, using, tasting, or contemplating, it surprises Desire by unveiling a decisive truth about its Desideratum. The desiring subject no longer views self-satisfaction as the ultimate goal. However, to feel, act, and be "for you" does not preclude my own happiness; on the contrary, it opens up a new dimension of possible meaning for me. It is possible to realize without egoism what Desire in me desires and still be content, even in face of the pains the realization costs.

What the discovery of the new meaning revealed by you means for the fulfillment of my other desires cannot yet be thematized here because we have not even begun a phenomenology of nature, art, politics, and religion. However, your resistance to my nostalgic way of Desiring, your call to conversion, has opened my heart to the possibility that other phenomena too might have more converting power than nostalgic interpretations of Desire are wont to concede.

From now on, I should be alert to other encounters that might de-center me. Neither consumption nor utility can constitute my dominant perspective; perhaps plants and animals and many other phenomena speak to me in a way that is more or less similar to the challenge of your face, thus refuting or relativizing my own centrality.

Nature

You, they, we, I myself demand that I respond appropriately to their and my being-there. Our mode of being, our characteristic existence—our "essence"—claims respect, reverence, service, and devotion. Your and our and my essence orients the behavior through which we respond to your, my, and our existence. They suggest an attitude, and if we are willing, they attune us to appropriate correspondence.

Can intersubjective correspondence be seen as paradigmatic for all moral responses? Does the universal principle of ethics lie in conformity with the essence, the *physis* or *natura*, of all beings to which we are related? Were Aristotle and his followers right, notwithstanding the difference between their conception of *physis* and our "nature"? Or must we shy away from all kinds of "essentialism" to save freedom, history, and difference in ethics? To begin with, let us look at the nature by which we are surrounded.

What Does "Nature" Mean?

The polysemy of the word *nature* is amazing. Having used it above in senses that are close to that of "essence" and "originariness,"[23] I will now focus on the universe of all nonhuman and nondivine realities. "Reality" reminds us of things (*res*), and these have often served as paradigms for thinking about nature, or even about being. It is, however, obvious that nature is much more than and different from a collection or system of things.

The perspectives of modern science presents nature as a play of particles in energetic fields that found all appearances of things, but nature is also the splendor of landscapes and seasons, the horror of cruel insects and rapacious vultures. Things can be studied as objects by curious but uninvolved observers; but our participation in the world of work and technology brings us in contact with nature through the use of tools, machines, electronic devices, and other sorts of equipment. Dissatisfaction with the reduction of nature to objectivity and utility has reawakened a retrieval of the Rousseauean and romantic desire for a return to nature itself, but even camping in the wilderness has become a highly technological (and commercial) business.

Not only does technology interpose itself between us and nature, but from the beginning of our history, art has also mediated our dealings with it. Are we at all able to maintain any immediate relationship with the inhuman part of living creatures? Even our awareness of prehistoric animals and cosmic occurrences is part of human narratives, reconstructions, museums, or learned discourses. Although we can imagine what happened before we arrived on the scene, we cannot erase our own, more or less frightened or otherwise affected presence as observers and potential actors on that scene.

However, neither art nor technology can bring us in contact with nature if we lack all sensitivity with regard to the ways of being and appearing in which nature and its parts emerge. Complete arbitrariness would suppress or destroy the appearance of all natural phenomena; but how could humans live without at least a minimal degree of obedience to the demands of nature?

Trees and Animals

Look at this tree in front of my window. The green of its well-shaped foliage has changed overnight to yellow, and soon it will shed its leaves, displaying the barren brown and black of its branches. We will have to wait five months for the return of its leaves, which again will form a glorious crown, greener and bigger than it is now.

It would "be a sin" to cut this tree. Its form, the shades of its leaves and its uprightness are impressive, beautiful, enjoyable. The wind seems to play as a friend with its leaves, whereas the storm of the other day ferociously shook all its members. There is a sort of alliance between the tree and our house; it reminds me of the linden trees in front of European farms in whose shadow the family rests after a day of harvesting. Together with the other ones, "our" tree gives the street its rhythm and style, orienting and measuring the space in this part of the suburb.

This description tries to show a tree in its splendor, thus emphasizing its aesthetic aspects and its function in the partly natural, partly civilized environment wherein we are at home. The tree is part of a natural constellation ruled by rhymes and correspondences. In its belonging, it is admirable, even lovable. It suggests and calls for an admiring and grateful response, and it forbids damage or destruction.

If the tree becomes sick and decrepit, however, as happened to that big oak on the other side of the street, its splendor gives way to the signs of its mortality. If I am very attached to it, I might still try to heal it, but if I don't succeed, I am not going to cause a drama, although my missing "that old tree" can take the form of mourning. A dying tree should be cut, consumed by fire, transformed into mulch, or whatever. Like all living and dead things on earth, trees are dominated by the destiny of generation and corruption, and this demands as much recognition as the glory of full maturity.

Is "the essence" of a tree only admirable and lovable, or does it, seen from other perspectives, show still other interesting aspects? For instance, trees are used for making furniture or paper; they are thus useful elements of a utilitarian economy. In certain circumstances, they serve to hide behind or to create an advantage in fighting. They function in children's play, and they play a role in many fairy tales.

Insofar as trees are useful, can we just ignore their admirable sides? Is it, for example, an appropriate, decent mode of action to sacrifice entire woods for heating or building? Why not? It has been done for ages, and it is hardly imaginable that such use will stop. Are trees and plants and stones not "for man"? But what does "for" mean in this context?

Using trees—first killing them and then using them as material for houses, furniture, heating, cooking, newspapers, and so on—is a form of consumption. We don't feel bad when we use stones, minerals, rocks, air, water, gasoline, and other inorganic materials for our consumption, although there may be limits here, too; but we feel uncomfortable when we realize how many animals are killed, not only to feed humanity, but also for gastronomic and cosmetic purposes. Don't we feel at least some guilt in killing animals when we do it without necessity or very good reasons? Even with regard to plants and trees, some feeling holds us back from useless destruction. What causes this feeling? Life as such? Is all life respectable, perhaps even sacred?

Consumption is always transformation, and transformation entails a moment of negation. Often, this moment is a form of destruction. Eating a steak presupposes the slaughtering of a cow. The reward for this killing lies in the feeding of another living being and the transformation of "cowy" meat into the flesh of a human body. Is this humanization a good reason, an adequate excuse, for the cow's violent death? Even if it is, a separate answer must be given to the question of whether an animal's life by itself deserves and calls for a certain kind of respect or awe, or, at least, a certain withholding of violence. Perhaps we must combine two theses: (1) Do not harm animals! and (2) There are cases where the general imperative (1) does not apply, for example, when human beings cannot survive or function well if they do not consume (certain) animals or kill them by way of self-protection.

Obviously, we must make distinctions between various kinds of animals. Although horses, cows, and domesticated dogs invite a certain kind of respect or even some sort of tenderness, sharks and scorpions rather suggest hatred. Monsters elicit fearful and aggressive behavior, as is illustrated by many myths about dragons and their sacred conquerors. However, even fighting with crocodiles and tigers does not eliminate a sense of awe and a special sort of "respect" with regard to these representatives of life. There is something forbidding and untouchable in them, even if they are perceived as symbols of harm and evil. The responses suggested in their appearance contain a moment of wonder that is close to admiration.

A phenomenology of the entire fauna is necessary to discover all the suggestions and appeals that lie in the appearance of various animals. For all of them, it is true that their emergence calls for an appropriate mode of responding, be this tender care or courageous fighting or some other behavior in between.

Can we state a similar thesis about the life of plants and trees? They do not provoke us in the same way as animals do because they do not show any behavior or awareness. Animals perceive and communicate in ways that we try to understand by comparison with human perception, feeling, and behavior. Many animals seem to feel pleasure and pain, to be driven by fear, desire, and devotion and by some sort of joy, gratitude, and friendship. Do they owe these emotions to their domestication? If so, they, too, like babies, can be civilized. Should we not treat them with care instead of harming or simply using them?

Since plants do not seem to feel anything, we do not feel accused by their "pains," but the vital and aesthetic aspects of their most impressive instances make us reluctant to destroy them without good reason. In creating a kind of awe, they do not exclude consumption, however, because we cannot live if we are not allowed to eat even plants.

The fruits of a tree are a good example of the multiple meanings attached to the vegetal realm. This apple is splendid, more original and better shaped than most jewels; but it also looks appetizing. If I eat it, I switch from an aesthetic delight to the enjoyment of its taste. The latter is not possible without destruction, while admiring contemplation can continue until the apple rots away. The switch itself is experienced as a light shock during the passing of a threshold: in peeling its skin away, I rob the apple of its splendor, thus preparing it for assimilation.

The tree offers me its fruits as simultaneously admirable and edible, forcing me to choose between responses that are not wrong but contradictory. To identify nature with its admirable qualities would cause our death; but to reduce it to a collection of consumer's goods would take away its splendor: nature's own art would be replaced by an ugly void, which would eliminate all poetry. By stripping nature of its beauty, we would also kill human sensitivity.

Notwithstanding big differences, the problem of animals' "fruits" is comparable to that of apples and peaches. Drinking a cow's milk or transforming it into cheese does not cause guilt feelings—unless, perhaps, such actions would lead to the calves' death. Can we say something similar about the eggs of chickens and ducks? By eating them, we prevent possible births, but we count on life's abundance to make up for our intervention.

Can the consumption of chickens themselves, as that of beef, pork, lobster, or fish, be justified through the argument that it transforms parts of those animals into constitutive elements of human bodies, thus actualizing higher possibilities of life? Instead of asking the cow to forgive us for eating its meat, it should, then, be grateful for being humanized, thus becoming intelligent and moral. Would this line of justification be more convincing if we argued that eating meat is redeemed by a *good* human life, whereas a bad life would make things worse? The elevation or "sublimation" of animal life does not necessarily lead to a higher meaning; it can also prepare a second, irreparable, death.

If the argument contains some truth, it might lie in the condition it tries to formulate: peaceful animals should not be killed, unless the killing, as a bad response to their suggestive appearance, is redeemed by a worthwhile form of new life. With regard to aggressive and dangerous animals, killing would be justified insofar as it saves the attacked life of endangered humans or animals. But is this line of argument not already too utilitarian?

When we see in a documentary how a leopard attacks a zebra calf, we are appalled by the bloody violence of the devouring. We humans feel that such killing is too "wild" and cruel. The cruelty does not so much lie in the killing as such, but rather in its mode. Death as such is natural and normal for all mortal beings. We can hasten and sometimes postpone our own or others' death, but we cannot avoid or abolish it. But the style of dying and killing does not leave us indifferent. However one feels about bullfighting, undeniably it can demonstrate that some killings are more tasteless than others.

Actively causing someone's or some animal's death determines the time and the mode of dying, which otherwise would have been determined by sickness, exhaustion, natural causes, or accident. The determination is arrogated by the killer: death has become the expression of another's "will." By deciding that someone here and now must die, a human will—in the form of an individual or an institution—gives a human meaning to a natural necessity. This meaning can be bad, for example, in a murder performed out of resentment; it can also be intended as a just retribution of awful crimes; or it can be the outcome of fighting for an honorable cause. Some deaths are glorious because they express dedication to a great ideal; heroic or saintly forms of dying, for instance, can compensate for their premature character.

If death as such is not the worst that can happen to a living being— if dying in a wild, inhumane, uncivilized, cruel, or meaningless way is worse—there might be reasons why certain kinds of death by human hands are preferable to certain forms of naturally passing away. If so, this does not yet answer the question of whether human individuals or institutions have the right to call for the death of other human beings, or even of animals. This question also involves the others' rights and the subquestion of whether one's right to life can be forfeited or sacrificed to other purposes. Do animals or some kinds of animals have rights in the sense in which we talk about human rights? This and similar questions cannot be answered until we have an insight into human freedom. Before we meditate on it in the next chapter, let us finish the meanderings of our meditation with a provisional conclusion about appropriate responses to the existence of living beings and an addition about nonliving phenomena.

The human face forbids us to reduce others to the use we can make of their qualities. Insofar as human beings have dignity, they escape the economy of use and consumption. Animals are different; some animals are good for company, others can be eaten, still others are dangerous, repulsive, monstrous, dirty. Different kinds provoke us to different reactions. With regard to some aggressive animals, it seems natural to many people that we kill them; other animals are so innocent and peaceful that we prefer to contemplate them. The responses suggested by all sorts of animals vary according to their character and the perspectives taken by the persons who encounter them. It is difficult or impossible to reduce all those suggestions to one denominator. Although animality or animal life as such has a normative character of its own, even in its lowest and most hostile forms, it demands a specific sort of respect and forbids arbitrary destruction. However, the same can be said about trees and plants: they, too, should not be destroyed without reason. What, then, is the ethical difference between animals and plants? Perhaps it lies in the fact that plants and trees do not respond but animals do. Perception and corporeal movements make it possible for animals to communicate with us through looks, sounds, and gestures, showing similarities to human behavior and expressions. The more similar they are, the more they appear to be related to us, populating the earth with us in various forms of familiarity, service, or accompaniment. Plants and trees, too, represent our surrounding life—how barren the earth would be without their greenery, how boring without their flowers, and how starving without their fruits!—but they have all their life in themselves, silent and fixed in their space, not interested in us, who may be interested in them. The kind of respect we owe a tree is closer to heeding than to communication. Plants have no interest at all, neither in an outside, nor in their own inside; they just are, achieving their growth in cycles, surviving, displaying their fragile or forceful beauty, inviting silent admiration.

Not all animals show interest in us, either, but many of them can "listen" and "talk" through "voices" and "gestures" when we address them. This draws us into a play with them, one in which the rules are suggested by the various characters of the participants. The truth of this sort of communication is symbolized in bestiaries and myths in which foxes, cocks, storks, wolves, and nightingales are the actors of our human comedy. If they can act so humanly, should we then not honor their claims to some quasi-human recognition?

An Ethics of Nature?

If it is true that all beings, through their being what they are, invite and challenge us to appropriate modes of responding, a complete philosophy of nature should explore the entire realm of nature in order to determine the whole range of such challenges. We could then go on in singing, as Orpheus did, the splendor and the terror of all kinds of animals, plants, rocks, mountains, planets, oceans, lakes, and stars.[24] However, we should not forget that nature is more than a collection of beings. The geological and geographical formations, the characteristic space and time of seasonal and biological cycles, and the various landscapes under different climates deserve their own phenomenologies. That the sciences may have a function in these, insofar as all natural phenomena have quantitative, physical and chemical, aspects, must be conceded, but that the sciences know better what and how nature *is*, is certainly not true. They have, for example, no sense for its normative aspects. These are experienced when we are confronted with the question of how we humans should deal with our natural surroundings, for instance, when we build a house. Not every type of house fits the landscape where we plan to live. Perhaps the desert allows for the most divergent buildings, but farmland in the low countries or lovely valleys among the mountains demand more adjusted dwellings than skyscrapers. Similar questions concern relations between landscapes and means of transportation, or rivers and bridges. The question of the right adjustment to the suggestions of nature is neither a merely utilitarian one nor a purely aesthetic one. Although we moderns have no strong sense of *belonging* to nature, we still are painfully affected by the discrepancy between the natural coherence of certain landscapes and the characterless constructions by which they are spoiled. Instead of showing that human cultivation can enhance nature, they offend our taste by the perduring contradiction of their mutual hostility.[25]

Ecology has developed as a concern about the human role in the fate of nature. The transformation of nature into culture cannot exclude all forms of destruction; a certain form and degree of violence is therefore unavoidable. Consumption, without which neither we nor animals can live, includes destruction, and using tools or employees wears them out. However, violence and destruction, if unavoidable, must be justified, and if a justification can be given, it also sets the limits for their use. If the destruction of the rain forest, for example, is a condition for the continuation of our printing culture, we must weigh the value of both the forests and the printed material we consume and find a balance between the two. Consumption and use themselves can become excessive compared to the value of leaving nature as much as possible unimpaired.

The reasons for our dealing with natural entities and processes must not be confined to utilitarian ones. Nature has a worth of its own that cannot be reduced completely to its serving our needs or wishes, or to our enjoyment of its aesthetic aspects. It is not easy to define what that worth is, but we experience it when we are overcome with awe for its unspoken secret, for example, when we see a documentary about the history of volcanoes or the life and work of bees.

Many tribes and peoples have venerated the vitality, power, and beauty of nature in the figures of gods and demons or as an all-permeating might. These gods and demons were experienced as more powerful than humans, threatening or friendly, generous or vindictive, punishing or forgiving. Even when monotheistic religions condemned all idolatry, the gods did not immediately disappear, because Nature could not be experienced as having no soul and secret of its own at all. Even in Christianity, many preferred to see Nature as ruled by angels or demons rather than give up all connections between Nature and the Divine. Only modern technology, conspiring with the modern economy, could convince an educated elite that nature was nothing else than useful material for human purposes. In the meantime, however, we have become suspicious about the ruthless utilitarianism that inspires that thesis. Some philosophers who see modern secularism as an aberration even reintroduce some kind of gods, whereas others try to retrieve the old tradition about the presence of the one and only God in all things.[26]

The thoughts expressed here are no more than hints for an ethics of our behavior (including our contemplative behavior) with regard to Nature. If correspondence has a meaning in this context, an enormous task awaits those who are convinced that the sciences offer only a very limited truth about nature. A more complete philosophy of natural phenomena is necessary for a more balanced relationship to nature than the scientific one.

Many people who accept, in theory, the scientific approach to nature combine it with an aesthetic approach when enjoying nature on vacation. Are they combining a scientific theory with an aesthetic practice? Or is the aesthetic perspective also relevant for an insight in the specific nature of nature? The relations between art and nature must be explored if we want to pursue the question of nature's transformation in culture and a culture's dealing with its available nature.

Art

The following remarks are still less systematic than those discussed above. They are meant as a possible preparation for a treatise on art in relation to nature and vice versa, insofar as both could or should play a role in a complete ethics of correspondence.

Art and Nature

Nature is amazing, splendid, wonderful; but it is also terrifying and demonic. The duplicity of nature is a mystery. As all mysteries, it attracts our curiosity while also scaring us. Science is one answer to its puzzling character. Contemplative fascination is another.

The aesthetic aspects of nature are savored in characteristic forms of contemplation and artistic practice. Nature's splendor and horror are embraced and tasted when art, taking up some of its suggestions, intensifies the ways in which nature impresses us. Poetry, music, visual arts, and architecture emphasize the signifying potential of nature's abundance in forms, lines, dimensions, sounds, colors, proportions, and contrasts. Radically different from the utilitarian perspective, to which nature can only show its consumable or instrumental sides, the aesthetic perspective either leaves natural phenomena unimpaired or transforms them into appearances that enhance their suggestions. Rather than treating nature's mystery as a puzzle that should be solved, the aesthetic attitude intensifies its duplicity by exaggerating, in the form of a particular presentation, the simultaneity of its immediate givenness and the meaning that remains hidden in its seeming candor. This exaggeration is beautiful when it follows the signitive indications of nature's splendor; confronted with nature's inherent horror, it offers us a possibility of coping with it, without, however, deciphering the what and why of its mysterious ruling. Thus, the aesthetic perspective stylizes nature as the mysterious mixture that it always already has been, although it needs artists to show this in all its aspects.

Nature as an Invitation to Art

Insofar as nature is impressive, amazing, wonderful, splendid or horrible, lovely or cruel, dramatic and poetic, it provokes our contemplation. We often dwell on its phenomena in amazement or terror and feel drawn to them without knowing what else to do in order to establish an adequate relationship. We follow the contours of the mountains, the vegetation on its slopes, the shifting of its colors under the sunlight and the changing shadows of the clouds. . . . We are caught by a dialogue between black-birds on a summer evening that brings peace. . . . We enjoy nature—but what shall we do with it?

Some of us respond to nature's splendor by hearing it as a call for re-producing it in a stylized form. Painting, poetry, architecture, and music are dimensions in which nature receives a manifold of humanized configura-tions, all of which recompose some of its features, as seen or heard by the artist and seeable or audible by others. Interpretations of nature by way of lines and colors, melodies, rhythms and timbres, images, words, and lan-guages emphasize in endless variations what nature in appearing suggests.

Not only nature's splendor, but also its cruel aspects are impressive: they slap us in the face. Their provocation can drive an artist to even exag-gerate their ugliness. It is true of both splendid and horrible phenomena that their contemplation causes a certain pain if we cannot somehow ex-press what they do to us. We want at least to express our awe when de-scribing to a friend "how beautiful, how dramatic, how awful it was." In-stead of embracing the mountains or kissing the nightingale, the artist composes a work in which the bird, the mountain, or the horse, reconfig-ured—that is, interpreted and transformed—can be seen in a new light or mode: Look how noble, strong, well proportioned, trustworthy—in brief, how "horsy"—this horse is!

Art as Displaying Nature

Not all art concentrates on nature, but when it does, it stresses na-ture's challenge by emphasizing selected features and patterns of its being there. Contemplation already selects and focuses on some aspects while ne-glecting or passing over others. Not only do seeing and hearing demand structuring and simplification, they also presuppose learning. Just like sci-entific observation, artistic perception implies a well-trained sensitivity. Likewise, new discoveries in art are only made by original ways of sensing and configuration.

All art transforms the given, at least by selecting and highlighting some and not all of its features. Emphasis and exaggeration are normal in art, and each great artist can be recognized by his own perspective and style. Does this "subjectivism" not make the poets and painters incapable of being teachers of perception? On the contrary. By selecting, focusing, emphasizing, exaggerating, reconfiguring, and transforming the given, they show aspects that have been covered up by average modes of perceiving and interpreting (for we always interpret and configure—even if we slavishly follow the "normal" way). Nobody will swear by one artistic view of nature (or, for that matter, of the universe); if we agree that the world of art encompasses innumerable interpretations, we will accept all that allow us to discover some of the reality that is evoked in the artist's reconfiguration, without identifying that reality with any of its renderings.

With regard to a philosophy of the given, art has at least two functions: (1) a phenomenological (or epistemological) one, and (2) an ethical one (in the broadest sense of the term). The first function follows from the explanation given above: if artworks show us things better than the average ways of perception can, they must be consulted by those who want to write a phenomenology of all that shows up. For instance, had you already discovered on your own the many ways in which flowers appear, revealed by the Dutch, French, and Italian still lifes from the sixteenth to the nineteenth century? Have Messiaen's works not given you a new ear for the songs of birds? How much more boring would the world be if art had not evoked and renewed it in its multitude of contrasting but complementary ways!

The second, "ethical" function of art lies in the exemplary way in which it shows us how we can respond to the challenge of natural and other phenomena. At least some aesthetic sensibility is presupposed to appreciate them the way an artist perceives and renders them, but once such a sensibility is awakened, all good artworks can guide us in finding our own mode of caring about appropriate, well-attuned perceptions and dealings with the polyvalent phenomenality of the given. Correspondence, as the appropriate attunement to and transformation of natural phenomena, can be accepted as a principle for an "ethics of nature." The aesthetic application of this principle falls under an ethics of refined sensibility and good taste. To act *comme il faut* is not obligatory in the sense of Kant's "rigorous duty" (*die strenge Pflicht*), but it belongs to the task of becoming "good and beautiful" in the sense of Greek *kalokagathia*. Aristotle's ethics, for example, is much closer to an aesthetic code of behavior than the modern separation of art from morality (which is much closer to legality and rights).[27]

The Aesthetic Universe

The aesthetic perspective is not limited to the contemplation of nature; it extends to the universe of all phenomena, including the moral, political, and religious. We can, for example, appreciate the good taste of innocent behavior or the beauty of religious rituals, even if we are not committed to their moral or religious meanings. Because of the modern separation between moral duties and aesthetic sensibility, the fascination typical of the aesthetic attitude expresses a rather different involvement than the moral one. A certain detachment from the fascinating phenomena seems even essential for experiencing them as impressive, splendid, dramatic, beautiful, and so on. The distance thus created explains the universality of this attitude. Not only crystals, mountains, birds, and trees, but persons, events, stories, communal histories can be observed, arranged, and (re)shaped without committing oneself to any scientific, moral, political, or religious judgment about their significance. True, art can be combined with the service of a nonaesthetic cause, and an artist can see herself as a moral or political propagandist, but such combinations do not exemplify the essence of the aesthetic dimension as such.

If the aesthetic perspective becomes the highest, all things and events—society, culture, history, and individuals' lives—are experienced as a drama. Even the most horrible events are then observed and evaluated in light of a desire for "beauty." Since life and history are mixtures of greatness, evil, and mediocrity, they form a combination of tragedies and comedies. We then try to redeem the human tragicomedy by showing how, despite its injustice, it is a marvelous spectacle.

Distance implies a certain irony, but irony does not necessarily include a total lack of involvement. Ironic artists, such as Nietzsche, can passionately be engaged in their descriptive and evaluative task. Instead of producing only decorative art, they then persist in showing us who and how we are in order to free us from illusions.

How various—for example, religious, strictly moral, legal, artistic, sportive, culinary—commitments can be distinct and still intertwined is a question that cannot yet be asked at this stage of our investigation. The primary task of distinguishing several attitudes that in some strict or broad sense can be called "ethical" must come first.

Community

Correspondence plays not only between you and me, nature and us, or artworks and us, but also between you, me, and us, on one side, and the various communities to which we belong, on the other. Although we are already involved in several communities before we can ask how we should deal with them or how they should deal with us, these questions must be asked from a certain distance, if we want to understand what we, as social and political beings, are and have to be. Are we able to take such a distance with regard to ourselves as always already involved in communal practices and institutions? Let us try to do it and see what the result of such an attempt will be. Perhaps it will be recognizable as an expression of the particular society in which we participate. If so, we may try to further overcome our particularization by a more universal approach.

Within the framework of this book, the main question here is how we should respond to the communal phenomena with which we are confronted. In a political extension of ethics, we should also include the question of how communities should deal with their members. Before asking these questions, however, we must clarify the relations that bind human individuals and their communities together. Once we have perceived how each person is involved in various communities, perhaps we will be capable of outlining an ethics of the appropriate attitudes and virtues characteristic of a good community member and—in a fundamental politics—of sketching the appropriate way in which the various communities take care of their participants.

Individual and Community

Too many social and political philosophies have taken for granted that a community and the individuals of which it is composed can be opposed as two poles of an opposition. This presupposition easily leads to the idea of a conflict between the two parties, each of which is fighting for its own interests. Such a conflict can then be resolved by mutual limitation or by subordination, but a sort of war underlies the balancing of the forces in play. Individualism and collectivism insist on the supremacy of one party over the other, whereas a compromise between the two poles veils the imminent outbreak of internal war.

What if we can show, however, that the concept of a human individual cannot be thought without communal features and that a community is nothing else than a specific constellation of individuals? Or even that individuality and commonality are two inseparable aspects of one and the same human reality—aspects that can be distinguished but not separated, not even in thought? The ideal of a synthetic philosophy would lie in a theory that shows how commonality is an internal element of human individuality and vice versa. If such a theory is possible, it cannot be demonstrated by staring at abstract concepts; it must be prepared by a phenomenological analysis of the ways in which individuals are engaged in various communities. To make a beginning with such an analysis, I will continue the study of the face to face that has been given above.

We (You and I)

I owe my ability to speak to those who, in the beginning of my life, spoke to me. My ability to address you is due to my having been addressed. When my mother smiled at the baby I was, I spontaneously smiled back at her. Slowly, I started imitating her speaking to me; now I can speak to you, thanks to all the educators who helped me to speak well— that is, to address myself to others in intelligible and appropriate ways. That you can understand me, we owe to our sharing a common language. This would not suffice, however, if we did not also share an entire universe of connotations and denotations, sayings, opinions, stories, literature, rituals, and so on. We share a culture or even a complex of several cultures and subcultures.

Without sharing a common culture we would not be able to communicate. But without being you and I, unique and different individuals, we would not say or hear anything else than the commonplaces that everyone can utter without thought or imagination of one's own. As soon as you and I express ourselves through the medium of common patterns we have incorporated, we make a difference. Thanks to the unicity of expressive individuals, a common heritage is varied, continually changing into updated versions.

In speaking to one another, we enact the linguistic potentialities of the community to which we belong. This dependence is not restricted to language and literature; it encompasses the entire range of thought, behavior, and imagination. Even our feelings are influenced and shaped by the particular culture in which we participate. The opinions and the ethos that rule our community, rule us; our attitudes and projects are mediated by the convictions and customs that characterize our civilization. Culture is indeed a "second nature,"[28] an "objectively" existing order to which we owe our manners. But how does this order "exist"? How is the cultural heritage of our community "available"? What kind of existence characterizes the commonality of our culture?

Communities and Cultures

Before we can give a precise answer to the question just formulated, we should specify the various cultures and communities in which we participate, as well as the different levels that can be distinguished in each of them. The following sketch may indicate a few lines of such an overview.

Each individual belongs to several groups, associations, or communities with their characteristic cultures or subcultures. An individual's abilities and character are formed by a particular confluence of those cultures, which thus are enriched with one more variation. Born into a family (or something similar), you were steeped in an emotional climate, a specific manner of laughing and crying, speaking and singing, doing and feeling. Your parents formed your speech and behavior; in school, your teachers further educated your mind; the church canalized your religious aspirations; in high school you began to appreciate literature and works of art, which inspired you to frequent museums and libraries; and at the university, you learned how to participate in the academic community. When you were sent to buy bread, you acted as a participant of the economic system, whereas discussions about political alternatives made you aware of belonging to the political system of your country. Because the world has become one, you now also feel solidarity with the entire humanity. Family, school, society, state, church, and humanity as a whole are only some of the communities that mark your individual existence as already civilized by a confluence of several cultures. Your way of undergoing and appropriating these is more or less your own. The more original you are, the more unique your version of the common culture is, but the result of your inculturation is always a particular blend of conservation and renewal. The extremes between which such versions fluctuate are reactionary conservatism, on the one hand, and rebellion, dissidence, or revolution, on the other. Retrieval of the ruling traditions in light of a hoped-for future is the law of all self-realization. Thanks to the existing communities, new generations can be civilized. That we became human we owe to cultures that existed before we were introduced to them. But how do they exist?

The Existence of Cultures

The culture to which I owe (part of) my humanization precedes my ability to speak, act, feel, imagine, and think as a human being. But no culture exists on its own, apart from cultured persons who enact or actualize that culture's potentialities. Abstracted from speaking, writing, playing, thinking, and acting enactors, a culture can be no more than a collection of traces without voice and real meaning. Their meaning—inscribed in books and monuments—is dead, fossilized, unreal until someone breathes life into them. The relationship between cultivated persons and the culture that enables them to produce meaningful actions, works, or speeches can be illustrated by the difference between the lines and notes of a score and the resounding symphony performed by live musicians. The traces of a certain past (for example, the past of a composer's imaginative "hearing" and producing) are given to us who, if we have acquired the requisite skills, can procure a future for them. Our performance actualizes the virtualities of inherited relics by a "presentifying" transformation. Similar analyses can be given for our use of language and our retrieval of existing mores: we imitate preceding speakers and actors by again enacting the patterns of a more or less fixed past in relatively new ways. We breathe new life into ancient schemas that otherwise would wither away. No language has ever spoken (*die Sprache spricht nicht und nimmer*[29]); no score has ever made music; no culture produces anything civilized. But it is also true that no person can speak or sing or act without the aid of patterns and traces inherited from an already existing culture.

It is not enough to state that the communities to which we belong, through their cultural traditions offer us a collection of traces or inscriptions that we can bring to life by breathing spirit into them. The ruling culture itself offers us examples and standard modes of retrieval; we are inspired and formed by models of renovation and heroes of "creative fidelity."[30] Once they have become parts of a culture, these heroes are recommended to us in the form of stylized types and laudatory texts. But even in the form of such traces from the past and possibilities that need breathing individuals to become actual, a culture cannot exist on its own, separately from persons who share that culture in practicing it. A trace would not exist if it were not conserved and offered as a possibility of life by parents, teachers, librarians, friends, or readers who recognize a possible promise in it. For them certain traces are reenactable and open to interpretation, even though they interpret them in ways that are different from their predecessors and successors.

"Culture" is a name for the ensemble of customary patterns and (re)enactments shared by the members of a community (family, school, association, society, state, civilization). A culture has its own time: the temporality of a past that, as tradition, is being transformed in the future shape of a community. Both community and culture are thus historical. Neither culture, nor community and history exist apart from living individuals; they are the common aspect, element, or moment of individuals who, despite the differences of their versions, share a particular mode of being human. This mode is theirs; it does not exist outside, above, behind, or before them, but consists of their manners of retrieving and preparing human possibilities that have been actualized by others before them. As a form of transforming imitation, retrieval keeps a culture alive so that it may have a future. Without imitation and repetition of that which is common to the participants of a culture, their community would disappear; but without change and differentiation, their culture—and therewith their life—would fossilize.

Community and Individuals

Through the prism of culture we have approached the commonality that holds civilized individuals together in particular communities. What they have in common—the customs, structures, patterns, stories, models, ideals they share—constitutes their community. This is thus not an independent entity, but rather the fact that the individuals who belong together (as their sharing shows) form an ensemble. How do they form an ensemble? By living in ways that are similar: they concretize and vary a common mode of being. Their ensemble, their community, is recognizable because together they display a characteristic constellation. A community is a specific constellation: a particular kind of organization, which, through its particular culture, characterizes the kind of life led by its participants; a specific kind of union with an articulation and style of its own.

When we say that individuals "belong" to the same family or the same national community, the temptation may be great to see their community as a totality that encompasses more than its parts or members. However, "community" means no more than all that which the composing individuals have in common. Besides their common institutions and monuments, they also own "things" that are not common, for example, the unicity that makes their individual lives radically different, unrepeatable, and nonimitable. That each life is only similar to other lives, and thus always the unique version of a common theme, expresses the noncoincidence of the individuals with any of their communities. Besides the commonality, without which no individual would be able to be human, there is in each individual also a private reserve or distance that counts for the possibility of making a difference.[31]

An individual can thus never be reduced to an associate, a family member, or a citizen; not even to a part of humanity. Individuals have a destiny of their own. Their death is the seal on their ultimate solitude.

However, although none of the communities enumerated encompasses the entirety of the individuals of which they are composed, must we not maintain that the latter are dependent on the commonality of the structures and contents, the organization and the culture, which precede their births? If it is true that no one can speak, act, imagine without retrieving an already available culture, does this not imply that no human individual can be prior to the emergence of the community that offers such a culture? Nobody has created language or the ruling ethos; they were already there before someone began to speak or act. If they are only traces, how can they precede all speech and action? The metaphor of the trace shows its weakness here. Speaking and language must always have been simultaneous, but language, as only an element, is less than speech, and action is more than ethos.

On the one hand, language and culture in general have been shown to be only subordinate elements of the individuals' unique ways of life; on the other, individual lives are dependent on the already available potentialities of a communal culture. There remains something mysterious in the availability of culture and civilization. Just as nature, the ensemble of all prehuman givenness, overwhelms us by its unexpected and amazing character, so the "second nature" of human culture and civilization makes us wonder about its origin. Although entirely human, language and ethos and all other cultural potentialities cannot be explained by some invention or creation for which certain individuals would be responsible. The givenness of our "second nature" appears as a gift, but the giver is concealed. The amazement that ensues from this gift might seduce us to see our cultural community as the giver, but this cannot be a speaking or acting subject.

If the community as the common mode of the composing individuals is not a subject, can it then be reduced to their "mentality"? It is certainly more than a mentality, insofar as it encompasses not only common conceptions, views, convictions, and beliefs, but also customs, uses, modes of behavior, symbolisms, stories, moods, and emotions. But even as an all-encompassing culture, the community of individuals that belong together seems to be more than the shared, communal, subordinate element of their self-realization. Not only does the culture they share somewhat mysteriously "precede" their actualization, their community is also a union, and this seems to be "more than the sum of its parts," as the saying goes. A union is certainly more than an enumeration or an addition. As we have seen, individuals share those elements that are at the same time constitutive for their community and their own concrete individuality. Their communitarian aspect cannot be hypostasized as an entity over against or above them. It can be contrasted with the thought of isolated individuals that would not share anything, but such a thought would be too abstract, or rather too unreal, to do justice to human individuality as such.

A union is not identical with shared commonality. Although a human union is not a hypostasis, a substance, or a subject, there is a difference between the union itself and that which is shared by the united persons. A community of individuals is not exactly the same as the common element in their lives. We can imagine a number of individuals who have a language or an ethos in common without forming a community. It is, for example, thinkable that Columbus might have discovered a people that already spoke Spanish (or, for that matter, Italian), but by itself, such would not have justified the conclusion that they belonged to the same community as he and his companions.

Forming a community presupposes more than similarity, commonality, sharing, or breathing life into a common element or fund. It also presupposes that the composing individuals *will* their union. This willing can be an explicit decision to unite or to maintain a uniting bond, but it can also remain implicit, for example, in the form of a scarcely self-conscious assent. In any case, however, the members of a community must will themselves as members, that is, as replacing their individual isolation by a chosen or consented coexistence, including at least a minimal form of willed living together, consensus, and cooperation.

Such a union necessarily takes the shape of an—at least rudimentary—organization: as united, the individuals accept or produce regulations that express and protect their collective unity. The organization of their coexistence demands institutions: limits that distinguish their community from other communities, laws for solidarity and mutual behavior, guarantees for each member's rights, limitations of greed and power, sanctions, and so on. Only an organized togetherness can be called a community. To share a culture is not enough because it leaves open the possibility that a culture is shared by different communities.

When considering an organized community with its own institutions and culture, for example, a family, tribe, or nation, the temptation to hypostasize it may even be stronger than before. When such a community is headed by one leader, some thinkers have seen the leader as the summation of the whole and interpreted his function—and therewith the function of the community—as the "more" or the extra that the union would add to the sum of the united individuals. A king or president can indeed be seen as symbolizing the entire nation he or she represents. When De Gaulle visited Chile, for example, he correctly began his main speech with the words "*La France est venue chez vous*" ("France has come to you"). Louis XIV was even more explicit when he said "*L'Etat, c'est moi*" ("The State, that is me"). It is obvious, however, that kings and presidents come and go, whereas nations perdure. Symbolic representation is not quite the same as identification. The temptation to personify the community and thus underscore its independence from its members remains strong, however. Durable or even "immortal" unions, cities, kingdoms, and empires have been venerated in the form of their protective gods. Apparently, the fact of being united, the foundation of the community as an organized union that precedes our participation in it, has been interpreted as a superhuman act and gift, similar to the gift of language and culture indicated above. The amazing character of such "gifts" need not be denied, but it does not justify conceiving of the community as an independent subject or "spirit."

When Herder or Hegel write about the *Volksgeist* (the people's spirit), they mean the principle that is responsible for the particular character of a people as it is expressed in its laws, language, vision, legal, social and political institutions, literature, art, religion, and thought. The spirit, which is the source of that character, permeates the whole of the people's community. As principle and origin, it is different from a mentality or cultural outlook. However, it can be neither a separate entity, nor a substance or subject that precedes the individuals that would be its accidents or modi, because their willing their communion with its characteristic culture and organization is constitutive for the spirit that binds them together. That "the spirit" of their community precedes and survives (in a modified form) their individual lives does not contradict the constitutive power of the individuals' willing, because their willed confirmation of the national institutions and culture will be taken over by the next generation—unless a very dramatic revolution occurs; but even then the survivors will build on the ruins and relics of the past.

Instead of attributing the uniting power to a superhuman spirit or god, most modern theories of the state have located it in the collective or "general" will of the united individuals themselves. They most often postulated a "social contract" achieved by all composing individuals to explain their organized cohesion, which is, however, more united than an agreement between private persons. The composing individuals themselves were then seen as sovereign with regard to their emergence as one people. This incorporation of the uniting principle into the individuals who create their union fits well into the modern wish of being the cause of one's own being, but it does not clarify the logic of the postulated transition from scattered individuals to a unified community, because the decision to unite into an organized community presupposes a prior commonality and communication.[32]

As we have seen, the imagined "state of nature," in which individuals, as atomic monads, are related only by competition and war, is an abstraction from the historical situation in which human individuals are always already involved in unitive structures and institutions. Rather than the reconstruction of a primitive or prehistorical situation, Hobbes' "state of nature" is a bugaboo used to deter the citizens of an existing "civil state" from abandoning the institutions that constitute their community—even if these institutions are corrupt and decadent. Do not regress into the chaos of isolated monads! Although the reasons given for this prohibition have often been utilitarian (you lose your safety and all opportunity for happiness), a more profound reason lies in the fact that total isolation destroys any possibility of being human at all.

Rather than being the product of a decision made by a multitude of individual wills, the collective or "general" will is the general consensus of already civilized members who hold on to the community in which they feel at home. Historically and in the development of a human life, autonomy (in the recent, non-Kantian sense of the word) emerges on the basis of a prior assent to the communal reality that makes individual survival and civilization possible. To exile oneself from such a "civil state" of affairs or to destroy its basis is generally understood and rejected as fatal by most actors who have not lost their head. Rebellion or revolution themselves are conditioned by the judicious use of the existing institutions. Beginning from scratch is impossible. Even the very planning and pleading presupposed by any contract and the commitment to its sanctioning would not be possible if the contracting parties could not speak the same language, make mutually understandable gestures, and appeal to a collective power to enforce the stipulations of their agreement. The sanctions that, according to social contract theories, result from the initial contract express a prior union of the many wills in their opposition to the scattering of completely separated wills. The idea of a willed union with others is presupposed in the wills of any civilized and civil individual. No one can live as an absolute stranger or exile. As Aristotle said, to live completely alone, one must be a beast or a god.[33] Perhaps he even expected too much from gods and animals; especially if his dictum regards the higher levels of animal life and the human, all too human gods of Greece.

The idea of an original contract through which we have invented and created the "civil state" of our sharing the institutions that regulate our lives is a way of imagining that we ourselves are the authors of our social, economic, political, and cultural existence, who keep it under control, ready to (re)adjust it as soon as we find it corrupt or unsatisfactory. Thus, we try to eliminate the role that fate and destiny play in our history and to forget that any contract, even the one we deem original or initial, presupposes a situation of relative peace in which it is possible to speak instead of only fighting, competing, or conquering. Some kind of realized sociality and respect—even if motivated by anxiety or desire only—must be given before individuals can come to an agreement about their distribution of power, authority, and rights. Any reflection about the organization of living together presupposes that a public order, however deficient, already exists. The foundation of a civilized community is never an absolute beginning; it is always the transformation of an already existent community, similar to art, ethos, or religion. Therefore, the suggestion that the communities to which we owe our civilized existence are only the products of our creative activity must be corrected: we must recognize their givenness by accepting them as coconstitutive of our own individual identity.

Ethics and the Community

The analysis of the mutual inclusion that binds the community and its composing individuals together seems to have carried us away from the central questions of ethics.

From the perspective of our focus on correspondence, the ethical questions concerning our existence in communities can be summarized in asking: How should we respond to the communal dimensions of human lives? Since communities are constellations of individual relations, sharing, and interaction, we must then also ask: How should we, while fulfilling communal (for example, familial, economic, and political) functions, respond to the claims and needs and desires of other members of the same or different communities? The latter question overlaps with the question of how "the community" must respond to its members, but we should avoid the danger of again hypostasizing the community as if it were different from the persons whose functions assure the union of the members' togetherness and thus totalize their plurality.

Although questions of community and commonality most often are studied in the context of political philosophy, we have already reminded ourselves that a family, a "republic of letters," and several other constellations are likewise communities. An ethics of the community must therefore specify the dimensions it intends to target. Because modern and contemporary philosophy emphasize the political constitution of the state, I will continue to regard it as the main paradigm, although further development of an ethics should also focus on the family, the various kinds of intellectual, scientific, and cultural communities, the realm of philosophy, and the communal aspects of humanity as a whole.

Several modern philosophers have treated the relations between ethics, rights, and politics as a question of the "external" behavior of citizens and states. However, a phenomenological analysis of motivation and behavior shows that the internal and the external sides of human action cannot be separated. Behavior shows its motivation, although a blind or half-blind observer may not be able to sharply distinguish all its revealing shades. Conversely, motivation cannot be genuine and appears as inauthentic if it does not express itself in corporeal, material, and "external" behavior. If, like Kant, we distinguish right, as the regulation of external behavior, from morality, we should not forget that law-abiding behavior that is motivated by immoral reasons looks radically different from "the same" but morally well-motivated obedience. Kant's statement that a system of right can be upheld by a devilish people[34] is therefore not only amazing but false. The "internal" *Gesinnung*, as an abiding "disposition," is decisive, especially in the long run, for the authenticity of morally based right. Besides, the word *disposition* is not clear enough to distinguish the mindset that Kant calls *Gesinnung*, for *disposition* can still be heard as a customary readiness or tendency to act in a certain way without being moved "from the bottom of one's heart." Ethics is interested in both the observable and the "cordial" sides of community and right; it refuses to isolate their "external" and "internal" aspects.

In focusing on right and rights, as social and political philosophers from Hobbes to Hegel did, we are drawn into the complex of questions that encircle justice: Is justice done? How should we be just? To what extent and how must we cooperate in the development of more just customs and institutions? Before we ask and answer such questions, however, we should reflect on a more immediate response to the fact that we are already born and educated in particular communities with their own institutions and traditions. The family and the state, for example, provoke us to acceptance, gratitude, critique, and emendation. How do we respond to this provocation?

Acceptance.   The general thesis about receptivity and acceptance argued for in Chapter 1 must be specified, not only with regard to the processes and events of nature, but also with regard to the familial and political, economic and cultural life we share with others. No less than the weather, the flora, and the natural disasters that determine our corporeal and mental life, our existence is shaped by the "second nature" or "objective spirit" of our social and historical world. We have not chosen the milieu or the culture that has become ours, but we cannot reject it, at least not at once (and probably never altogether). We are forced to accept the language, the mores, the mentality, and the history we unavoidably share with other members of the same community. Neither did we choose our parents, nor the tradition that has become ours. To accept the ethos of our community is to accept those aspects of ourselves that have been civilized by socialization and inculturation.

Gratitude.   Since I would be no more than a monkey, if that, if I had not been civilized by representatives of the communities to which I belong—my parents, teachers, social and spiritual guides, politicians, police, and so on—gratitude seems to be an appropriate reaction: I owe my civility to the care that they, thanks to a shared culture, took of me. In them, I thank the community.

At this point, we can apply all that has been said above about the necessity of conservation, tradition, handing on, creative fidelity, and retrieval and about the past as an indispensable but generous gift that makes civilization possible. Nature and second nature, as the context and externality of my body, have made me human—albeit in a particular and individual way (but individualized particularity is the only possibility of being universal in a human way).

Notwithstanding all the gifts we have received by being born into an already civilized world, much of it is so deficient and disappointing that some people reject the thought of any debt of gratitude. Should we not rather condemn and reject this bad, unfair, cruel universe? Below, I will consider the role of evil and ask what kinds of response it deserves, but for now I presuppose that at least part of the world that is given to us can be enjoyed.

Acceptance and gratitude regarding our heritage concretize the fundamental receptivity that characterizes the finitude of our fate. As we have noticed, this receptivity is no mere passivity, but it would degenerate into a stubborn conservatism if it were not animated by a devotion that recreates our heritage in new ways. Such a recreation presupposes critique and an orientation toward something as yet unknown that provides the inspiration for promising changes. In the meantime—despite critical disapprovals and doubts that might assail us—we cannot refuse to cooperate with the other participants of our community and culture in maintaining the established mechanisms and processes of our shared existence.

When it is said that we should be grateful for the gifts of our community, to whom exactly do we direct our thanksgiving? We thank our educators, but most of what they taught us belongs to the traditional culture they themselves received from other representatives of that culture. Does this fact not indicate that "the culture" (and thus the cultural community) is the giver to which our gratitude should be directed? Again we must repeat that "the culture" would not touch us if it were not brought to life by receptive as well as productive people who make it speak, act, influence, form, and so on. But it is nevertheless true that these people do not possess or create the culture; they can only transmit and to a certain extent transform or *re*-create it.

The question acquires a more critical edge when it is reformulated as a question about gratitude with regard to the heroes of our culture: the classics of art, literature, morality, politics, religion, science, philosophy. Are they not the great creators of newness, or even the founders of our civilization? Insofar as we have enough data to reconstruct the genesis of their "creations," history will always show that their exploits were not creations ex nihilo. They did not stand at an absolute beginning, but rather at critical points of history where the original form of their retrieval gave a revolutionary twist to the received tradition. Their renewal was as much conservative as futuristic. If they had not heeded anything old, nobody would have been able to understand them; their message would have disappeared without leaving any trace.

Critique.   The analysis of experience has shown its reflective and self-critical character.[35] Experience is always accompanied by an experiential self-evaluation, which may lead to readjustment. Experience is oriented by a desire to do (more) justice to the phenomenon with which we are confronted.

Involvement in communal processes is a concrete aspect of our experiential awareness. We share in the experiences of the communities to which we belong: what their average members feel, opine, imagine, deem decent and just has permeated our education and thus is part of our own experience, although we may have transformed it into a highly original variation. A sociological analysis of our dependence on the average experiences, opinions, myths, and mores of the existing culture should carefully distinguish the different groups to which we belong and the levels of our sharing. Obviously, a society and its culture are not monolithic; they are composed of many, often contradictory, levels of experience and conviction. It is, for example, possible that some citizens swear by the predominant public opinion as expressed in the media, whereas others, whose contempt is fueled by academic standards of description and interpretation, feel that the media give a distorted picture of the reality. Still others may look down on average scholarship, finding themselves in agreement with a contemplative tradition that honors much higher standards than academic performance. These and other levels of experience and perspective belong to the various communities in which one can feel at home. Most often we live on several levels at the same time, which forces us to integrate all of them in a personal way.

The example just given focuses on possible modes of knowledge and evaluation with regard to the world in which we live; but many other perspectives have their own multiplicity of experiential levels. In literature, art, morality, religion, housing, fashion, gastronomy, and the like, we share opinions and tastes with others who belong to the same group, class, church, or sect, but all these groups are related by some affinity, insofar as they together form one overall culture.

Besides the distinction of experiential levels just mentioned, we can also distinguish the formal differences between authentic and fake, deep and superficial, or serious and frivolous experiences. For instance, individuals can share a Christian or Islamic outlook and practice, although some of them are serious about it while others take it lightly.

What does all this have to do with a critical response to the community in which one is involved? Critical self-evaluation implies evaluation of my sharing certain experiences and spontaneous reactions that are deemed "obvious" and "correct" in my community. If my evaluation results in criticism, whence does the principle or criterion come that prompts me to criticize the shared experience? A new mode of experience is burgeoning; apparently, the phenomenon at issue, together with my desire for justice, urges me to attempt a better mode of responding to it. But how can I feel or see that the situation or structure I am evaluating is not good?

Often, perhaps always, the principle of my criticism, even on the most basic level of experience, is already present in the communal culture that I share. The criterion that allows me to criticize a vulgar ethos, for example, might be given in the ethos of a more noble or refined group than the vulgar one with which I was familiar until now. In conversing with a new circle of acquaintances, or in reading texts that testify to a different type or tone of experience than the average one, I might awaken to a more fitting responsivity. The very criticism and its criterion is then offered to me as an already available possibility.

Is the principle of my critical experiences always borrowed from an already past or present heritage? As we said above, even rebellion and revolutions owe much to the potential for transformation that is a feature of the criticized culture. One can no more reject the whole of a culture than one can create it. Every break is a transformation. Often a change is made by a group whose *doxa* and ethos were obscured by a more powerful or famous, and thus more public opinion. The leaders of national and world historical movements have a genesis; they do not emerge from the forehead of Zeus. Even if they are inspired by God, their deeds and words betray their debt to the communities that took care of them.

Are originality and unicity then meaningless words? Do all individuals owe all of their doings to a past or present that welcomes them? A new version of an old truth or tradition is neither a repetition, nor the simple realization of a possibility that, as a ready-made blueprint, is waiting for realization. The inherited possibility that is made manifest in an original artwork or action is more than a realization: it not only discovers but also invents the possibility that was already there, although it was neither recognized as such, nor simply given-but-hiding. The possibility itself is retroactively coconstituted by its surprising actualization. The potentialities of the past depend on the ways in which ulterior realizations reveal that they contained unsuspected promises. Even as unfulfilled promises, they would not exist if they would never be fulfilled. Would they still be (albeit undiscovered, forever concealed) possibilities? Who could tell? To recognize them as such, someone must already have imagined or thought them as possibilities of representable realities.

Revolt and Patience.   We have not emphasized enough how much injustice and corruption have damaged or prevented and often ruined the gift of an already socially and culturally organized world. Disappointment, indignation, bitterness, and revolt seem more appropriate responses to the real situation of human society than gratitude. Is all talk about acceptance not a mask for quietistic and reactionary kinds of conservatism without vision and courage? Revolution is certainly necessary where corruption has emptied all institutions and manners of their meaning, but even there, a revolt fails and thus loses its meaning, when it cannot count on some form of communal cohesion that can replace or transform the general disorder. If a society has lost all elements of solidarity and justice, there is no other hope than trust in the power of words and guns, but is it still possible to listen, or even to speak? As long as there are relics of cohesion and justice, these must be revived and developed, but that is not enough: the chance of winning in the name of justice—or, more modestly, of rebuilding some sort of social framework—must be real enough. Beginning a combat that risks turning into universal slaughter is not always better than enduring widespread corruption. Impossible and unfulfilled promises of liberation have made many peoples more miserable than they were before the revolution, but this observation is not an excuse for letting corruption grow along its own tendencies. An appropriate response to injustice demands a balance between conservation and radical change, and this balance cannot be found without selective cooperation with ongoing processes. Few reforms can be accomplished immediately; some shifts take even ages. What cannot be changed within a generation, even if it is unjust and cruel, must be accepted as an evil, but actual condition of the obligatory struggle for a better future. Patience does not condone any injustice when it suffers with and for the victims of economic and political corruption. If it is courageous enough to fight when this is necessary, patience has more compassion with the victims than hopeless freedom fighters, although compassion, in more promising situations, might demand that a life and death struggle be risked. The justice of the cause is not betrayed by a patience that accepts inevitable suffering as preparation for the right kind of revolution.

A certain degree of injustice has always accompanied and partially corrupted the many attempts to build a just society, and there is no guarantee that this situation will ever change. If we, enlightened westerners, boast about our moral standards and human rights, we should not forget that many of our "civilized" nations have initiated and continue to organize and achieve systematic robbery and exploitation, slavery, oppression, torture, tyranny, and destruction.

Critical Cooperation.   Since we are indebted to our communities for almost all the economic, social, political, linguistic, and cultural elements that made us civilized, we are grateful, but since they are nothing else than unions formed by our intertwined destinies, they owe us their continued existence and development of what they are. Through the diversified process of complementary functions, we present and represent our communities, keeping them alive by mobilizing their possibilities, holding open their promises, educating new members, inaugurating new institutions and practices, and handing on the traditions of our heritage. Before we existed, these tasks were achieved by other generations, who thus assured the survival of their and our communities. In expressing gratitude to the society that "made" us what we have become, we thank those representatives who were closest to us during our education: the family members who taught us how to speak, the teachers who trained us in writing and calculation, the guides who cared for our souls, the colleagues who recognized our worth, the critics who suggested that we correct our behavior, the judges who protected us against crimes, and so on. In us, the community thanks former generations (that is, its own past) for surviving and procreating itself. This procreation sometimes means progress, sometimes decadence; most often it develops as a mixture of progress and regress, or rather as a continual shifting that is too varied to be pressed into the schemas of progress and regress. The main point, however, is that we, the actual representatives of the community to which we belong, owe our communal life to the "we" of former generations while ourselves being responsible for a "we" that comes after us. Our generation took the place of our fathers and mothers, and other generations will replace our efforts to continue the tasks of the same, although incessantly changing, community.

The temporality of generational sequences conditions the identity of any community (civilization, nation, family, religion, church, club). The births and deaths of different generations condition the nature of our tasks, insofar as we form a communal *we*. The primary task is always the same—namely, the survival of our community and the realization of its essential purposes; but the ways in which this task must be concretized depend on many varying factors, such as the influx of new members, the relations with other communities, and historical changes.

Against the backdrop of communal identity made possible by the historical difference of generations, the question of how we should respond to a community of which we are members receives a first answer: We are responsible for its ongoing life. This responsibility encompasses at least the following tasks:

1. Insofar as belonging to a certain community (for example, a nation, a religion, the academic community) is experienced as necessary for living a fully human existence, we must accept it as the context and point of departure of our social and cultural life. This may mean that we have to take responsibility for specific tasks of a community to which we already belong, or that we must enter into a community without which we cannot exist in a fully human way. It can also mean that we must quit the community of which we have been members and enter another one. This happens, for example, in emigration and conversion to another religion or when we try to identify with another language and culture.

2. Acceptance includes a certain degree of cooperation and shared responsibility for the survival and development of the community. This responsibility involves us in some communal functions: each member has some specific rights and duties while the officers have the additional responsibility of their governing and administrative tasks. Here lies the foundation of an ethics of communal or public virtues and rights.

3. Acceptance and cooperation do not exclude critique and criticism. Just as an individual life is always accompanied by critical self-evaluation,[36] each nation, church, university, or club needs self-critique in order to remain focused on its essential purposes and weed out inevitable corruption. Responsible critique is not easy, but no community can preserve decency without it. It is thus a basic function of any community that respects itself. Any nation, church, or club should be grateful for those internal critics whose judgments are motivated by the authentic orientation of their union.

This orientation encompasses in any case the following purposes: (1) communal survival; (2) a meaningful life (whereby the meaning of "meaning" each time is determined by the specific—national, religious, academic, artistic—horizon of the community in question); and (3) an enjoyable life. The third purpose is subordinate to and perhaps already included in the second, but I distinguish it here in order to give a place to "happiness," which often is proposed as the highest purpose and criterion of a good society. I agree with Kant in considering the modern idea of happiness a confused representation instead of a clear concept,[37] but it can be clarified—in a more Aristotelian vein—as the enjoyable side of a meaningful and virtuous life. That this kind of enjoyment cannot be missed—especially on the level of public activities, follows from the impossibility of imposing meanings on community members who cannot sympathize with them.

Critical evaluations of existing communities cannot remain at the level of condemnations; they are not fruitful unless they propose concrete modes of emendation. For both tasks, they need a criterion. This is to be found in the original or essential purpose or purposes of the evaluated community, but often these purposes are only implicit, concealed by distorting interpretations and twisted by corrupting ideologies. The critics may not come to an agreement about the correct interpretation; moreover, they might discover that the criterion hitherto accepted by the investigated community no longer can be considered fair or humane. But what gives them the right to appeal to another criterion than the one that the members apparently have accepted—and often for many years or even centuries?

We meet here again with the question of whether the ethos of a nation or culture or other kind of community can guide ethics or not. If ethics does not want to be lowered to the level of ideology and propaganda, it must at all costs attempt to maintain its distance toward nationalistic or otherwise particularistic standards. But where can it find supranational and supracultural criteria?

With regard to the political community, this question has expressed itself in the ancient opposition of the king and the prophet. In the best situation, the king could appeal to the revered principles of traditional politics, whereas the prophet challenged him in the name of higher principles whose validity he often attributed to revelation. However, if our world no longer is ruled by religion, who can still speak in the name of higher criteria than those of the prevailing politics (or economy)? Should we trust the intuitions of the critics? Can we confide the task to philosophers, the academic stars, the media, the people? Have we then not seen enough proof of *their* corruption? If there are no geniuses of wisdom left, or if we cannot (or do not want to) find them, how can we avoid appealing to subjectivistic intuitions and "prophetic" but publicly unwarranted criteria? Is it then not wiser to stick to "business as usual," even if such a conservatism cannot purge all corruption? Without solving the political problems that emerge at this point, I will later come back on the ethical dimension of the tension between factual and ideal criteria (including that between ethos and ethics); for now I indicate only the need of reaching beyond the publicly recognized ethos in order to find a trustworthy criterion for the evaluation of praxis and ethos.

Tradition. By critically cooperating, we maintain our community in life through various styles of recycling its traditions. We amend its institutions; we retrieve our heritage in unforeseen ways, while fashions and customs change. An ongoing reformation is inevitable. Our responsibility for the present produces a different future by reproducing the communal past. Present responsibility thus includes responsibility for the future: those who live afterward must be educated by handing on to them (our version of) the common past. Because nobody can live without culture, we must prepare the next generations for their tasks. In this respect, at least, we live beyond our death. The criterion we are seeking should in any case include the demand that the communal and cultural life of those who survive us should be meaningful—if possible, even more meaningful than ours. Handing on our heritage, in a critical way, and proposing emendation cannot be achieved in a dogmatic way. We can neither impose nor predict the ways of life that future generations will adopt; the education we offer therefore has the character of a proposal rather than that of a dogmatic conservatism or liberalism. It is true that we here and now are already deciding in which language and with what manners our children will live; we mark them as members of a particular culture, but the alternative lies in a total lack of civilization. The impossibility of being educated as a "universal" human (who later on may choose a particular form of culture) is part of our finitude, but belonging to a particular (and to that extent biased) community is better than being nothing in particular (for example, mute).

Our responsibility for the future can be unfolded in a philosophy of education. Devotion to our nation, church, or "republic of letters" can be motivated by care for those parts or aspects of our own lives that are shareable within the horizons of particular communities, but it cannot avoid devotion to the future members whom we do not even know. In both cases we are not devoted to "the community" or its government as a sort of superperson, but rather to the present and future persons whose lives are conditioned and made meaningful by the communities whose survival we deem necessary. The ancients, those whose mortal lives were dedicated to the civilization of our lives, deserve thanks (and some of them deserve veneration). Responsibility thus implicates us in history.

Politics

How should a community behave with regard to its members? Since a community is not a person, this question cannot be understood as a specification of ethical questions about personal duties and rights. If "community" is a name for us, insofar as we share parts and aspects of our lives, we cannot express ourselves through one voice or action unless we agree on certain forms of representation and delegation. Political philosophy studies the conditions of their possibility and the various forms of their concretization. How "the community" must respond to the claims of its members is then equivalent to the question of how those who represent its public functions must act in order to respect the social worth of its members. The personalization of collective structures is the condition for saving the human dignity of persons, who, as persons, are more than components of a systematic whole.

Intersubjectivity and Community

Because it is impossible to draw clear-cut boundaries between ethics and politics, this chapter could not avoid broaching some political problems while focusing on the ethical role of correspondence in different (and analogically congruent) dimensions of phenomenality. However, the purpose of this book is not to develop a complete treatise of ethics in the broad sense that encompasses also the normative aspects of politics, art, and nature, but rather the testing of some principles that seem to be basic for morality and ethics in a more restricted, but fundamental sense. A complete treatise would have to do much more. One of its difficult tasks, which follows from the preceding analyses, would be to disentangle the intertwining of face-to-face relations and communal or communitarian ones. How does correspondence between *you* and *me* relate to the unity-in-difference of collective processes in which *we*, as sharing a common life, are involved and which normative consequences follow from the issuing connections and tensions?

Another question that should be treated, even if we only want to complete a basic reconnaissance of "the analogy of should," concerns the ethical character and role of religion. Because this issue is even more controversial than the ethical relevance of art or nature, I will postpone an answer while being aware that this chapter remains not only elementary but also fragmentary. I hope, however, that it may be read as an invitation to meditate on the ethical relevance of correspondence on all the analogically similar levels of the good.

CHAPTER 7

Unity and Universality

The preceding chapter was a first reconnaissance of some types of phenomenality from the perspective of ethical correspondence. A complete overview of all the dimensions of "ought" or "should" and "correspondence" was neither achieved nor targeted. However, we cannot wait for completion in order to ask—again in a provisional way—how all the analogically similar dimensions and phenomena make up one all-encompassing universe. The unity and universality of phenomenality and being, along with their varied claims, must be sketched if ethics and an ethically justified life are not to fall apart by fragmentation. If those dimensions remain disconnected, we cannot determine how conflicts between them must be resolved or how they can form one ensemble in life and theory. In the absence of a unifying principle, our combinations would become arbitrary.

Is it possible to "be fair" to the universe in its totality? Can we gather all the dimensions of "should," notwithstanding their analogical differences? Can we discover a certain unity in the plurality of claims of which an open mind is aware? Let us try to find an answer by unfolding the question from two sides: (1) by asking to what extent the universe is a whole, and (2) to what extent the very person confronted with the question of unity and universality is the gathering center that orders all the varieties of "should" into an overall unity.

Nature and Culture

Having surveyed several parts of the universe in quest of appropriate responses, we must now ask how the universe formed by those parts appears as such and provokes us to correspondence. As we said before, we are not simply confronted with a natural cosmos of things, landscapes, vegetation, animals, and other persons; few phenomena show up in their natural, prehuman, precivilized, and precultural state. Most often, we encounter nature in gardens, parks, well-kept fields or woods, whereas tigers, bears, snakes, and monkeys are met in the zoo. If we do not cultivate flowers ourselves, they delight us in bouquets. Human beings, in particular, meet us in civilized forms: clothing and cosmetics enhance or spoil their natural phenomenality. We perceive the cosmos through layers of civilization: a host of linguistic, aesthetic, symbolic, and ritual (re)shapings mediate our contact with nature. Each culture cultivates and stylizes the cosmos in a particular way, thus constituting a responsive pattern of its own. Correspondence begins with inculturation: by adopting the habitual patterns of perception, imagination, speech, handling and so on, a child already responds to the phenomena in culturally preformed modes. Responding to the universe as the totality of all phenomena includes a response to the characteristics of the particular culture in which one is educated: we can conform our behavior to the responsive pattern of everybody around us or vary it in a personal way. The adoption of a radically different mode of responding requires either conversion to another culture, which is very difficult, or a revolutionary uprooting of our own culture, which is perhaps even more difficult.

Since we are in touch with the natural universe through its cultural (re)shaping, correspondence to the cosmos has at least two levels: our attitude is a positioning with regard to nature *and* to the particular culture that presents nature to us in a characteristic form. The actual situation is more complex, however. A culture is neither simple nor homogeneous; it not only encompasses an ensemble of layers and perspectives, but it also contains elements of other cultures. In the modern western culture, for example, the scientific conception of the universe is only one way of perceiving the cosmos; it coexists with other, for example, artistic and religious views, and it has integrated innumerable tools, customs, symbols, and thoughts from other cultures. None of its views is purely natural, although certain poetic or commonsensical views might be more natural and less sophisticated than that of physics.

Since we have become aware of our cultural determination, philosophy now involves the task of characterizing the variety of worldviews invented or adopted by diverse societies in different epochs of history. It is an endless task, for the description itself represents only a particular—albeit erudite—perspective, and no human being has the eyes of a god. Each metacultural characteristic must therefore be supplemented by a multitude of other characteristics, all of which represent peculiar perspectives on the culture under consideration. Yet this diversity does not preclude truth. Not every view is equally perspicacious or wise, but serious approaches are bound together by an affinity with the truth of things, and we may hope that they converge somehow somewhere. The only way toward "more truth" lies in the purifying cultivation of the approach that appears most promising to the researcher.

Cosmic Claims

The phenomenological quest for the most hospitable approach to the phenomena themselves necessarily implies a critique of the cultural patterns that have imposed themselves on our minds. Without these patterns, we would see very little; with them, we only see aspects. But how rich and marvelous these are!

Insofar as particular cultures show the world in a special "light," they also illuminate its claims: we must inhabit, use, enjoy, abhor, and cultivate this universe in specific ways. Most often, however, a worldview does not confront us with the total universe at once, but rather with parts of it. For example, in the western world, cows are seldom admired (although they were by several painters in the seventeenth century) but instead are generally used as producers of milk and meat. In India, on the other hand, cows deserve respect and gratitude: how dare you eat the animal that so generously feeds you with her own milk! Monkeys, likewise, are venerated, even though they eat a considerable share of the harvest. Both incorporate the presence of the divine. Obviously, two cultures clash here, but each of them brings an entire worldview with it. Their ethoses with regard to cows and monkeys cannot be isolated from the other elements of their attitudes toward animals, human customs, and religion. Despite its composite character, a culture has a coherence of its own.

In addition to conflicts with other perspectives, each worldview must also deal with internal conflicts. These are caused by the tensions between the phenomena that demand attention and the attitudes people take regarding them. If, for example, people ought not be killed, situations will arise in which we must kill certain animals. Plants must be sacrificed for food, stones must be used for building, and so on. As an ensemble of all things, the cosmos suggests an order and requires us to respect its components according to degrees of importance and subordination. Consumption is fundamental, but it cannot constitute the whole meaning of our inhabiting the universe. The splendor of sunsets, flowers, and birds asks for admiration; a life without beauty is poor; the lack of social relations causes agony. How shall we combine our attention and respect for all the elements and events that compose the world? A solution to this problem is provided by the ethos of each culture, but various individuals, belonging to various subcultures, create their own version of a solution: some people focus on food, clothes, jewels, mansions, vacations, others are obsessed with moneymaking; intellectuals take time for literature, museums, and concerts; religious people adore and enjoy the presence of God in all things; and moralists are concerned with the decency and decadence of our relations. The way in which the universe appears runs parallel with our attunement; our interests reveal corresponding aspects of the surrounding reality. A glutton perceives a cosmos different from that of an artist, whose view differs also from a thinker's; a politician sees the world as a field of forces within and between communities that must be ruled, whereas saints love the universe as the creation of the God they adore.

Are all of these attitudes and worlds equally valuable? If they were, the universe as such would not demand any specific response. Ethics would then be confined to aspects or parts of the totality and to the specific ethoses of particular cultures and worlds. Does the totality of all beings suggest, demand, or impose a certain attitude that is fundamental and, in that sense, universally valid? Is not such an attitude the basis of all morality?

Beyond the Cosmos

Can we understand morality as appropriate correspondence toward the phenomenal totality of all beings viewed as a cosmos? We see phenomena as composing wholes through a variety of connections, such as similarity, association, coordination, subordination, and domination. Do we, can we, should we, experience all phenomena as components of one over-all universe? If so, what kind of configuration does it have? Does this question suggest a certain hierarchy that should be respected by our feelings and behavior? It does suggest that we should appreciate the various phenomena according to their proper worth or dignity and observe the correct proportions in harmonizing our responses to each of them. All things together would then form a well-ordered cosmos, and a good person would respond to it by expressing a well-proportioned appreciation. Under God, as the highest being, humanity would be the summit of an earthly pyramid of all kinds of beings, the lowest level of which would be represented by an entirely indeterminate "stuff" or *hyle*.

Are these suggestions defensible? Can we gather all beings in one synthesis of which they are the parts or components? Can we conceive of their relations as a sort of glue that unites them in one whole? Below, when we consider the links between religion and ethics, I will argue that God does not belong to a hierarchically construed universe, because God is neither a being (and therefore not either a supreme Being) nor the being that is common to all beings.[1] With regard to human persons, Levinas has shown that the face, as a "hole," does not fit into any cosmos.[2] Neither you nor I are parts or components of any whole; we protrude above any synthesis because we do not coincide with any of the aspects that characterize our involvement in consumptive, aesthetic, social, historical, or religious systems and processes. Insofar as we are free, we do not entirely belong to any economy, and this difference constitutes the dignity that is at the core of our essence. Since culture is also an economy, one can state that you and I do not ultimately belong to culture, although we are profoundly involved in it. The conflation of our cultural involvement with our most radical belonging—that is, the confusion of inculturation with responsibility—is a fundamental mistake, especially in ethics. If you and I cannot be imprisoned within the boundaries of a cosmic totality, the reality of "all things" (*ta panta*) does not coincide with the *synthesis* or *universe* of all "things." "Synthesis" suggests a structure that is not wide enough to respect all that exists—in particular, neither people nor God fit into it. We can and must formulate this fact in aporetic ways, for example, by stating that the totality of all beings is not total, or that the universe is not universal, or that all beings together do not form one whole.

Levinas and some of his followers, who have accepted Plato's use of the word *being* (as *ousia*, or essence), have renewed the Neoplatonic tradition insofar as it points toward the possibility of something (the Good) that "is" or exists "beyond being." Although this line of thought deserves the highest regard, the aporias in which it is inevitably entangled encourage me to maintain the universal use of the word *being*, which seems to be typical for Indo-Germanic languages, although I am well aware that this preference entails the loss of being's univocity and thus generates other aporias and paradoxes.[3]

The Human Universe

If people are not parts or elements of the universe, how then can we speak about the "universe" in terms of the human world and history? What becomes of correspondence as an answer to the togetherness of all phenomena? The combination of attitudes suggested or required by their multitude must, as a kind of nonsynthetic totality, mirror the phenomenal "universe." But how do you and I and all others form a quasi-whole with the rest of the phenomena? Through our faces and speech we surpass homogeneity, but our involvement in the physical, chemical, and biological processes of nature and the economic, political, linguistic, aesthetic, and other processes of culture show that we also function as components of a worldly system.

Should we honor the exceptional status of human beings by regarding them as the extraordinary rulers of all other beings, including animals, trees, plants, mountains, seas, stars, stones, elements, and atoms? The universe would then be divided into two main classes: rulers and ruled beings. Although animals would be ruled by humans, human beings themselves would be ruled insofar as they are determined by natural and cultural laws.

The picture of a ruler is a political metaphor employed to illustrate the relations between humanity and the world. Does it give too much credit to the ruled? Ruling presupposes that the ruled are somehow able to listen and to obey or rebel; but can this be said of nonhuman phenomena? By adding the economic metaphor of property to that of mastery, Descartes projected the image of man as "master and possessor"[4] of the world. He thus gave a modern twist to a tradition that saw the human race as the all-important being among finite beings. All other beings are "for man," as material, tools, nourishment, protection, toys, and ornaments. Humanity can dispose at will of everything else in order to maintain and develop itself. Other beings, from planets to worms, have meaning only insofar as they are valuable for humans. Correspondence would then consist in the subordination of all things to the human will. It would also imply indifference to useless things, because the law of the world is expressed in the imperative: Make humanity powerful, great, happy, and satisfied.

If it is true that animals, trees, plants, and even mountains, lakes, and skies evoke specific kinds of awe, the portrait of a human proprietor amidst materials and instruments is wrong or incomplete. Even emphasis on the aesthetic aspects of the cosmos would not do full justice to the nonhuman phenomena, unless it at the same time recognized their proper dignity. The rediscovery of the nonhuman respectability through which natural beings surprise an open mind does not necessarily bring us back to a cosmos in which rivers and bushes are inhabited by gods. Besides polytheistic versions, there are atheistic and monotheistic versions of respect for the natural and cultural cosmos in which we live. If a person is an image of God, animals and crystals, too, symbolize or trace God in ways of their own.

Recognition of the varied worth of nonhuman beings does not necessarily exclude their usefulness for us. Being ruled and used can save their independent dignity if it simultaneously fulfills their own destiny. A well-ruled dog, for example, is—at least in some respects—more dignified than the wild animal it would have become without a master. Recognition of nonhuman dignity differs from abuse insofar as it resists reduction of the cosmos to human utility. As I stated earlier, art is the domain in which this difference is abundantly expressed: painted horses, mountains, lakes, for instance, have their own secrets and destiny. They demand contemplation, but contemplation is not necessarily useless, even though it cannot and should not be bought. Are there no limits or conditions for respectable use? This question brings us back to the question of how we are supposed to relate to the "totality" of phenomena, including societies, cultures, histories, persons, animals, plants, landscapes, mountains, skies, and stars. Which kind of unity and "universality" is required for a good relationship to the entire universe as a (quasi-) whole?

The answer can be found only in a complete unfolding of the correct responses to the various kinds of phenomena and their (actual or possible) relations of encountering, association, combination, competition, conflict, and exclusion or inclusion.

My Universe

The many levels and instances of "should" seem to form an uncon-
nected multitude rather than a universe. However, I can bring them together through my awareness of them. This includes not only my involvement in all the dimensions distinguished above, but also my being
challenged by their different appeals. I am part of nature, civilized by a specific culture, speaker of a particular language, citizen of a certain nation,
where I am subject to a code of law; I am a member of a family and participate in a worldwide economy, while having my personal friends and
ideals about the future of our world. All these engagements, with their obligations, find in me their unity. I am the center that they affect. As such, I
am not necessarily a master or owner, nor an infant or Narcissus, but I cannot escape the necessity of ordering the confusing manifold of the whole
to which I belong

One of the beings that affect and challenge me is my own self: I find
myself as the one who I have to be, that is, to become, develop, accomplish. I cannot escape from its demands, although I can disobey them. In
being aware of my fundamental task, I discover the limits of my capacity:
I, who must achieve that task, am conditioned by natural, cultural, historical, and personal factors that exclude many possibilities that are open to
other persons. Within the range of my own obligations and possibilities I
must create some sort of unity, because that is the only way to prevent
paralysis or fragmentation. Can I find a unifying principle in myself?

Saint Augustine advised his parishioners: "*Ama et quod vis, fac*"
("Love, and do what you want"). But do we know what *amare* means?
Since "love" is perhaps the most worn-out word, we cannot at the beginning take it as our guide. How could we distinguish between true and false
kinds of love?

In Chapter 4, we presented Desire as a fundamental dynamism that
orients human lives, even if individuals choose not to follow it. But can we
trust it? Should not *all* our desires, including the most originary one, be
measured by a higher standard? Augustine's dictum seems to suggest this
when it subordinates desire to love. But if we do not know what and how
to love, neither can we know how to regulate desire.

When arguing that Desire precedes freedom,[5] I have also insisted on
the difference between the radical Desire and the many particular desires
for such concrete desiderata as food, music, science, and friendship. Al-

though the radical Desire orients us even before we become conscious of it, its orientation is not given in the form of a definable movement toward a concrete desideratum. As the dynamic principle in all desires, Desire originates and encompasses them all, but this overdetermination appears as indeterminate and abstract. Thus, human self-consciousness remains puzzled by Desire and incessantly seeks to bring to light the origin and ultimate purpose of its own motivation. The quest for unity is a search for understanding the movement that makes us human.

Theory is not enough for this search; it coincides with the experiment of an entire life, that is, with a series of various attempts to adjust and respond to the multiplicity of concrete challenges that affect each individual. Such attempts unify the challenging dimensions and phenomena by tentatively gathering them in the form of an experimental configuration, thus transforming their multiplicity into a testable universe.

Experimentation implies evaluation, and if life as a whole is at stake, self-evaluation. Thus Desire itself can learn whether an attempted configuration is really what it wants: does the universe, thus configured, respond appropriately to the question of how the many challenges can be accepted and lived as a proportioned whole?

The ideal would consist in a configuration that is perfect from both the perspective of the challenges that affect us and that of our Desire. If a certain ordering of the world is such that Desire recognizes it as both fair to the phenomena and agreeable to its own orientation, the experiment has been successful because a complete agreement is reached. Until then, dissonance and tensions urge us to change any disappointing configuration into a better one.

To give an example, many ways of dealing with the multifarious universe are narcissistic. Because they do not respect the challenges of the face, they run into a conflict that must be overcome. Either all faces are wiped out by a murderous version of egoism, or one tries to ignore the others' claims by avoiding any contact. In the latter case, an essential dimension of life is excluded, which causes loneliness and spiritual poverty. Narcissus was so concentrated on his own image that he could not see the faces of the others; he never learned that his kind of autism was not really Desirable and he paid for this ignorance by dying. Desire needs open minds to recognize the various claims that might lead it to its unifying Desideratum. It must learn which configurations are compatible with both "the facts" (including their claims) and its own orientation.

The original orientation of human lives is not a fixed staring at one particular goal. Although preceding—and thus independent of—any choosing, Desire, in its overdetermination, is indeterminate enough to adjust to all the calls and claims it may encounter. The unity each of us creates by configuring these claims as elements of a universe, characterizes each station on the way to the longed-for perfection. The latter is reached when the sum of all claims perfectly coincides with the most desired situation, that is, when the "justice" demanded by all persons and things is exactly that which someone Desires most—or, in other words, when we fully desire nothing else than that the good—"justice" or appropriate correspondence—be realized.

I Myself

In adjusting to the universe, I try to be fair both to all things and to the self in me. Insofar as I have neither created this self nor decided what it demands from me, the actor whose freedom we still must consider, I am subjected to the appeal and the tasks my self imposes on me, somewhat analogically to the appeal and the tasks through which other individuals affect me. I must, for example, respect my self as having a dignity or "height" that I have neither caused nor provided with its basic demands. I am charged with this individual life and ought to take care of it. This charge includes not only the responsibility for all encountered beings according to their different appeals, but also my responsibility for the unification and ordering of a livable universe and for an identity of my own. I must heed my self, the origin of my desires and duties, by realizing what it wants me to be/become/desire/feel/think/do.[6] My self is my own other,[7] and since it is the closest (*proximus*) of all who are very close (*proximi*) to me, service and charity begins with me. This need not scandalize anyone, if it is true that being myself essentially and unavoidably implies both being-for-you-and-all-others and being-for-me.

CHAPTER 8

Freedom

From "Ought" to Self

In Chapter 2, we saw that the ethical "ought" has been experienced differently in different cultures and epochs. To illustrate this diversity, I contrasted Greek *kalokagathia*, medieval obedience, and Kant's sense of duty.[1] Chapters 5 and 6 showed that different kinds of phenomena direct us in different ways toward appropriate responses: some phenomena—for example, human faces—challenge us with a mode and rigor distinct from others. In addition, the experience of obligation and decency can change within the course of a life: our conscience can become more strict and refined or more sloppy, dull, or lax. There are many shades of "ought," "should," and "shall," but all of them challenge a subject that could not respond to them if it were not already responsible for such a response. For an order to have meaning, it must be addressed to someone who is able to obey and execute it. Obedience and its contrary, disobedience, presuppose a self that can accept the order as its own. Appropriation (or rejection) is the expression of having some sort of own-ness: I cannot make anything my own unless I am already something of and on my own. Thus to hear an order implies that I, of my own or as a *self*, can accept and follow it—or not.

Kant's argument for freedom, expressed in the formula "I can, for I ought,"[2] does not mean that all morally desirable ends can be accomplished in all actual situations by every individual or collective agent. Obligations do not automatically entail the physical, psychological, or social means and conditions necessary for their accomplishment. For instance, the obligation to abolish all hunger and injustice does not guarantee the capability to achieve this instantaneously. It does not even guarantee that we will be able to fulfill this task in the future. However, as an obligation that, for now, demands too much from our capabilities, it orders us to be seriously dedicated to the task and to start doing all that is in our power to progressively realize it. It urges us to adopt a favorable attitude and orientation toward a goal that might turn out to be utopian, while demanding, here and now, that we at least fight injustice and hunger on a less than ideal scale. Each person's concrete obligation is measured by the available talents and circumstances, but within these limits the personalized ought would be nonsensical, even absurd, if it did not appeal to the freedom of a will that is capable of preparing its actualization.

Conscience

An order would be meaningless if it were not addressed to some kind of self. If ethical obligations can be understood as orders, they always concern an addressee. The voice that summons me addresses me, but it does not necessarily come from outside; if it is the voice of my own conscience, "I" am at the same time the one who addresses (namely, insofar as I coincide with my conscience) and the addressee (insofar as I am the self that receives and ought to fulfill the order).

The commanding voice "speaks" to me; but even if it is the voice of the Father, the State, a friend, humanity, or God, my conscience must recognize its pronouncements as its own before it can hear them as authentically obligatory. As we will see in the next chapter, all valid orders are mediated by my own conscience. If I do not recognize them as supported by an inner voice of my own, my obedience does not surpass that of a slave; my execution of the order would then be the result of coercion and fear, not the expression of a conscientious attitude. As a moral being, I must obey my own conscience. This insight includes the obligation to develop an accurate and fine-tuned conscience, although it does not exclude that my own "voice" may echo the voices of God, society, my neighbors, and my friends. It "only" affirms that all moral orders are also orders that "I" (my conscience) address to myself.

The orders and demands of morality must be "authorized" by me. Although I am not their origin, I recognize them as my own if I discover that the imperative, even if it comes from elsewhere, expresses something that is essential to me. By adopting the commanding voice as my own, I begin to "have" or to "own" a conscience. But how can I appropriate it if I do not already have a conscience that orients and guides this appropriation? The conscience that precedes all acquisition and recognition must lie in a demand that is not divided into an outer and an inner voice. The initial call must come from a voice that does not yet make this distinction.

A conscience cannot be chosen, but it can (and must) be awakened, experienced, purified, and refined. Insofar as I "am" my conscience, "I" precede "me," the self that reacts to it. It is almost impossible to avoid using the word *I* for the ensemble of my mind and body, intelligence, desire, and conscience. They constitute "me," but "I" (my self) have not had any say in this constitution, although I can respect or distort it in my practice or theory. Insofar as I make choices and decisions, the imperative "I" presupposes the "I" that is capable of choosing. This capability is presupposed as a necessary condition for the acceptance or rejection, execution and meaning of all orders that are given to me. If I could not choose to obey, the order would be an inner contradiction. Commanding a tree to bear fruit, for example, is a magical, not a moral or political, act, while commanding a domesticated animal belongs to the twilight realm where shadows of freedom are at home.

"I Can, for I Ought"

Kant was right: true obligation presupposes freedom, whereas absolute determination precludes responsibility. Human liberty is discovered through the awakening of one's conscience; as a condition for its possibility, freedom is tied to morality.

The awakening of conscience is not in the first place the discovery of a debt; rather it makes me aware of a demand neither caused nor escapable by me.[3] Whether this demand comes from a face, a law, or an inner voice, I recognize it as a (pro)vocation that orders me, this unique individual, to respond. Insofar as the provocation encompasses my entire life, my obedience cannot be substituted with another's. Singular plans and actions can be delegated but nobody can take away from me the "provokedness" of my life. I discover myself as always already "in demand."

The natural and normal response to an order that emerges from my own conscience is obedience—unless considerable obstacles or counterorders make me hesitate or force me to disobey. Freedom is primarily the possibility of *pro-hairesis*[4]: taking advantage of an opportunity for being good or bad; dedication or devotion of one's self to a demand, a task, a way of life. Such devotion is often hampered; if so, it demands the conquest of the obstacles. Some obstacles find accomplices in our own constitution, especially those tendencies that do not fit a conscientious orientation. Conscience forbids one to follow these tendencies insofar as they cannot be reconciled with its demands, or rather—to put it in positive terms—it urges us to bend and habituate these tendencies to the orientation of our conscience. Resolve and *askēsis* are required to maintain one's orientation. One can, however, give in to hostile forces, "letting oneself go" through complacency and indulgence, but such weakness is experienced as a defeat. Remorse and shame follow, but they do not exclude a return to conscientious dedication.

If this all too brief summary of the moral situation is correct, it cannot be represented by the confrontation of an entirely indeterminate subject with a plurality of competing possibilities from which the subject must choose. Such a model might work in the supermarket, but it does not do justice to the struggle for moral decency. When conscience is awakened, we are already involved in characteristic habits and practices. Most often, we have been doing what "everybody" does, yet some of our actions, past or imminent, might create problems for us: remorse, doubts, and scruples begin to plague us. Can I continue doing this? Shouldn't I have refrained from enjoying that? In retrospect, I regret and condemn my behavior; with an eye to the future, I decide to change the course of my life. I try to replace an old pattern of action with a new one. I must detach myself from the inclinations that lead me back to the old habits and I must reinforce the new orientation. My decision is indeed a choice insofar as I adopt a new pattern while rejecting the old one; but this choice is not made from an indeterminate standpoint, and the patterns in question are not just a variety of possibilities displayed as equally choice-worthy. I am already committed to a distinct way of acting, but when spurned by my conscience, I twist myself loose from it by trying to engage in another way. The idea of an uninvolved subject facing similarly attractive possibilities of behavior is an abstraction that ignores the reality of the moral struggle. The demands of my conscience affect me while I am already engaged. If they conflict with the mode of this engagement, they call for another, better mode. Such intervention might require reflection on various lifestyles observed in others or read in books, but the decision to live otherwise does not have the structure of a freestanding will sovereignly selecting one possibility out of a number of equally possible possibilities. It is rather the transformation (or conversion) of one involvement into another on the basis of loyalty to one's own history: the history of an always involved but conscientious subject. Marked by all the formerly chosen and unchosen elements of my past, I am challenged by demands that do not entirely agree with the loyalties of my factual engagements. Called to appropriately respond, I discover my solidarity with styles of action that do not quite conform to the calls of my own conscience. Instead of a series of free choices, a conscientious life is the attempt to hear the moral appeal that urges me to leave all my betrayals and distortions behind.

Selfhood and Originality

Freedom is not identical with the ability to choose. It is the ability to be involved as a self in actions, habits, relations, rights, property, and so on, which thereby become my own. A moment of choice is implied in the free appropriation of authentic demands, insofar as concrete solidarity with my conscience demands the rejection of some attractive but inappropriate practices of my own and others around me. Rejection is then a condition for positive identification with the "voice" within me: I cannot "own" an authentic conscience unless I separate myself from its corruption. Conscience itself calls for its own authentication.

Obedience is possible insofar as a certain future can redeem the past. Without time, we would be paralyzed; as an instantaneous decision for or against, morality would not involve any struggle. In fact, conscience calls for a lifelong combat against false imitations through katharsis.[5]

When I accept the demands of conscience as guidelines for an entire life, I recognize that I am neither its creator nor its sovereign legislator, but rather a co- or subauthor who must accomplish the "work" prescribed by it. I am responsible for the success or failure of a lifelong task and no one can take this burden away from me. This responsibility constitutes my unicity.

In which sense and to what degree am I the author—not of my own life, but of the way in which I live it? So many elements and aspects of my behavior are determined by my educators and the given culture that the question of my responsibility is a messy one. Inculturation, training, imitation, and influential role models have formed me, but I am the only one who owns this specific blend of determinations, which is the result of a unique life story. On the basis of my formation, I repeat many patterns inherited from others, but once in a while, I do or say something original by inventing a remarkable variation. Rather than through singular acts, words, or works, I am unique through the style of my acting, thinking, speaking, gesturing, imagining, and feeling.

A style is an individual's mark on his or her activities. It is similar to that of many others, but the extent to which it is personalized makes it original and unique. Individual styles would be impossible without selfhood. Originality expresses the ownness of an origin of appropriation, but all originality is full of legacies and borrowings.

Choice and Self-Determination

Freedom is the selfhood of a self that, as such, can appropriate and thus can give responses of its own. *Pro-hairesis*, preference for a certain line of conduct, is first of all a positive attitude: dedication and devotion to a cause that is worthwhile (and thus corresponds to a desire). It is not a wholly indeterminate neutrality vis-à-vis contrasting possibilities. If such a neutrality were basic to freedom, how then would we explain that the more dedicated someone is, the more determined *and* the more unhampered or "free" one becomes in accomplishing one's goal? If freedom as such were neutral, becoming more intensely attached to virtue and thus less likely to commit evil acts would render one less free.

A person who has grown in benevolence over many years cannot be considered undetermined with regard to the choice between benevolence and cruelty. With a very high degree of probability, we can predict that this person will not try to kill or wound anyone in the near future. Would we call this person unfree? If the determination that results from constant dedication makes a person more inclined to behave appropriately, this person has become better equipped, less impeded, and more free to do what has to be done. Thanks to practice and habituation, a low degree of determinateness has been replaced by a highly determinate mode of doing and being. Freedom is here not opposed to determinateness because the determinations are willed and embraced or engendered by the dedicated person in question. This freedom is located at one end of a spectrum whose other end is occupied with the undecided indeterminacy of one who plays with possible lifestyles without commitment to any. Even in the latter case, however, the noncommitment can become a rigid commitment to non-commitment. The freedom of devotion overcomes the arbitrariness of an empty liberty by filling it with the content of an engaged career. Instead of continually choosing between contrasting possibilities, one pursues a promising orientation with confidence, although not without the critical curiosity that belongs to all serious life experiments.

A perfectly virtuous person has (almost) reached the stage where obedience to the voice of conscience has become second nature,[6] that is, a well-established, ongoing, "normal" identity of conscience and action. One can quite well imagine human beings so perfect that they cannot betray their conscience—not because of any mental or emotional paralysis, but because they have become accustomed to confirming the demands of conscience through a basic and total Yes and Amen while concretizing this Yes in a perfect life. The freedom of a saint is the opposite of indeterminacy, but it is an exemplary form of grateful self-affirmation and self-determination.

Self-determination does not exclude a manifold of determining factors coming from society, history, nature, and culture; neither does it exclude the possibility of divine providence as creation and salvation of the human self. As divine, providence cannot be played off against human decisions—as if God were jealous or hostile toward humanity—but insight into the relations between God's infinity and human finitude presupposes a theological context.[7] The finite determinations that come from nature and culture do not destroy the human capacity for self-determination (that is, the individual's will), because the will is not one factor among others. Having an essential distance from all determinations, whether these are the effects of outside influences or one's own past actions, the self cannot avoid taking a stand toward what it has become. It assimilates or sublimates its own factuality and tries to bend or eliminate the determinations that do not fit. Even if I am unable to change my behavior and desires to conform with the demands of morality, I remain free and obligated to take a stance with regard to my own mixture of willingness and inability. The self has the last word, but what it says and does is for the most part borrowed from other actors. Self-determination encompasses influences, traditions, and authorities; instead of a neutral standpoint, it is the ultimate "form" and the decisive initiative or *archē*, which is always already involved in a particular way of life.

I am responsible for the unique style of my life insofar as I own or disown what I have become through my own and others' doings. Even if I disown parts of my lifestyle, it still takes time to transform them into more fitting elements; and if I approve of them, they can still be refined. Freedom is the possibility of ongoing self-transformation; its ideal is complete adherence to a conscientious way of life. Indeterminacy must be absorbed by concrete rulings of the Good.

Appropriation

Appropriation begins with acceptance and consent: I have to accept myself as I have become, including my character and customs, career and skills. Some of my manners and parts of my past do not please me. Can I change them? As for my manners, I can try, but my past seems fixed. Its effects on the future and its meaning are not set in stone, however. Through remorse, amends, or penance, for example, my sins can receive a new function in the course of my life. By reminding me of my weakness, they humble me and teach me caution. If they are recognized and forgiven, they may deepen my gratitude.

Acceptance of what I have become develops through ongoing care: revision, correction, further unfolding of a personal style, and so on. Being mortal, I am responsible for a limited future that is partially uncertain and partially determined by the results of my life so far. Since my life is interwoven with other lives, my responsibility encompasses more than an isolated destiny: my behavior influences my family, friends, colleagues, and several communities. They belong to my life, as I belong to theirs. To be myself therefore includes the awareness that they compose a world of my own. How big this world is and how long my influence in it will last, I cannot know. I am therefore responsible, or rather *co*-responsible, for a larger world than I can determine. Freedom makes me a unique and irreplaceable center of the world, but I cannot estimate the extent of my influence. This fact already renders any utilitarian calculus impossible. However, it does make me aware that my responsibility stretches farther than I can oversee.

Although freedom does not provide the answer to the question of how a human life can be good, it makes all lives "owned" by selves. It contains a strange imperative that can be formulated in various ways: "Own your life!" "Be yourself!" "Be responsible for what you do and are!" The strangeness of this imperative lies in three facts: (1) I have not created myself, but rather found my life, including its freedom and responsibility, as already there for and in and as me; (2) the particular course and manner of my life is the result of a host of influences and determinations, many of which were not initiated or even willed by me; and (3) I cannot refuse to obey that imperative; whatever I do or refuse to do, I will be appropriating and owning my life as mine, my own, the one for which I cannot escape responsibility.

Even if I let myself and all things go, this "lack of responsibility" is itself my manner of accepting my unavoidable being-free. The refusal of my own freedom is a free decision, even if it is expressed with the utmost laziness of one who tries to abstain from all action. Such passivity is a rebellion, but since it rebels against the self, it is defeated before the first attack can unfold. Simply letting things run their course is a form of praxis, as are all the lazy, tired, cowardly, sick, resigned, and languishing modes of authoring one's own life. Responsibility cannot be rejected; it can and must be accepted and it is practiced necessarily. However, its good and bad modes are not fixed but chosen. Not being a *causa sui*, a human individual is responsible for the manner of its owning what it has become and will be.

From Involvement to Correspondence

Always already involved in particular worlds, we are awakened to questions about this involvement by Desire, which drives our feeling and action toward its desiderata. What we desire is not a thing or an event, but rather specific engagements and enjoyable unions. Enjoyment cannot be found, however, unless we respond appropriately to appearances and possibilities. Correspondence requires the right attunement. However, the ethos of the particular society in which we are involved has already decided which responses are "normal"; these are endorsed by public opinion, politics, and education. Through our involvement, we have already adopted this normalcy and expressed a certain trust in the righteousness of our community and tradition—until Desire shakes us from our doxastic sleep by making us ask: do I really desire and approve of what my ongoing involvement cultivates? Desire then becomes critical; it wants us to decide whether our own desiderata and those of our communities concord. Consent becomes more problematic than before; it is no longer obvious how we, how I, should live. Although I cannot start from the beginning—I am not the creator of history—I might discover that I should be engaged in other ways. I must then transform my commitment and modify the powerful desires and habits that rule my situation. Life is no longer a matter of "going with the flow"; it is an experiment, which, although led by Desire, is circumscribed by historical circumstances that cannot be denied.

Freedom is the human possibility of accepting the task that is composed of Involvement, Desire, and Correspondence. I am responsible for the Experiment, and thus for the Critique, the Katharsis, and the Reform of the ethos in which I am engaged. It is time here to reaffirm what was stated at the end of Chapter 2 as the nucleus of ethics. Desire and Freedom demand the ongoing Transformation of our inescapable Involvement in History.

However, before we focus on the kathartic aspects of ethics, two rather popular opinions should be discussed in order to further clarify the concept of freedom: (1) the postmodern thesis that morality is always linked to a certain degree of violence, and (2) the Hegelian thesis that freedom is best understood as self-realization.

Freedom and Violence

How often have we experienced that conscience or the Law painfully contradict what we have done or plan to do? Are they not dictatorial and does their despotism not imply violence? When a legal or moral power forbids me (this self-aware and independent person) from following my desires, I feel uncomfortable. The prohibitive voice is perceived as having a strange sort of authority; although lacking physical force, it insists on my conquering the most spontaneous and "natural" moves of which it disapproves. How can I agree with this voice? How can I embrace, want, will, desire its prohibitions? Would I not, like a coward, betray the sovereignty of my will, my self that must choose its own life? Moreover, would I not harm or destroy my affective spontaneity and the exuberance of my vitality? Is the enthusiasm of my emotions not an essential part of my liberty?

Kant and others have argued that the voice of authentic morality cannot be reduced to an external injunction, because it always also originates in our own conscience, which to that extent can be called autonomous (or "original" or "*archa-ic*"). Whether conscience should be interpreted as (practical) reason (with a priori universality and necessity as its attributes), as Kant would have it, or rather as a call of being, is not the question on which I will concentrate in this section. But if we agree that moral normativity emerges from our innermost self, it becomes difficult to understand how we can commit ourselves to a voice that declares itself hostile to spontaneous wishes and typically human tendencies. Must we not experience that voice as a repressive and hostile power? Must we not accuse it of condemning the most vital part of our lives? Does morality include violence? Does it necessarily split us into warring parts? Does the moral perspective reveal the human essence as a battlefield?

If it were possible to love the moral voice so much that my inmost self becomes identical with it, I would become my own *daimonion*[8]; but have I then not killed the entire realm of my passions and "natural inclinations"?[9] Is it possible that my most profound Desire and the moral norm coincide? Or is a good life identical with a life in which morality excludes happiness? Does it reduce us, without appeal, to being innerly divided without hope of unification? But even Kant recognized that ultimately, "in the end," goodness and happiness must be one.[10]

Various attempts have been made to resolve these questions. The Stoics, for instance, aim at *apatheia*; they recommend insensitivity toward our emotions because these prevent wisdom. They do not abandon all hope of a happy life, however, as an eros other than that of the passions remains their guide. We cannot live without desire, but how can a desire that sympathizes with the moral voice make peace with contradicting desires? Can the latter be converted into concretizations (instruments? servants? expressions? particularizations? instantiations?) of the former?

The Epicurean resolves the tension by interpreting the moral call as a recommendation to satisfy the ensemble of our desires in the most harmonious way. The opposition between a morally justified desire and other desires is resolved here on the basis of a homogenization of all desires. However, suffering and death, both of which are unavoidable in any life, contradict the realization of such happiness, which is why Epicurus insists on the phenomenal unreality of dying: when death is present, we are not; when we are present, death is not.[11] However, death is always present, because we cannot live without continually eliminating desirable possibilities. All our choices are accompanied by the denial of many goals that could also have been pursued. A host of partial deaths is the condition for each individual's self-realization.

The recognition of our mortality and the sufferings in which it is foreshadowed belongs to moral realism; it should not be repressed. The "violence" of unwanted suffering is part of human life and the love of life demands its integration. The pain that emerges from erotic conflicts reveals our imperfection, but at least some form of reconciliation is necessary if we want to avoid the destructive dualism of an endless fight between conscience (or enlightened Desire) and passions (which remain unenlightened as long as they avoid all alliance with conscience). Integration of mortality and its forebodings is a normal and "natural" condition of a well-lived life. The imminence of death and the reality of suffering are coconstitutive of life's highest enjoyment, and a good life includes a good way of dealing with the unavoidable.

Self-Realization

In the trace of Kant, freedom has been presented here as the possibility and necessity of responsibility. Because we are responsible for the way in which we deal with things and events, others and ourselves, we are able to determine ourselves with regard to the obligations imposed by their occurrence. Freedom or liberty is thus discovered as a (transcendental) condition of our being called to appropriate responses. Since this call encompasses all the imperative aspects of our relations to other beings, it is the normative side of our "transcendence." However, we must not forget that "transcendence" includes an essential relationship to our own being. If we accept these assumptions, freedom can be defined as the possibility of determining (that is, particularizing and concretizing) the demands of our "transcendence" (understood as the origin and summary of all our relationships) in situated behavior. In line with this perspective, Hegel and his followers have sketched an ethics of "self-realization,"[12] but how must we understand the "self" and the "realization" to which they refer, in order to justify their position?

As openness or "transcendence" toward all phenomena, the self can be compared with (1) an open space where all beings can present themselves. This space is (2) mine; I *am* that openness; or rather "I" (as free) am responsible for it (the human space and transcendence granted and imposed on "me"). (3) I must accept and embrace this space ("me") which enables "me" (as the responsive and responsible receiver) to welcome (or flee or reject or fight) all the phenomena (including "myself") with which I am confronted. (4) In this ability, as the origin of specific attitudes and individual acts, I take initiatives that cannot be reduced to any play of drives or forces. In my behavior there is always an element of initiative, originality, and creativity. (5) Since all my initiatives are dependent on the primordial givenness of my transcendence and transcendental freedom—that is, since I have not chosen but must embrace my responsibility for my own transcendence—my originality is relative: it is a "given" or "founded" initiative. (6) By accepting myself (that is, my own freedom and transcendence) as given, I avoid the extremes of arrogance and "selflessness"; the recognition of my selfhood's givenness combines authorial pride with the modesty of radical (that is, noncreative) dependence. If this characterization of "the self" is correct, what then does the "realization" of this "self" entail?

Something can be realized insofar as it is not yet real but only possible. Even without entering into a discussion about the difficult concept of reality in its relations to actuality, existence, and being, we can point out that focusing on the transition from the self's possibility to its realization does not sufficiently clarify the specific nature of this realizable possibility. If we do not delineate the "content" (or the "program" or "plan" or "project") of the self that should be realized, only formal structures—that is, a kind of pure logic of ethics—can be developed.

Another difficulty consists in the fact that the possibilities of each self are always already restricted to the particular and individual circumstances (the situation) of the one person in question. The (possible) self that ought to be realized is in fact a highly determined reality, although it still has some unrealized possibilities. The more an individual has realized his or her initial possibilities, the smaller the range of still unfulfilled possibilities. The full realization of someone's possibilities seems to lie in their exhaustion: in the end, the initial range of possibilities would be reduced to a fully determined reality without further surprises or adventures. But is this not the definition of a corpse?

One answer to this difficulty could be attempted by noticing that the concept of a self between mere possibility and full reality (or actuality) is a transcendental schema that—more or less comparable to the modern Cogito—reaches back to the initial, merely possible idea of an as yet empty self and reaches forth to the idea of a fully actualized (that is, completely particularized and individualized) self. However, what does the idea of a "fully actualized" self mean?

One can perhaps defend the thesis that the human mode of being (the essence of being human) is a universe (or "multiversum") of possibilities, all of which can be realized by the entire humanity over the course of its history. One of the difficulties that this line of thought must overcome, however, is the question of whether history can be understood as a process that has an end. If history is necessarily and essentially nonterminable, how would a complete realization of all human possibilities be thinkable? If history cannot be thought as a totality, we cannot even talk about its result.

As for a human individual, it is all too obvious that the idea of an "*uomo universale*," understood as the complete realization of all human possibilities, is not even possible as a dream: how can one, at the same time, be an accomplished politician, a boxing champion, the best violinist, the summit of philosophy, and the most dedicated receptionist? A completely realized self, in this sense, is self contradictory, as a few experiments in imagination can show. Choices must be made to realize any individual self, but if an accomplished person can develop only a few possibilities (for example, being an excellent violinist, a loving husband and father, a generous host, and a reliable friend), how then can we say that the human "self" has been realized—and not only a few possibilities of this self? Why should we not say, with the same right, that such a person has failed to realize himself insofar as most of his possibilities have been left unrealized? If "self-realization" is an abbreviation for the realization of the best or the most personal possibilities of the self, what is the criterion for distinguishing these from other possibilities? Why, for example, should a self not be realizable by developing a nasty character or criminal behavior? It is true that the situation and the individuality of a person strongly restrict the range of human possibilities, but normally many paths remain open. In addition to these questions, we must not forget that the self's possibilities not only regard *what* one can realize, but also the *how* of its performance. There are many ways of being a violinist or a boxer, and only all the possible and realized ways combined would represent the full realization of the particular possibility indicated by "being a violinist" or "being a boxer." And finally, what does all this have to do with ethics? Why should the realization of possibilities be good or bad? Does virtue not include the wisdom of leaving many possibilities of human selves unrealized, or even preventing and eliminating them? Must we not already know which possibilities are good or bad, or morally neutral, before we can recommend or condemn their realizations?

To begin with the last question, the answer that is implied in the ethics of self-realization suggests that to realize the self is itself the fundamental or highest norm for all good life and behavior. "The self" then stands for the fundamental possibility of human beings that must be realized, whereas other possibilities—for example, murder and slander, cruelty and greed—must not be practiced. To what extent, however, can we interpret bad actions and attitudes as realizations of "non-self-ish," "anti-self-ish," or "self-less" possibilities or as destructive with regard to becoming an actual self? What is meant by the emphatic, authentic, true, original, or good self that must be realized instead of the arrogant, greedy, dictatorial, or egoistic ("selfish") possibilities of the human self? Are these other possibilities seen as alien to our "authentic" or "true" self? If so, the theory assumes that we can and must distinguish a true or authentic self from an inauthentic or untrue and false—perverted or perverting—self. Or must we consider all human selves authentic and good, while all evil originates in an alien power that besieges and often conquers what we ourselves do? The latter version of the theory would abolish freedom, unless we can show that freedom does not coincide or overlap with selfhood, while the former conceives of freedom as the power that ought to realize the true self against the temptations of another, equally present but bad, self. If we do not want to sacrifice freedom, we must justify the dualism of two selves that make a human being at the same time potentially good and bad. Neither the difference between the possible and the real nor insistence on the "self-ish" character of our behavior are then able to function as moral criteria, because they do not help us to distinguish a good self (and its possibilities) from an evil self (with its possibilities).

The entire discussion of self-realization suffers from the confusion that surrounds the concept of self: is it limited to the concept of free will as self-positing power and practical self-affirmation or does it include a content, a program or project, a projection of specific ends, a set of rules? If the latter, as suggested or assumed in the above considerations about a "true" or "authentic self," which ought to be realized, the self includes the freedom of the human will insofar as this adopts the ("true") essence or idea of being human as the program for its realization. If selfhood is limited to the self-positing character of the will, without having a program of its own, only a mere formalism can be justified, unless one can deduce a normative content (that is, particular ends and manners) from that formal principle. Both Hegel and Kant tried but failed in making this transition and more recent attempts have not succeeded either, except, perhaps, when they smuggled in another more substantial principle, such as an appeal to the normative aspects of human nature or certain conventions of human history.[13]

Even if we are able to discover which essential possibilities a truly human self entails, we still must justify the thesis that it can be realized through the realization of only some of its possibilities, while condemning others to *un*-realized possibility. What rule or principle allows us to specify and individualize the general rule of self-realization and to thus exclude many of its possibilities from realization? And with what right can the violinist and the boxer claim that they have realized "themselves" instead of only a few possibilities of their selves? Must we, for an answer, appeal to a unique call of conscience or a vocation? Even then, it does not sound right to say that someone who follows his individual vocation realizes his self—unless selfhood encompasses not only universal and situational demands but also the unique destiny of each unrepeatable individuality. This idea of selfhood is acceptable, but does it not imply a rationally unjustified element: vocation? In any case, it does not answer the questions of (1) how the entire self can be realized by limiting it to only a few of its possibilities; (2) why some of the self's possibilities ought to be realized while others ought to be excluded (in other words, why the exclusion of certain possibilities is not bad, but good); and (3) which criterion guides our preference for certain possibilities, or—if we accept the appeal to vocation or destiny—how the authenticity of the call can be recognized.

The central problem with the identification of a good life as a life in which a self has been or is being realized, is that one must show why the (possible) transition from mere possibility to actuality is something good in the case of the self as such. Even if we may qualify the proposed principle as an imperative to realize the "true" self while avoiding the realization of the bad possibilities that also inhabit us, we still must justify the assumption that the possibility of this self's actuality is or entails an imperative. Does our self-experience reveal a commanding voice? It does, but the source of its imperative nature does not lie in the self's possibility, and the imperative does not order us to realize all that is possible for a (true) self.

If "the true self" is another name for the "me" that is invited to correspondence, the ground of all ought is found in my "essence" as free transcendence. This essential self is the law of laws. As such it commands me to realize only some of its possibilities, most of which are not chosen but imposed on me by factors and events over which I have little power.

A Note on Fulfillment and Completion

Self-realization is often explained in more or less Aristotelian terminology.[14] The actualization of human possibilities is then seen from the
perspective of a principle (*archē*) that develops the various possibilities (*dy-
nameis*) implied in it. Full development (*entelecheia*) would coincide with
the complete realization or actualization (*energeia*) of that principle. From
this perspective, a good life is understood as the completion or fulfillment
(telos) toward which the original and all-encompassing *dynamis* is oriented.

To a large extent, this conceptual schema is appropriate for a study of
living beings. Growth, for example, can be understood along the lines of
an *archē* (for example, an acorn or egg) that develops itself into a full-
grown tree (an oak) or animal (a chicken). The possibility of applying this
schema to the moral perspective on human life is much more limited, however. Human beings certainly grow and develop their abilities, but what
has this fact to do with their morally good or bad behavior? Some well-de-
veloped skills are murderous; an accomplished musician can be a nasty person; a saint can be primitive or foolish. Unfolding and completion, perfection and imperfection are normal results of vitality: if the situation and
everything else cooperate, people become competent adults; but why
should this make them morally good? To become a perfect violinist might
be someone's destiny, but excellence in playing does not imply excellence
in morality. Moreover, what does it mean to say that full actualization,
completion, or perfection count for a morally successful life? What is complete in it and when is someone "fully actual"? As we saw before, a human
life is complete when it is over, but when we look for a perfect man or
woman, we think of someone in the prime of life. The end (telos) about
which Solon spoke does not coincide with the flourishing of Aristotle's *eudaimonia*.[15] Can we not continue to be good after having reached the high
point (the *akmē*) of our life?

In many respects, the approach of death is a process of decadence,
but is it impossible to become better in a moral sense during such a decline? If it is possible, we must distinguish between moral excellence and
other kinds of perfection and ask whether the idea of a fully developed and
flourishing being, which seems adequate when applied to a bulb or seed, is
applicable to the ways in which a self relates to all kinds of realities, including its own mind and corporeality, and, if so, thanks to which modifications. Again, our goal is not the completion of the greatest number of

initial potentialities, but rather the precision of our responses to reality and the excellence of their style.

Free self-actualization, as thematized by Kant and Hegel, is certainly an essential element of moral life. It can be unfolded into the formal framework of universal and reciprocal human rights and obligations, but how these must be filled in can only be discovered if we may appeal to one or more principles that concern the concrete phenomenality of the world we have to deal with.

Virtue

Above, I argued against the opinion that morality necessarily implies violence, repression, self-destruction, or alienation. However, no one can deny that conflicts and fights result from the different directions that our inclinations and obligations impose on us. In some people, the tensions are stronger than in others; they vary on a scale that runs from slight discomfort to a feeling of internal division. Most people have learned to subordinate various wants and wishes to the rules and customs of some ethos, but rarely are all moral tensions completely overcome. It is, however, possible—or at least imaginable—that a person has become so strongly attached to the demands of morality that her entire existence—soul and body, heart and head, reason and passions included—expresses an overall harmony of its many components. Through education and self-training, such a person has become what Plato calls a *mousikos*. A "musical" person's passions and inclinations have lost their wild and arbitrary character through subordination to a morally justified orientation. Instead of being repressed, the resisting tendencies of such persons have shown enough flexibility to be integrated into their Desire for goodness. Harmonious behavior has become habitual: it is now the normal way of acting and reacting, imagining, planning, and feeling. Although seldom if ever realized, the idea of an entirely unified and morally good person is, as an ideal, entailed in the idea of morality itself. The all-encompassing demand typical for morality triumphs when it pervades the entire person—not only an abstract, besieged will, but all of the individual's tendencies. Such a person is virtuous in the emphatic sense of human perfection. All desires have been transformed into differentiated expressions of the original Desire that as yet could not name its Desideratum because of its vague, all too universal, ultimate, and therefore simple, nature. Fully incarnated morality would terminate the intrapersonal struggle, insofar as it transforms the main task into the acquired spontaneity of a "second nature." A person's goodness has become not only trustworthy and reliable, but even "natural" and (almost) indubitable. Of course, as long as she is not dead, she must still keep her good habits alive—and the vicissitudes of life may still demand renewed efforts to stay the course.

Virtue must be understood as excellence in moral self-determination; it consolidates a good use of freedom by concretizing it in a habitual (for this person, "normal" and "natural") way of dealing with the universe. As an established way of life, a virtuous life is a refutation of the view that freedom is equivalent to neutrality with regard to all possible choices. A good person, accustomed to behaving well, is really, concretely free—more so than one who, uncommitted, postpones a definitive decision. The neutrality of indecision might seem attractive to those who prefer romantic irony or the experimental omnipotence of a universal possibility over the unavoidable limitations imposed by every realization. Perhaps they do not realize that it is impossible to live without being already engaged in a determinate course of life, be it an experimental, ironic, cynical, traditional, original, or reactionary one. The choice for a merely potential omnipotence is impossible; it realizes a particular style of life in which nothing can be serious while at the same time remaining attached to it. By choosing to be as "free" and unrealized as possible, one does not take a stand with regard to the factual powers and circumstances of the real world. To remain outside, on some Archimedean standpoint, is impossible. Whoever attempts it is unable to withstand the currents and trends that sweep away all those who do not freely determine their own mixture of participation, protest, and transformation. Freedom, as self-determination, is self-limitation; as the realization of good possibilities, perfect freedom is the exclusion of many possibilities that would make us bad.

However, if the summit of freedom is reached through total attachment to moral laws, how, then, can it be differentiated from a conservative, anxious, or lazy fixation on particular customs and routines? If freedom does not lie in choosing amongst the range of possibilities that are still open, how can we distinguish it from determinism?

We already saw some examples of facts we can neither refuse nor change: our being born, the earliest education we have undergone, the historical situation in which we become aware of our existence. These facts are basic; they precede our awakening to self-consciousness and our ability to choose or decide. They must be embraced (albeit grudgingly instead of joyfully). Embracing presupposes freedom, but there is no alternative. The core of freedom lies in self-determination, but determination does not necessarily entail the presence of more than one pregiven fact or fate. The variety of possibilities that open up before someone who is confronted with unavoidable facts lies in the various attitudes and modes of acceptance that can be adopted. We can enjoy or merely tolerate our existence; we can love or hate our fate; we can be puzzled by it, hesitate to call it enjoyable, and so on. The specific attitude we adopt codetermines the character of the facts that precede our response to their inexorable existence. Gratitude, for instance, implies that we interpret them as welcome gifts, whereas anger converts them into cruelty.

If virtue is a habitual mode of morally commendable behavior, it differs from bad habits insofar as it combines (1) the perdurance of self-determination with (2) the self's orientation toward the good (that is, toward that which makes the self's life good). Of course, customary behavior can also spring from a good or bad character or from a merely external adaptation to the manners of a specific society. Although it is not always easy to distinguish between virtue and good character, true virtue includes a free and passionate love for the good that is realized around and within the virtuous person. The dynamism of Desire must be perceptible in virtue, whereas character is compatible with immoral purposes.

Reason

Noēsis, logos, ratio, raison, Vernunft, and *reason* have played decisive roles in ethics since Plato. Kant identified freedom as practical reason and distinguished it from the ability to choose (*liberum arbitrium, Willkür*). In his view, the "matter" or content of behavior is borrowed from sensible inclinations, but the criterion for its moral quality lies in its being motivated by reason. Insofar as reason is practical, it is not only the source of all goodness but also free: as will, it is a principle that transcends the empirical causality by which all parts of nature (in the modern sense) are ruled.

Is reason indeed the highest criterion of morality? If so, how then must we understand its superiority over our passions and emotions, and in general over all other elements of our earthly existence?

If reason itself is practical, it has a practice of its own. To "have" or inaugurate a practice presupposes a purpose, an end, or a goal. That Kant himself recognized the teleological structure of reason can be demonstrated in several ways. The main object or end of reason in its practical use is an "end in itself" (*Zweck an sich*), namely human dignity. Even more clearly, the Dialectic of the second *Critique* shows that reason itself both desires and demands the realization of the highest and complete good, which consists in the synthesis of goodness and happiness.[16] Reason itself is thus driven by a Desire that differs from the desire of happiness and all the drives and inclinations connected with it. The principle and criterion of morality is a Desirous reason or a reasonable Desire.

Eros or Desire, as presented in these pages, encompasses not only reason but also those particular and individual desires in which it can recognize or infiltrate its own orientation. If reason is taken to be a purely formal faculty, it functions as a "logical" criterion for the adventures through which Desire discovers what it wants. But this discovery primarily relies on the irreducible eroticism that precedes all use of reason; it appeals to the recognition of that which is most authentic, "pure," and originary in our being moved and motivated by primary (or a priori) drives. Of course, this recognition presupposes and demands a wise discernment, and this must be acquired by experience and purification. Reason is involved in the genesis of discernment, but it would be blind if it were not supported by the trial and error of a Desire in search of its own secret.

Several topics for further investigation have thus emerged: the relations between reason and desire, authentic and inauthentic desires, logic and teleology, the growth of wisdom. These must be analyzed before we can sketch a critique of "pure" practical reason.

CHAPTER 9

Conscience

One of the dangers an ethics faces is its propensity for idealization. The course of a life is a mixture of good and bad, beautiful and ugly, pure and impure actions, institutions, rules, customs, attitudes, and structures. In attempting to sort out this mixture, we risk contrasting unrealistic pictures of pure virtue with their opposites while forgetting that human reality is most often transitional, unfolding somewhere between both extremes.

That we do not entirely fulfill the obligations we acknowledge is a sad but trivial fact. What is more significant is that the very truth of our obligations, the criteria that rule them, and the dispositions that make us good are not given once and for all, but must be conquered through the transformation and purification of the dispositions with which we begin the struggle. What we initially take to be a decent disposition, basic to the moral quality of our life, is forever shifting; our conscience itself is involved in a course of growth and change. But how can we know whether we are making progress at this most basic level of morality? How is the amelioration of a conscience possible?

Experience and Self-Critique

All experience experiences something other: even if I experience a pain or a hidden wish or a thought still immersed in feeling, my subjectivity is outgoing, transcendent. At the same time, however, I am aware of my experiencing that something: I have an experience of my experience. Experiencing my experiences, engaging in the preconceptual reflexivity of my involvement in the universe, conditions the possibility of profound change. If I completely coincided with my experiences, without being able to "have" them in an at least minimal kind of nonidentity, I could not change anything of their mode or character. Because I do experience them from a certain distance, however, they may develop into criticism and change.

The reflexive experience that accompanies each experience is not a mere observation; it is also an evaluation. In experiencing what and how I experience, a "metaexperience" evaluates the appropriateness of my experience of—and thus of my initial response to—the phenomena that appear to me. Although I may at times approve of my habitual responses, as given in my perceptions or treatments of the experienced beings, I sometimes or often feel uncomfortable with them. A suspicion emerges in me concerning my dealings with things or persons: is my way of perceiving or handling them correct? Am I biased, thereby distorting that which tries to tell me how it is? Such suspicions can initiate a growing discontent and disapproval. Behind or beneath the world with which I have become familiar, another manner of being touched and surprised, and along with it, another picture of the world, is budding.

Once I have discovered that my habitual mode of experiencing may be deficient, none of my experiences can be simply taken for granted. This discovery has lead some modern thinkers to a generalized suspicion and doubt, even to skepticism. Perhaps their "all or nothing" attitude is not the wisest, but maintaining some distance and a certain level of caution are appropriate reactions to the loss of naïveté triggered by that discovery. From now on, all experiences are accompanied by a metaexperience that tests their adequacy.

This testing is not accompanied by a clear standard that I could formulate and apply to ongoing experience, however. The standard, which must somehow guide the evaluation, is not simply given. It remains hidden, although it is already operative, as my suspicion or unrest shows; it inhabits the testing, but it must make itself explicit before I can distinctly experience how it rules me.

Each experience is a kind of experiment with regard to an appearance: can I see or feel it this way, or does it resist such an approach? Is my way of perceiving refuted by the thing itself? Can it give itself as it is if I persist in this mode of reception? Each experience is thus accompanied by a wider perspective whose rule is the following: give any phenomenon the best chance to express itself! This rule cautions our spontaneous observations: Did you see it accurately? Look again!

Desire for the truth imposes this rule. Appropriate correspondence, accurate adjustment of my openness to the phenomena is what Desire wants. Inauthenticity and distortion spoil the desiderata. Desire carries with it the confidence that it is oriented toward the pure and genuine being of all that appears attractive, but we also know that many desires make us biased. The struggle to deliver the appearances from distortion by purifying and authenticating one's own outgoing drives encompasses the entirety of erotic life, from the most basic and elementary dimension of experience to the highest level of illuminated speculation. Correspondence is therefore not merely a matter of propositions and rational proofs; it demands an adjustment of the entire person, including moods, senses, feelings, tastes, and corporeal postures. *Askēsis* has become the name for the exercises in purification that are required to move from crude modes of being to authentic and well-attuned modes. In order to correspond well, we must learn to conquer our inauthenticity by freeing the moments of truth in our relations to the universe. Loyalty to the phenomena presupposes a certain purity of life; one must become more true to the being of things by loving or hating, admiring or despising, welcoming or fighting them more appropriately.

Aquinas uses the mysterious word *convenientia* to indicate the originary affinity between the human mind and the being of all things. Desire is rooted in a love (*amor*) that is "pleased with" (*complacens*) all beings insofar as they truly are, and thus are good. Desire directs human lives toward various kinds of union because of the essential "convenience" of the various kinds of being with the soul.[1] This basic friendship and familiarity is not recognized, however, unless the soul is purified from narcissistic indifference.

The Voice of Conscience

Self-purification is guided by conscience, but conscience itself must become more perspicacious and pure. How can an impure conscience discover and acquire greater purity? Two factors are required: (1) a voice that challenges the average conscience by pointing to a more genuine mode of conscience, and (2) exemplary persons whose impressive appearance sheds light on the impurity of average consciences. The voice can be an inner voice or the outer voice of another's pastoral, therapeutic, or prophetic word. Or rather, both voices work together: without the challenging voice of others, my inner voice will probably remain asleep, and even a prophet cannot have an effect on my conscience if this does not recognize the agreement of his words with its own appeal.

Moral heroes and saints can be perceived as voices that speak to me while I am still discovering the authentic core of my own conscience. I can hear the tone of another's behavior as proof of that person's genuine goodness through which I can gain access to a conscience more genuine than my own. The converting voice must come from a prophetic voice that resonates in the heart of my conscience.

The voice of an average conscience is a flat translation of the original voice by which all consciences are most profoundly inspired. The moral struggle is in the first place a struggle for coincidence with that inspiration; conscience itself should become as pure as it is originarily meant to be. Conscientious self-critique is therefore the basic task of a serious life.

Conscience and Culture

Since one's conscience is formed by the particular culture in which one is educated, the self-critique of a conscience is ipso facto a critique of the cultural elements integrated in it.

By living in a certain epoch and participating in a subculture of a general culture, we share in a particular ethos. We are farmers, salespersons, intellectuals, academics, journalists, cooks, gardeners, and so on in this country and in this time. Each profession has its own customs and institutions; adherence to one of them may make a difference for our moral conceptions, but the general ethos of a country seems to have more bearing on the formation of individual consciences. Insofar as I have assimilated the general ethos, my conscience agrees with the average participant, "everyman." "Everybody" is convinced that human rights and democracy must be promoted, that adults must be free to arrange their own lives, that devotion to justice is good, and so on. Some "general" convictions, however, are contested by minorities, who propagate another ethos in the name of new ideals or the mores of other times or countries. For all people, however, a critical judgment about their own conscience presupposes that it has already been formed. At least parts of the prevailing ethos are already incorporated, not only in our convictions, but also in our reflexes. Moreover, each conscience has already developed a personal style: it can be rigorous or lenient, narrow or wide, accurate or sloppy.

Once we discover that our conscience, as it has developed, cannot simply be taken for granted, the critical task begins: we must test our conscience and the cultural elements it has integrated. The self-critique of one conscience thus implies the critique of the culture in which it is steeped. Cultural criticism begins with the experiential self-evaluation described above. We critically experience our experiential reproduction of the "normal" emotions, habits, beliefs, and demands. Moral growth implies a distance from the normative ethos that we share with the communal (sub)cultures and traditions to which we adhere.

Often we can criticize the prevailing rules and opinions of a society by pointing out that they harbor contradictions (compare, for example, Marx's critique of capitalism or Nietzsche's critique of moralism). It is more difficult to overcome an ethos that is coherent yet founded on false intuitions or experiences that are widely proclaimed valid and normal. One must then develop a sense for more genuine experiences that contradict the prevailing belief. The most difficult task lies in the search for a more originary genuine conscience, as this is a rarity hardly recognized by "everybody." Conscientious self-critique demands conversion from the prevailing corruptions of a particular culture to the rare purity of authenticity.

Ethos and Conscience

There is no other rock on which an ethics can build than conscience, but the average self-consciousness and self-interpretation of conscience is quicksand rather than granite. Insofar as a conscience has already been formed by education and growth, there is no guarantee that its formation was not simultaneously a (partial) deformation. Moreover, the conscience that issues from today's inculturation is a confusing and sometimes contradictory multitude of guidelines. And here we must correct the suggestion implied by our references to "*the* ethos of our culture" and "*the* average conscience." Indeed, we are confronted with many ethoses, and it is not possible to live in the world without concocting some mixture of elements from different moral traditions. Confronted with a variety of cultures and subcultures that differ, conflict, or overlap in the postmodern world, we must adopt a position with regard to very diverse traditions and theories about good and evil, all of which imply a determinate conception of conscience. How should my conscience react to conceptions that are different?

The ethos with which I have become familiar is a particular synthesis of the various ethoses of my country, the family into which I was born, the Church to which I belong, the workplace where I meet with colleagues, and the ideological community in which I feel at home. However, there are still other ethoses I can share, for example, the ethos of the wealthy, that of the (upper or lower) middle class, or that of the poor; the ethos of academics, intellectuals, or the media; Catholic, Protestant, liberal, humanist, stoic, hedonist, utilitarian ethoses, and so on. Within every ethos there are also different levels (for example, the level of the ideal and that of the practical) and modes (for example, an average, mediocre, exemplary, or decent but not excellent mode).

Refined studies in the sociology of culture and social psychology are required to map all the varieties and combinations that form the "ethical multiverse" in which we participate. A philosophy of conscience must answer the question of what this multitude of factual consciences means for a true and authentic conscience.

The existence of a specific ethos and of the conscience implied in it does not guarantee that they are good. How shall we respond to the plurality of factual consciences and the multitude of ethoses to which they can appeal?

Philosophers are wont to consult with the classics of their own discipline in order to create clarity and prepare a solution for their most difficult questions. In ethics they preferably turn to Plato, Aristotle, the Stoics, Aquinas, Kant, Hegel, Marx, Nietzsche, Ricoeur, and Levinas. (Whether the widespread neglect of Epicurus, Plotinus, Saint Augustine, Spinoza, Fichte, Schopenhauer, and Marcel is justified, will not be decided here.) It is obvious that each classical ethics confronts us with a particular ethos that is (at least somewhat) different from ours, although affinities and partial continuities cannot be denied. Familiarity with the classics and sensitivity to the climate of their world are needed to characterize the conscience that speaks to us from their texts. The Platonic and Aristotelian *kalokagathia* fits well in a Greek celebration of the divine cosmos, but it is much more aesthetic than the Stoic *ataraxia* or Kant's rigorous view of rational obedience. Thomas' natural subordination of sensibility to reason and of reason to

God's law reflects a more peaceful conscience than the romantic longing for unreachable bliss, and so on. Each ethical philosophy is the conceptual instrumentation of a fundamental conscience that seeks a clearer understanding of itself.

In addition to philosophical works, the entire range of dramas, poems, and novels presents us with specific types of morality, while evaluating them explicitly or implicitly. The diversity of factual consciences and ethoses, as presented in literary, philosophical, psychological, pedagogical, theological, and other interpretations, confronts a philosopher with at least two important questions: (1) How must we interpret this manifold of interpretations in order to determine a morally and ethically justified response (attitude, action, or plan)? (2) How can the search for authentic conscience succeed, once it is confronted with its own dissemination into such a manifold?

Several responses to the first question are possible. Because at least some of the existing ethoses (and the consciences unfolded therein) contradict one another, attachment to some of them necessarily excludes others. On the basis of this insight, one can adhere to one (simple or composite) ethos and condemn the incompatible ones. This can be done thoughtfully or dogmatically, in a reactionary or progressive manner. Although the reactionary way is inclined to appeal to the past ("the tradition," "the ancestors," "the origin"), the progressive mode appeals to the future ("history" as progress and providence).

A second answer was given when—especially in the eighteenth century—the plurality of moral cultures was interpreted as a series of variations on a common theme: human nature. Some universal convictions and moral norms were singled out, which seemed to represent the essential (nonposited or "positive" but "natural," that is, universally human) stock of all consciences.

The belief in a common essence or nature is no longer popular among intellectuals. But how do we interpret the similarity between the various ethoses? One popular position claims that not only all persons but also all convictions and consciences ought to be respected. But how can one respect those that flagrantly contradict one's own? In fact, those who defend this position exclude all positions that disagree with their own imperative of universal respect for any ethos or conscience. Many of them would deny that the many ethoses are separated by real contradictions. In their interpretation, the variety of consciences entails only differences. The apparent or seeming contradictions veil a deeper similarity or contrariness that makes the conflicting positions incommensurable rather than mutually destructive. According to these interpreters, the opposition between consciences is more or less analogous to the differences between Dante and Milton or between Velazquez and Rembrandt.

Perhaps the empirical scattering of consciences can indeed be interpreted as the effect of an underlying unity. If all the expressions of conscience are only attempts at capturing an ideal, their differences and obvious exclusions can be understood as deficient expressions of a common search or quest. All of them would then point to the idea of a most pure and true conscience (that is, the most true and pure knowledge of good and bad that can be attained), which at the same time motivates us and makes it extremely difficult to capture it adequately.

The presence of an ideal conscience in all its interpretations can be compared to the light that illuminates the originary Desire that forcefully moves us, although our wish of possessing it in the clarity of conceptual language cannot be fulfilled. Our many attempts at elaboration show how that light—through the prism of our urge for insight—is broken in partial and biased exposures. If this metaphorical description of true conscience and its inseparability from Desire is valid, we must penetrate the surface of its more or less shadowy translations into a variety of ethoses. The question remains, however, whether and how we can find another access than the conceptual one to the "knowledge of good and evil" that enlightens the heart.

In any case, it is impossible and immoral to adopt the position that all convictions deserve the same degree of respect. If that were true, anything goes; there would be no reason to search for adequacy of conscience and arbitrariness would triumph. Against this form of immoralism we must maintain that factual consciences, ethoses, and ethical theories can be incarnations of evil, as Hitler's *Mein Kampf* and Sade's fantasies demonstrate.

Education in a corrupt culture is not easy to overcome. At the very least, it demands a conversion. But the problem has a more general dimension: since we are drawn by conflicting inclinations, we must *learn* how to evaluate their ends and the combinations suggested by them; we must learn how to distinguish between good and evil, even after we have already been accustomed to a certain kind of conscience. Despite its actual concretization, conscience pushes us forward to a revision along the path of self-critique and purification. The basic task of moral self-consciousness precedes all obedience to norms and application; it demands that we detect and overcome all corrupt elements that have spoiled our conscience. *Katharsis* is the ancient device that names this task—a task almost forgotten in modern and postmodern ethics.

Before we consider the difficulties involved in moral purification, however, we must answer the question of how we are able to discern what is authentic and pure in the existing kinds of ethos and conscience?

Recognition

If Desire is seeking what it desires and conscience longs for an insight into its own most genuine "knowledge," they are on the way to the ideal of fully self-conscious and enlightened perfection. If correspondence is the law, this perfection consists in an ongoing life that is well attuned to all good and bad "things," constellations, situations, and events with which the individual in question is confronted.

To translate these generalities into a more concrete portrait of moral excellence is a task so difficult that no individual could achieve it on his own. For millennia the authority of mythological, religious, philosophical, or ideological traditions have aided in this task. Adherents of Judaism, Buddhism, Christianity, Islam, or Philosophy knew about good and evil because they learned from their religious, Platonic, Stoic, or hedonistic communities.

Since the beginning of modernity, autonomy has replaced authority: I, this singular individual, must accept full responsibility for my thinking and acting. No other, individual or collective, consciousness or conscience can take away my fundamental sovereignty. There is an element of truth in this thesis—the acceptance of authority cannot do without personal recognition—but if we really were completely and singularly responsible for the justification of all our thoughts and rules, we would fail miserably. A symptom of such failure may be seen in the widespread agnosticism and skepticism that is the result of the modern experiment in autonomously demonstrated truth. Fortunately, however, people, including all philosophers, have continued to rely on the authority of communities and traditions for the moral, aesthetic, literary, and philosophical trends and manners that rule their lives. Only the bearers of authority and their quality have changed: instead of the biblical traditions, for example, Descartes and

Hume or Nietzsche and Heidegger, and some more ephemeral stars have acquired extraordinary power in the philosophical world, whereas other circles are more impressed by novelists, journalists, pop singers, or other celebrities. There is an enormous inflation of authority in the "democratic" adulation of all sorts of heroes, but the idea that everybody has or should have a personal opinion has not died. Even in philosophy one often hears a disparaging tone when a reviewer remarks that an author "only" explains what Plato or Kierkegaard thought without forwarding his or her own criticisms. However, it is rare that someone who does criticize the classics proffers thoughts that are neither popular or traditional, nor borrowed from other classics. Important criticism is the flip side of positive insights that can be unfolded into impressive thoughts, but fault-finding without any attempt to renew traditional questions and answers is seldom productive.

Personal freedom and responsibility imply that, whatever interpretation or norm is proposed or imposed, an individual must at least be able to recognize it as reasonable, (probably) correct, and good. We would not be capable of justifying our thoughts and practices if we could not begin by relying on opinions and codes that are offered by classics and traditions; but we cannot freely adhere to opinions or codes unless we recognize them as (partial or approximative) expressions of what we "somehow," "somewhere," "deep down," always already have "known" and sympathized with as being "on target" or "right."

Although all of us are committed to the customs of a characteristic way of life, the freedom of this way presupposes that we recognize the rules of our behavior as justified. Recognition or *anamnēsis* is a necessary condition for a free conscience and personal virtue. External voices and words may be required to wake us up, but if they do not conspire with an already present, albeit sleeping or dreaming, conscience, they cannot make us free.

Recognition of truth or goodness in a proposed theory or code would not be possible if we were not guided, inhabited, obsessed, or possessed by a preperceptive, prepropositional, precognitive, and preexperiential sense for goodness and truth. A pure—albeit embryonic—conscience wants to become concrete in all our desires, ideas, criticisms, attempts at reformation, and conversions. A full unfolding of this conscience would give us a picture of ideal virtue: a person who most perfectly responds to the phenomenal "multiverse" by heeding its splendors and fighting or correcting its horrors. All finite phenomena would be respected and abhorred according to their own nature and proportions, whereas the infinite desideratum in light of which they are perceived would be honored as such.

From the above it follows that the texts and traditions to which we appeal for help in our search for an authentic and authorial conscience cannot have the last word. Hermeneutics, as the ensemble of repeated and retrieved interpretations of moral experiences, is a necessary but insufficient condition for a successful search, because the decisive phase lies in the recognition through which those who are involved in this search identify a proposed interpretation as a more or less accurate expression of the most authentic but deeply hidden conscience. If we take this conscience to be identical with the source and core of all authentic experiences in the dimension of morality, we can state that the significance of all hermeneutics primarily depends on the authenticity of the experiences to which the various interpretations refer and so, indirectly, on the quality of the conscience implied in them.

The experiences of one who is fortunate enough to have a lucid and accurate conscience are morally appropriate; if she is a sensitive and skillful interpreter, she can write an excellent ethics. But how does one become good in experience, perception, sensitivity, genuineness, conscience? This question has often been neglected in modern philosophy. A widespread misunderstanding of autonomy, together with the relativistic "democratization" of perceptivity and evaluation, has fostered the belief that all individuals are equally able to establish how the most difficult phenomena must be perceived and appreciated. Experience itself has been delivered over to common sense, which Descartes and his followers—perhaps incorrectly—considered generally shared by most people. But, like all human activities—and especially the basic ones—experiencing implies difficult tasks and can be achieved in many ways. Superficiality, sloppiness, lack of concern, anxiety, arrogance, indifference, and many other obstacles can hide or distort the look or sound or touch or worth of the phenomena. Not everyone is a specialist in aesthetic or moral or religious experience. Anyone who is not blind can see that this plant is not a stone, but as soon as we begin talking about its details, its relationship to the surroundings, its significance for human beings, and so on, the experiences of those interviewed begin to differ. In science, much energy is spent on establishing norms and methods for accurate observation. No scientist would tolerate being corrected by the common sense of unskilled observers; why, then, should the accuracy of moral experiences be left to just anyone?

Many think that moral experiences, together with aesthetic and religious experiences, are too "subjective" to serve as the basis for any universally valid theory. Some even deny the possibility of distinguishing correct from faulty experiences in these domains. Insofar as an ethical theory is an interpretation of moral experiences, it only expresses a subjective perspective, which then might resonate with other individuals who share that perspective. The relativism that accompanies this position can take two forms: either it sees the various perspectives as complimentary—and perhaps partly spoiled—perspectives that point to a complete and unspoiled truth, which may or may not be discovered as such; or it considers all perspectives equally subjectivistic and unreliable. In the latter case, it implies that experience as such should be distrusted and that the attempt to describe authentic experiences is futile. We should then not be concerned about experiential purity and progress in the art of experiencing.

If anything goes, not only empiricism but all phenomenology is condemned. If ethical theory is still possible at all, it should be limited to the logical investigation of formal structures while leaving all other questions to the subjectivistic sense that is common to all individuals.

The exclusion of moral sensitivity from the realm of universally valid observation is one cause for the disappearance of an indispensable insight that dominated the history of philosophy from Parmenides and Plato until the end of the Middle Ages. If one experience differs in quality from another experience, if one person is better in experiencing than another, if one can learn to experience in a more accurate way, if one's way of experiencing can undergo radical conversions, then an experiential propedeutic is a necessary condition for any phenomenology and for philosophy in general.

Katharsis

No sympathy for rationalism or idealism can annul the necessity of a certain empiricism in philosophy. We must at least recognize that the search for knowledge and evaluation must begin with empirical data, which then should be conceptualized through analysis, reflection, synthesis, and so on. Not all data are equally apt to function as the basis for theoretical elaborations; experiences differ in quality. Modern philosophers have distinguished the experience of "primary" and "secondary" properties and focused their attention on the influence of the observer's subjective conditions on the appearance of observable objects. At least implicitly, they recognize that some experiences are more reliable and better points of departure than others, but rarely do they acknowledge that experiencing is a difficult task that demands education and refinement. The philosophical treatment of experience often gives the impression not only that everyone's experience is good enough to build a theory upon, but also that experiences do not change. However, both suppositions are false. Like all other tasks, experiencing involves trial and error, experimentation, advancement or regression, growth in openness and perspicacity; it demands orientation, reorientation, critical revision, ongoing practice, and theoretical reflection. All these elements must be dealt with in a theoretical as well as a practical propedeutic.

Such a propedeutic would constitute an ethics of experience. But should this (part of) ethics then precede the rest of ethics? If so, where would the propedeutic find its own experiential support? Does it presuppose its own results or even those of the entire ethics? Are we turning in circles? Perhaps. But the fear of being in the midst of a circle should not deter us from exploring the a priori conditions of what we are doing; for circularity characterizes the most important realities, such as freedom, responsibility, existence, being, and God.

A propedeutic of human experience has many branches. One of them concerns the cultural characteristics and historical transformations of collective types of experience (for example, in everyday life, science, art, religion, and morality). This branch would involve a theory of hermeneutics, insofar as various types of experience (1) are decisive for the interpretations that have emerged from them, and (2) imply embryonic interpretations. In this chapter, however, I want to focus on the propedeutic practice of individuals who have become aware of the need to replace their half-blind or distorted experience with a more genuine and truthful one. As it was said before, even on the level of perception and originary evaluation, we must "do justice" to all things, but how can our actual way of experiencing become "just"? The transition from corrupted modes of experiencing to better ones is part of the purification that was a basic element of most philosophies from Empedocles to the late Middle Ages.[2]

In an epoch where the idea of formation of the entire person, humanistic education, role models, and discipleship are replaced with the selling of information and the quickest possible technical training, a plea for katharsis must seem odd: are we not all equipped with the same capacity for observation? However, it is an undeniable fact that the modes of perception depend on the modes of life lived by the perceiver. This is especially true for the perception of moral phenomena. The moral experiences of a bandit do not feel the same as those of a saint. But the saint is not born a saint; she had to grow in honesty and devotion before becoming a saint. The "*via purgativa*" stretches from the most evil or polluted conscience to the purest one; but how can such a way begin, which stages must it go through, and whence comes the guidance that prevents going astray?

Katharsis begins in experience itself, insofar as an experience always includes an evaluative experience of itself.[3] The apperceptive structure of each experience includes a critical self-evaluation. The criterion implied in this self-critique can only lie in the most open, unbiased, precise, unspoiled, clear, and encompassing experience of the phenomenon in question, which thus can "give" itself in the most real, unhidden, and undistorted manner possible. The decisive question is, of course, whether the specific being of the phenomenon comes to light genuinely and fully, but a merely formal analysis can at least distinguish the formal properties of ideal experience. The experiencer should be entirely open (and in this sense tabula rasa), not narrowed by limits other than those belonging to finitude as such; pure, such that the phenomenon can clearly be perceived as it is, not obscured or colored by interfering appearances; benevolent, so that he can welcome the being that appears; alert, so that he also recognizes the appearance of evil as deserving hostility; perspicacious and precise; and nonidolatrous, to prevent the experienced phenomenon from being taken to be the absolute or infinite itself. All these properties must be present in any experience, at least embryonically, if the experiencer should be capable of evolving in the direction of the ideal. Their ensemble functions as the—albeit merely implicit—standard that motivates the experiential self-evaluation and self-critique. It thus motivates a possible departure from any less than ideal mode of experience.

Often, such a departure—and the adventure inaugurated by it—presupposes that one is awakened to another, in some respects better, manner of experiencing, as expressed by other observers in words or texts. But, as we said above, no such recognition would emerge if it did not appeal to a possibility that, although dormant, is already present and eager to become active.

Purity

The history of katharsis shows that three contexts have been important for the meaning of "purity" as characteristic of a morally good attitude.[4] A first use of "purity" occurs when it is opposed to a mixture—for example, in referring to pure (nonpolluted) water, pure thought (not mixed with sense impressions), or pure experience (not yet informed by a priori concepts). This use sometimes passes over into an evaluative use, in which the opposition between purity and admixture is associated with the opposition between the good and the bad. Roughly speaking, the latter use takes three forms: (1) in a medical, psychological, or environmental context, people or things can be pure or polluted; (2) in a religious context, purity before God is opposed to sin; and (3) in an ethical context, purity is contrasted with the impurity of bad intentions, attitudes, inclinations, or deeds. Ethical impurity and sin are often seen as two aspects of the same impurity, not only in the Jewish, Christian, and Muslim traditions, but also in the philosophical texts of, for example, Empedocles, Plato, Aquinas, and Kant.

By focusing here on the ethical meaning of purity from the perspective of katharsis, we are inevitably struck by an old tendency that has prevailed in western ideology: the tendency to identify the polluting factor with sensibility, corporeality, and materiality. Many texts of philosophical and religious spirituality present the necessity of purification as the need for overcoming the desires of the body and its senses. Instead of living a brutish, animalistic life, we should become spiritual. The soul should turn from the material to the spiritual; the *nous* (spirit) alone can save us from drowning in the illusions of sensibility. Spirituality as spiritualization has been called a Greek heritage, whereas the genuine tradition of the Bible is said to be free from such dualism. It is, however, certain that much of the Christian and modern literature has adopted the combative schemes of an opposition between the body and the spirit. Abnegation, discipline, *askēsis*, self-castigation, and so on, have often been understood as a struggle against corporeality rather than the flip side of a self-respect that encompasses body and soul as well as head and heart.

From Plato to Hegel and beyond, philosophy has been seduced by the assumption that pure thought would purify us with its quintessential light; but fortunately its spiritualistic tendencies have been contested by another contrast: the contrast between a good and a bad orientation of the entire human person. In Plato's work, especially in the *Phaedo* and the *Republic*, one can see the shift from an ethical meditation on the contrast between a wise (that is, just, happy, and philosophical) way of life and an unwise (and therefore unhappy) life, to a theory about the ontological difference between the soul (*psychē*) and the body (*sōma*). Both contrasts are intertwined, but the ethical problem, which was the original one, has often been forgotten or seen as dependent on the ontological theory.[5]

If katharsis consists of progressive spiritualization, angels are the example of pure intelligence, whereas the body ties us to the company of animals. As hybrids we are then condemned to the unhappy existence of not fully belonging to any realm at all—unless we destroy our body or abolish the spirit. Whereas the latter has been accomplished by some modern and postmodern empiricists, the former has been attempted by some stoic and pseudo-Christians; most people, however, unbothered by theory, have appreciated the overall unity of their finite—and on the whole rather enjoyable—life without seeing how they could distinguish between purely spiritual and (im)purely corporeal activities. Aristotle is on their side when he remarks that the body is animated and informed by one soul only: the human (not animal, but noetic) soul. Corporeality cannot even be thought without including the spirit in its concept. On the other hand, we do not know and cannot imagine what a human spirit without body would be, because we do not have any experience that shows it in a bodiless activity or presence.[6]

In moral practice, we never experience an opposition between body and spirit if we take these words to mean what dualistic theories tell us. Many oppositions we experience within ourselves suggest that we are not spontaneously unified, but all our "states of mind" are empirical (which does not exclude that they are at the same time spiritual). When, for example, a thinker is thinking about the most abstract problems of logic, he experiences his own activity as a process that occupies his head (where he feels it), is driven by a felt desire for clarity, and uses bodily energy (the strength or exhaustion of which is also felt). "The experience of thinking," of which Heidegger speaks, is a specific experience of our entire, empirical and corporeal, existence ("our body") by itself. Such experiences are distinguished from other experiences, such as eating, boxing, digging, money making, and warring, by differences in density, intimacy, gravity, urgency, or sublimity. We can try to describe them as high or low, deep or superficial, sublime or abject, highly "human" or brutish and "bestial," even as "spiritual" or materialistic; but all these differences display themselves within the "multiversum" of the corporeal and psychical phenomenality of the humanly empirical.

The word *spirituality* can indicate (1) a specific phenomenal dimension, where religion, morality, philosophy, and literature are at home; it can also be used to point to (2) "higher" elements of that dimension in contrast with "lower" ones. If it is meant to indicate a metaempirical (or "metaphysical") principle or component of our existence that, together with another component (which then in any case cannot be a human body), makes up our (phenomenal) being, it should not be mistaken for the description of an experienceable phenomenon. And it certainly should not be declared the moral ideal that human beings should try to realize at the cost of the other component.

The unity of human existence excludes any possibility of opposing body and spirit, but it does not license the rebellion of brutish, crass, superficial, or "materialistic" inclinations against the noble or sublime capabilities that distinguish human beings from animals and trees. An ethical theory according to which a contemplative way of life is better than a farmer's life may suggest that the spirit, in the form of thinking, can be opposed to the laboring body, but both ways of life are active modulations of corporeal spirits or spirited bodies. Moreover, it is obvious that an excellent thinker can be a nasty person and the greatest concentration on intellectual or other "spiritual" activities can go together with extreme arrogance. Moral purity is equally attainable in "higher" (more "spiritual") and "lower" (more "corporeal") life styles. Immaterial spirits can be devils, and intellectually poor or handicapped persons can be saints.

If purity and purification are still significant for ethics, they should be thoroughly dissociated from the long, stubborn tradition of anthropological dualism that has ravaged western civilization. Only then can the pro found opposition between good and evil show its true colors. Only then can the kathartic process toward a purified life avoid the pseudomoral attempts at repression that litter the road to authentic spirituality. Ascetic violence is a degeneration of the praxis (*askēsis*) that precedes virtuousness. If the body (understood as the ensemble of our spontaneous affects and activities) is seen as an entity that must be fought against by another entity, the "spirit," repression is inevitable, with all the violence and disappointment that follow; if, however, spirit (Desire) and the body (the totality of our emotions and desires) converge toward one entirely human desideratum, experimentation and negotiation are better metaphors. Each life, in its own way, is an attempt at coordinating its various dimensions.

Via Purgativa

The premodern literature on the kathartic process is abundant, as, for example, the dictionaries referred to in notes 2 and 4 show. Ancient wisdom and Christian spirituality continually express the conviction that a life cannot become good unless it passes through a decisive turn or conversion, which is then followed by further purification. The purifying or purgative process thematized by Greek philosophy and Christian spirituality is one aspect of the process one must go through to acquire the right attitude: a stance so sincere that it is governed only by love of the true and good. Although often associated with the spiritualistic dualism criticized above, the best elucidations of the kathartic process—and of the propedeutic way in general—did not present it as a kind of flight from the real world into an angelic existence. In Plato's sketch of the search for the Good, for example, the emphasis is not placed on the ascent alone: having been purified and illuminated, one is finally able and obliged to redescend into the worldly reality of an impure people with its corrupt customs, opinions, officials, and politics.[7] The Christian theologians and mystics who inherited much of their theoretical models from the ancients were certainly tempted by spiritualistic tendencies, but they overcame them by loyalty to their faith in the resurrection of the entire human being, "soul *and* body," and the all-encompassing commandment that identified the love of God with love for all humans.

Traces of kathartic awareness can be found in modern philosophers, such as Descartes (especially in his *Discours* and in the *lettre-préface* of *Les principes de la philosophie*), Spinoza (*Treatise on the Emendation of the Intellect*), and Hegel (*Phenomenology of Spirit*). By way of generalization, however, we may state that philosophy has abandoned the question of katharsis to psychology, which, in its turn, has transformed it into a question about mental health. Clinical psychology and psychoanalysis have taken over the task of ancient and medieval guides for life and conscience. Some of them have maintained the links between health and the spirituality of which theologians are supposed to be specialists, but many psychologists have further restricted their task by interpreting katharsis as a variety of medication.

A critical history of the western praxis and theory of purification would presuppose a thorough analysis of the distinct meanings and mutual relationships of health, virtue, perfection, happiness, and salvation. This cannot be accomplished here, although it would be important for a metatheory of ethics, as distinct from and connected with various medical, psychological, and theological disciplines.

Becoming Virtuous

The goal of ethical purification is a good, excellent, virtuous life. This is not found in a specific job or type of work, but in the most appropriate manner of relating to the world, others, oneself, and God. The center and source of a good life is the attitude of "the heart" as the affective and dynamic organ that rules all the movements and expressions of the entire person. Few persons are perfect, perhaps even none, but many are engaged in a process of amelioration. We can learn to become better in action and knowledge; we can form and reform ourselves. Between a sudden conversion and a slow, almost imperceptible, transformation, there are many forms of becoming better that should be studied within philosophy. The contributions of psychology and pedagogy cannot be ignored, of course, but the entire study cannot be abandoned to them because that would exclude philosophy from the study of movement and mixture in the dimension of morality. However, mixture and movement are so constitutive of the human reality that ethics would become unreal if it neglected them.

If the goal of katharsis lies in the best possible realization or approximation of the moral ideal (the perfect life), the change of attitude that is required of morally imperfect individuals must be approached by a way of life that is not yet wholly good, but at least in some respects and degrees similar to a wholly good life. In its similarity, such a life "imitates" the ideal, but as an imitation, it necessarily falls short. Between equality and difference, it is an approximation.

If it is true that the decisive "factor"—the heart—of a good life lies in its fundamental (or originary) attitude (whose sincerity is expressed in its actions), the approximation with which one tries to imitate the ideal must consist primarily in a change of heart, that is, a change in the basic orientation and intentions rather than in a mere difference of deeds— although, of course, different hearts will always express themselves in different deeds and words. But how can one change one's attitude? Thinking and representation or inner dialogue are not sufficient; we do not possess our heart as an instrument that we can manipulate. In order to change our orientation, we must not only consider, test, diagnose, reconsider, and speak to ourselves, but also anticipate the deeds and gestures that are part of the good life toward which we are moving. Here, we encounter the paradox that Aristotle pointed out in his theory of the *askēsis* (exercise) that is necessary to acquire virtue: in order to become virtuous, we must act *as* virtuous people.[8] We must act in a way we are not yet capable of. Is this *as* an *as if*? That depends: an actor imitates and plays the role of a dramatic persona, but he does not let it affect his life, whereas one who is training in virtue is seriously engaged in the attempt to become what he is trying to represent. The mask that is displayed on the way to real virtue is a hybrid of "good intentions" (which, in fact, are not yet fully good, because they are still intertwined with and fighting against less-than-good intentions) and acts that would be wholly good if they were the effortless and spontaneous expressions of a virtuous attitude (or heart). The ascetic way of acquiring virtue is to act "virtuously" before the virtuous attitude is fully established; one begins with the fruits before the roots have developed. Of course, the beginning of roots must be there, because otherwise the entire *askēsis* would be a lie; but a dialectic of action and intention rules the time between the awareness of a person's impurity and the achievement of excellence. If this period lasts an entire life, it remains a mixture, although the good may come to predominate over time.

Did we use the right word when we said that the ascetic process is dominated by "imitation"? What exactly is imitated? If the moral ideal is not a determinate action, job, or person, but rather the excellent manner in which a person relates to the "multiversum" of the world, others, the self, and God, the ideal is a "form" or pattern rather than a human figure. A figure, even an idealized or nonexistent but imagined hero, can be imitated, but can we "imitate" a form or pattern? Should we then rather speak of "applying" or "concretizing" or "realizing"? Whatever the answer may be, the abstract character of an ideal requires the supplement of ideal persons whom we can call to mind as models or examples that show us what excellence means *in concreto*. Examples can be imitated, but they must be known *as* examples of less concrete and more formal ideals. In imitating an exemplary person, I should not copy the features that distinguish that person's unique individuality, but instead find my own style of moral excellence. This distinction presupposes that I can compare the examples and my own lifestyle in light of an idea(l) of moral excellence that has become concrete in the other's unique life and should become differently concrete in mine. Without copying the other's unicity, I should become *similar* insofar as both of us are called to embody the same (abstract) excellence.

Askesis

As a change of heart, the road to virtue is a painful enterprise. Like all forms of training, the transformation of an ingrained ethos demands great effort, and changing the manners of doing, moving, desiring, and imagining in which I was at home causes discomfort. Since morality goes deeper than most other dimensions, we might expect that the pains of a moral transformation are more profound: the course of a life has become addicted to mores that must be left behind; it resists an exodus. Detachment is very unpleasant. The word *suffering* might be more appropriate.

The painful aspects of a moral transformation awaken protests. *Askēsis* and asceticism are accused of being repressive, alienating, violent. What is more natural than to follow one's spontaneous inclinations, such as hunger, thirst, the desire to earn money, to be respected and praised? Is *askēsis* not a systematic repression of such inclinations in the name of a moral or religious ideal? Is it not a dualistic perversion of our natural desire to be fully human? Mortification and sacrifice are associated with hatred of the body. Are they not symptoms of decadence? Does spiritualistic hostility toward the senses not propagate a culture of death?

Nothing is wrong with natural inclinations unless one or more of them become harmful to their own goals or other inclinations. The desire for eating, for example, can be so overbearing that nothing else matters anymore, but its exaggerated satisfaction destroys the body that it otherwise seems to sustain. The need for money can degenerate into insatiable greed, which destroys loyalty, friendship, contemplation, and a peaceful mind.

The tendency to inflate our natural inclinations and the difficulty of ordering them are old topics of ethics. Kant thematized them under the heading of "happiness."[9] Radically different from *eudaimonia* and *beatitudo* as thematized from Plato to later scholasticism, Kant's *Glückseligkeit* represents the overall satisfaction human beings are longing for. As the maximal fulfillment of the ensemble of our (sensible) inclinations, it presupposes a successful combination of our desires according to appropriate proportions. Kant points out that happiness, understood in this typically eighteenth-century sense, has too many subjective aspects to allow for a universally valid specification: some people need wine or delicacies to feel happy, and others can easily do without. The criterion we use to determine what we consider our happiness is satisfaction, which Kant—alas!—identifies as pleasure (*Lust*), but pleasure is experienced differently by different individuals. Kant concludes that happiness is a vague representation rather than an objective concept.[10] It cannot be the ultimate end or object or idea of ethics, because it is too subjective, too multiple, and too sensible. However, it is an essential, but only material, component of the ultimate end that orients ethics. Happiness represents the empirical part of human existence, whereas the formal, "objective," truly universal, and a priori element lies in practical reason, that is, reason insofar as it contains an a priori imperative that ought to rule or "form" our (sensible) inclinations. This "formation" occurs when reason's practical rationality creates a (rational) order in the conflicting multiplicity of our drives. At that point, our "naturally necessary desire" for happiness is elevated to a rational level, thus being transformed into an empirical expression of human loyalty to reason.

Kant, whose ethical theory is here summarized in a way that shows an affinity with Aristotle,[11] defends here a traditional answer to all those who protest against the ascetic aspect of morality: Reason (*nous, logos, ratio, Vernunft*) must order the many desires and passions that drive the human self to action. However—and here we must correct Kant—reason cannot govern any dynamism if reason itself is not dynamic. When reason is understood as a purely "logical" and "formal" principle without orientation and end of its own, it is impotent vis-à-vis the erotic and passionate tendencies that seduce it to obey their particular ends. Reason cannot command, it is incapable of uttering an imperative, if its logic is not a *teleo*-logic. In other words, reason must have or be its own desire, its own passion and pathos. Reason and Eros must be one and Eros cannot be reduced to any of the many desires striving for the whole or a part of "happiness." As Chapter 4 has shown, Desire is the origin of *all* movement in a human being; its Desideratum is not an end in the sense of the finite ends of our desires, but rather its ultimate horizon: that which "in" all finite ends (but radically different from them) is the most loved "end" beyond and "before" any end. Desire is enlightened by a light that has been identified as our originary conscience. Conscience then is the origin of reason and rationality in their more derivative capabilities and functions. The teleological structure of reason should not be understood as striving for a supreme (and thus still finite) end above all other ends, because its infinity "ends" all ends insofar as it "makes" them (or creates them as) desirable, without losing its own infinity.

As we saw, infinity cannot be opposed to any finitude (not even to that of the entire universe and the "whole" of history), because such an opposition would place the infinite within an (onto)logical framework where it would fill only a part of the available "space," thus becoming finite. If human Desire is indeed a longing for the infinite, it follows that a contradiction between Desire and the ensemble of all finite desires is impossible. Seen from the originary "level" (which is not a level), Desire and desires are more united than anything else, for we could not have the slightest desire or inclination unless these were already permeated and activated by the Desire that is their "ender."[12]

The response that is provided here to the accusation that katharsis and *askēsis* are repressive is unconvincing to those who file all talk about infinity under the heading of wishful thinking or metaphysical nonsense. They prefer to restrict the discussion to the struggles between finite drives and desires. But even on a medical level, some *askēsis* can be recommended. It is, for example, obvious that diet and exercise—with the accompanying sacrifices and pains—are necessary to restore one to health following sicknesses caused by overeating or excessive drinking. To repair the damage, return to a healthy diet is not always sufficient; it might be necessary to do the exact opposite by fasting or abstaining temporarily.

In our strivings, we all must manage an erotic field of competing forces. Although such management has been prepared by education, we still must solve the problems of an individual life story, and especially the overall problem of how unique persons can become happy. There is no universally valid pattern of happiness that can be advised for all people. Although certain jobs exclude it, many others are compatible with it. We cannot even prove that happiness presupposes satisfaction or fulfillment in all the dimensions of human life, such as visual art, sports, poetry, or science. It is not necessary that *all* our desires be fulfilled or that all desires receive equal attention; but it is inevitable, and at the same time a task, that we order their conflicting claims. Thus emerges an erotic "economy."

There are various types of such an economy. From an ethical perspective, we cannot say that the life of a philosopher is better than that of a house cleaner, or that it is better to concentrate on contemplation rather than to volunteer for Amnesty International. As Kant understood, desires and happiness, as well as the multiple constellations generated by them, do not by themselves determine the moral worth of a person. If reason is not as formal as he claimed, but rather coincides with a light that is oriented by Desire, we must agree that the economy of human desires ought to be ruled by the conscience of that Eros to which all constellations of desire owe their moral significance.

Against the preceding considerations, most postmoderns will raise the following objection: If Desire possesses and obsesses us rather than being possessed or willed by us, does this not imply an essentialistic belief in human nature, with all its dogmatic and authoritarian sequels?

Many objections against the insight that human beings are characterized by a typical mode of being (*ousia, essentia*) are in fact motivated by an aversion to particular interpretations of the human essence, not by valid arguments against the thesis that "humanness" is an indispensable component of all human individuals. It is true that western civilization has often identified the human mode of being with a peculiar conception of it, for instance, a conception that had disastrous consequences for slaves, serfs, women, the illiterate, and people of color. The multiculturalism of our time is an antidote against forgetting that the idea of a universal essence is precisely meant to affirm the fundamental identity and equality of *all* human beings, notwithstanding their innumerable particularities and (equally universal) unicity. Theories that identify the human essence with some culturally concrete model are indeed dangerous. When they become powerful (as certain versions of "Platonism" and Christendom have been), they are prone to impose that model on the adherents of other cultures, thus degrading them to second-class specimens of humanity. However, nothing in such a mistaken conflation of the universal essence with a particular interpretation militates against the truth of the distinction between essentiality and particularity. "Essentialism" is a nickname; instead of clarifying the discussion, it most often confuses and obscures it.

Returning to the question of whether an "essentialist," kathartic, and ascetic conception of ethics is necessarily repressive and alienating, I answer that it is not, if at least the following conditions are fulfilled.

1. The human mode of being, as constituted by enlightened Desire, must be understood as an origin (*archē*) that precedes and generates (and therefore cannot coincide with) various (theoretical) interpretations and practical concretizations in some economy of finite desires. The (erotic and

conscientious) way of being typical for humans (including their Desire and Conscience) cannot be captured in any formula, but it can and must be lived, experienced, and evoked through the best possible approximations.

2. The moral commitment of a person, a group, a society, or a culture implies loyalty to the (approximate) concretization of Desired goodness that appears to them the most trustworthy (appropriate, reasonable, enlightened). In thinking and living according to one's own ethos, one always runs the risk of committing injustice and violence against the true human essence (one's own and that of others) and the ethoses of others; but it is precisely the task of morality and ethics to invent a concrete universality that as well respects as embraces many languages and different practices.

In a political community it is extremely difficult—perhaps even impossible—to abstain completely from imposing a specific ethos on the entire range of its subjects. A certain amount of "violence" seems inevitable on this level, although conscience demands that it be as limited and reasonable as possible. Moreover, the inevitability can be recognized as such; to a certain extent, it can be accepted and integrated into private lives as part of the unchosen and unwelcome facts and forces that have to be accepted with or without protest (unless the price becomes too high).

The political problem that arises from the clash of ethoses within one community cannot be solved by the liberal device of reducing the state to the rational management or merely administrative coordination of many individual choices for varied life styles. The administration itself is not an amoral outsider; it adheres to a specific ethos that is founded on a specific interpretation of liberty. Liberalism is itself a particular interpretation of the human mode of being and the ought implied in it. Its imposition is therefore as authoritarian as other impositions—except that it tries to respect everyone's right to responsibly discover by one's own endeavors the right interpretation of the common good. Liberal politics mirrors, on the level of the community, the dialectic of individual freedom as choice with regard to private desires indicated above. It is possible, although not justified, to deny that universality of a certain ethos is essential, while at the same time dogmatically affirming that choice as such—and consequently the coexistence of contradictory ethoses—is the only human good.

3. So long as I—as a private person—realize that my own interpretation and practical concretization of the Desired good (in the form of a specific constellation of desiderata and desires) is only an approximation—albeit the best I could discover until now—I am aware that I ought not

treat other attempts at interpretation with contempt or violence. Even if I could be certain that my own ethos is the best possible or a better approximation of the conscience that is constitutive of the human essence, I cannot forcefully impose it on others or myself, because this would destroy the responsibility (and thus the freedom and morality) of the person whom I would like to convince. I cannot make another good, not even through early education. Training and repetition may be useful (depending on their method and style), but by themselves they do not create a moral attitude.

To resume, I do violence to others not only when I impose my theoretical or practical interpretation of Desire on them, without allowing them to take responsibility for accepting, amending, or rejecting my view, but also when I seduce them—for instance, by propaganda or teaching—into accepting a particular ethos as simply identical with the voice of conscience. On the other hand, my commitment to the ethos that seems to me the best approximation of human goodness obliges me to plead for it in discussion with others. With regard to my own freedom, I commit violence if I entrust myself to an ethos that is suspect, even if it is the ethos of the prevailing authorities, or if, agreeing with a correct interpretation and practice, I force it on myself without judiciously and ascetically bringing my life into a well-attuned disposition.

CHAPTER 10

Adventures

Katharsis and Conversion

Katharsis is the elimination of impurity from a particular course of life. A characteristic way of life has been developed, but it is mixed with unfitting deeds and words and emotions. Askesis is required for a life to become genuine, uncontaminated, pure.

In addition to its primary meaning, the word *katharsis* is also used to indicate a more radical change in attitude and lifestyle. Plato's *Phaedo* is an illustration of this secondary meaning. What is called a turning around or conversion in the *Politeia*[1] is interpreted in the *Phaedo* as a purification for which one owes a cock to Asclepius, the god of healing.[2] In this dialogue, Socrates shows how a trivial life, obsessed with food, sex, babble, and superficial praise, can and must be transformed into a philosophical life, dedicated to spirituality and hope.[3]

Plato was not the first to compare different sorts of lives: Hesiod, Pythagoras, Empedocles, Parmenides, and Heraclitus had also contrasted good and bad, wise and unwise lives by presenting them in stylized portraits. Aristotle followed their example when he compared three types of *bios* in his search for *eudaimonia*.[4]

The comparison of characteristic ways of life has remained an important genre in the psychological, literary, and religious classics of western civilization, but it has disappeared from the handbooks of ethics. The rediscovery of Aristotle and the Platonic tradition, together with Hegel's *Phe-*

nomenology of Spirit and Kierkegaard's *Stages on Life's Way*, might convince the moralists of our time that a consideration of lifestyles is more urgent than endless discussions about rules or actions and cases.

Models of Life

Whether one distinguishes, like Aristotle, between a life of pleasure, a life of honor, and a life of wisdom, or like Kierkegaard, between an aesthetic, an ethical, and different kinds of religious life, or like Nietzsche, between the lives of a lion, a camel, and a child,[5] or as I tried to do in *Before Ethics*, between an egoistic life, a just life, and a life of service,[6] one always presents the reader with stylized paradigms. Hardly any individual's life fits within such paradigms because they abstract from all elements that complicate their unambiguous simplicity. The relevance of paradigmatic "descriptions" does not lie in the fact that they present a realistic psychology, but rather in their usefulness for distinguishing certain tendencies and possibilities of which the lives of real persons show various mixtures. The portraits of different lifestyles are philosophical constructions comparable to the "ideal types" used in psychology, sociology, and cultural anthropology. They simplify the ethical fauna by sketching them as variations on a limited number of basic principles. As such, they are close to a philosophical classification of moral types.

Journeying

In addition to the classificatory perspective, another perspective emerges when we ask how the transition between different forms of life is possible. A response to this question must clarify first the sense in which the question is asked, and second the sort of movement that links the different forms of life.

The question can, for instance, be psychological. In clinical psychology, one asks, for example, how a neurotic person can live in a more healthy way, whereas developmental psychology deals with theories about the stages of a human life and the transitions between them. Philosophical anthropology and ethics should not ignore what psychology discovers—applied ethics, in particular, must take into account the psychological conditions and (im)possibilities of moral demands—but a sequence of moral stages does not necessarily parallel psychological growth. A child can be more just—or in Kierkegaard's terminology, more "ethical"—than many egoistic adults. Nonetheless, the psychological study of moral phenomena also encompasses the investigation of developmental aspects that are immediately relevant to ethics. For example, the emergence of remorse or fundamental changes in moral conceptions present philosophers as well as psychologists with material for reflection. Whereas philosophers must learn from psychology, psychological research must be informed by the descriptive and conceptual analysis that is the specialty of philosophers.

Insofar as lifestyles mirror the various ethoses of particular societies and epochs, they can be studied in sociology, cultural anthropology, and history. But here, too, we must avoid a hasty identification of these perspectives with the philosophical point of view. Hegel's identification of the logic of history with his ontologic has not yet lost its impact on contemporary thought, but it is a great obstacle for understanding the many varieties of premodern wisdom that were neither infantile nor primitive. However, despite his unwarranted assumptions, and especially his faith that logic sovereignly rules the universe, the second part of the *Phenomenology of Spirit* gives us the admirable—albeit amendable—example of a philosophical theory of spiritual development via experimentation and conversion. The ideal of a fundamental ethics lies in a philosophical narrative in which various moral constellations can be shown to be worthwhile and coherent up to a certain point, but oriented toward more desirable attempts at living a good life.

Hegel knew that his philosophical history was a retrieval of the Platonic and Neoplatonic ascent from lower to higher figures of life, but he did not stress another old tradition according to which each individual essentially and per se is a pilgrim in search of a fundamentally better life. This tradition, which forgets neither head nor heart, is documented in many "ascents," "ladders," and itineraries from Origen to Cusanus and beyond.[7] One of ethics' most urgent tasks lies in a thorough reflection on the typically human movement toward greater goodness that is generated by unsatisfied Desire.

Stages

All human activities must be learned, even eating and drinking. Skills, language, manners, character, and the style of a life presuppose periods of training during which they are not yet fully formed: one tries to act as if they were already mastered, but the acting is still awkward, tentative, not quite "natural," still out of tune.

Training in virtue is the moral version of learning how to act well, or rather how to become willing, able, and accustomed to act well. Vice, too, can be the result of training, but most often it is the outcome of a certain abandonment to spontaneous desires. A person's ensemble of virtues and vices determines his or her moral character. Because virtues are rarely perfect, further exercise is required to develop and refine them; and because a character can and often does change, a person's life is a moral adventure.

The changes that occur in a human life can be studied from several perspectives. A psychology of moral phenomena is possible insofar as morality can be considered in its relations to age, temperament, intelligence, and so on; but the dynamism inherent in the search for goodness is as much a subject for philosophy as is the structure that coordinates the moral elements of a person's stance and development. Ethics must combine a synchronic study of the moral structure with a diachronic study of the process that characterizes moral life as a journey.

That morality cannot be detached from the experimental process in which it discovers and develops its own genuine core has been emphasized by both ancient philosophy and Christian spirituality.[8] In philosophy, the best known example is perhaps Plato's *paideutic* sketch of the twofold path that leads to complete virtue: the ascent through dietetic, gymnastic, athletic, military, literary, musical, religious, scientific, and philosophical education, followed by a descent into the frightening world of corrupt politics and perverse culture, into which the well-educated philosopher must instill wisdom and virtue.[9] Aristotle's oeuvre, as we have it, insists much less on the diachronic aspects of a good-and-beautiful life, but his short analysis of *askēsis*, his distinction between novices, disciplined (but still struggling) individuals, and perfectly virtuous persons, and his attention to the political significance of *paideia* contain the rudiments of a similar theory.[10] Plato's theory of the upward and downward path has infiltrated the West through its Neoplatonic retrievals and the medieval "ways" of theory (*trivium* and *quadrivium*) and spirituality (*via purgativa, via illuminativa,* and *via perfectiva* or *unitiva*), in which religion replaced Plato's emphasis on politics.[11]

Why did the diachronic study of morality recede in modern philosophy? One factor lies in the modern idea that science and philosophy, or in general all "objective truth," presupposes a completely certain and neutral standpoint, which must be established before the theoretical enterprise can begin. An "unshakable"[12] fundament must be discovered before experience and logic may be consulted. No "subjective" or mixed viewpoints are admissible; if the standpoint of a theory is not universally and absolutely valid, the rest cannot be worthwhile. Consequently, the question of a well-established beginning is decisive, whereas processes without certainty can have no more than propedeutic significance.

Descartes and his contemporaries may have thought that it was relatively easy to secure the principles of objective and universally valid observation and thought, but the history of modern and postmodern philosophy has shown the impossibility of their dream. The conviction that the *principia* of philosophy had to be guaranteed before proceeding to other questions led to transcendental reflection on the necessary and contingent conditions of the scientific and philosophical enterprise as such; but each attempt to establish a safe beginning was immediately attacked and replaced with new attempts to solidify the basis for further constructions— until despair overwhelmed philosophy.

In the course of modern history, the connections between the theoretical and the "spiritual" (religious and moral) aspects of human lives have become very thin, and the necessity of an ongoing purification of the basic attitude from which experience and thought arise has been forgotten. The all-or-nothing demand for an unshakable foundation has lead to complete disappointment: the optimistic enthusiasm of the modern revolution has changed into a generalized skepticism. May we interpret this skepticism (and its relativistic varieties) as the inevitable outcome of a promise that could not be kept?

What if, in ethics (and even in philosophy as such), the exigency of an absolute, noncontextual and nonperspectival, completely pure, authentic and truthful point of departure is too much for human beings? If ethics is based on experience, and if experience is as situated, historical, (in)authentic, (im)pure, and (un)true as the experiencing subject, are we then able to isolate an unsituated, unbiased, completely pure, authentic, and true core in ethics? If not, should we wait until we are perfect before beginning our ethical research? Or, extending the question to philosophy as such, should we postpone all thought until our perception, feeling, and taste are so unhampered and refined that the phenomena can fully display their genuine reality?

In actuality, ethics and philosophy in general have developed their thoughts on the basis of mixed experiences and ways of life. Implicitly, they have conceded that even impure beginnings should be tried out in taking them as the basis for theoretical research. What they have often overlooked, however, is that all their research is conditioned and only provisional, so that it will need to be redone as soon as a better, more genuine, and perspicacious basis has been reached. If we maintain this awareness, we will demand that all treatises on ethics (and philosophy in general), as tainted by imperfect experiences, represent only stages of an ongoing history, and that their authors' primary task lies in the amelioration of the experiential basis from which their ethics emerges.

The amelioration of experience, especially in ethics, demands more than logical tests or phenomenological refinement. The conceptual analysis of a basic experience can show its positive content and check whether it contains hidden contradictions. Incoherence can function as a criterion for the refutation of certain points of departure. Phenomenology can refine self-awareness about our own experiences. But neither logic nor phenomenology can guarantee ethical purity. How pure is the experience from which the phenomenological description emerges? If there is no universal, noncontextual, unbiased, and unhistorical experience, a guaranteed standpoint from which all experiences can be viewed seems impossible. The viewer himself is involved in the history of a particular standpoint with its own perspective and experience.

As we have said before, the particularity and relativity of concrete experiences does not preclude the presence of a universal element (or, as Hegel would say, moment). It does not even preclude the idea that many or all particular experiences contain that element, point to it, or converge in trying to express it. What we are not capable of, however, is describing *the* universally valid but at the same time concrete (situated and historical) picture of perfect (complete, completely genuine, and appropriate) experience.

In ethics, to become better at experiencing means that, through appropriate means of katharsis, one continues the search for the best possible conscience that can be given or acquired. This amelioration of an individual conscience cannot be wholly separated from the individual's moral practice, because the latter is an experimental testing of actions and motivations in which conscientious recommendations are probed. Moral praxis is part of the exploratory process in which a human life tries to discover its own best way.

The last sentences refer us to several questions that are fundamental for ethical theory, although they are not often discussed, even in the methodological parts of most ethics: (1) To what extent is morally good praxis an indispensable condition for an authentic and truthful ethics? (2) To what extent is moral life an experiment?

The Ethics of Ethics

The modern conception of philosophy postulates a faith-free, theory-free, and value-free point of departure. Although modern philosophy may be dead, as many say, the idea of a superparticular, transcendental standpoint cannot be given up if we want to maintain that a universal (that is, worldwide and historywide) discussion in philosophy is possible. However, being only an element of the philosophical reality, that idea cannot eliminate the situated and historical contingencies of any concrete standpoint. As for the value-free character of theory, in the preceding chapters, I have argued for the unbreakable tie between perception and evaluation or between being and being-good or being-bad. The question on which we must focus now concerns the practical conditions of moral experiences and judgments: must we be morally good persons and behave well if we want to know the truth about morality?

It is tempting to draw a comparison with art: must I myself be a good painter to have a good judgment about the aesthetic quality of paintings? The negative answer seems obvious. Yet, although being able to paint is not necessary, I must have good taste, which is something that can be developed. Taste has a (personal and collective) history, but its development (unfolding, refinement, and so on) is not necessarily due to the practice of painting, whose results are evaluated by it. The process through which a good taste is developed is one of well-guided and repeated looking and contemplating. Likewise, a taste for music is refined by attentive listening and comparing. Others, who already have good taste, can help by pointing out certain structures, transitions, contrasts, and emphases that I had not noticed, but in the end it is I who must see or hear how beautiful, impressive, dramatic, or shattering the artwork is.

One could surmise that the evaluation of morally good persons (and thus of the features that make someone good) runs parallel to the appreciation of art. Do we not learn discernment by contemplating exemplary actions and heroes of morality? There are, however, big differences between aesthetic and moral worth: (1) while a life without aesthetic involvement, although perhaps poor, cannot be called a failure, a wicked life is worse than death; and (2) no one can exempt him- or herself from morality; different from art, science, sports, erudition, business, enology, and gastronomy, the struggle for moral goodness is unavoidable, a constitutive part of all human life. This means that everyone is inevitably engaged in moral practice and that this practice is a question of life or death with respect to a life's ultimate success or failure. Morality is thus much more serious than art; to succeed in it is to succeed in life.

However, this fact does not yet answer the question of whether, in contrast with art, moral evaluations presuppose a morally good praxis. Could not a person's judgments about good and evil be true, while that person's behavior is condemnable in the name of his own judgments?

To some degree, a certain difference between judgment and practice seems to be the rule in morality: who can genuinely affirm that their practice completely conforms to their conscience? Does the frequency of such differences mean that moral sense or "taste" is wholly independent of moral practice? No; even if it is possible to lucidly condemn one's own behavior, it remains true that the unwavering accuracy of a truthful conscience is strongly aided by an ongoing attempt to live as well as possible while it is constantly threatened and obscured by the opposite practice. Not only are we inclined to justify our bad actions by bending our conception of the rules instead of defending them, but we also miss the chance of acquiring an experientially concrete acquaintance with the full worth of virtuous behavior if we are not engaged in it. Indifference or indulgence in moral deviance tend to rationalize their irrationality, whereas the concordance of practice with conscience provides the latter with a concrete experience of the desired kind of life it projects. This experience is peaceful, even if it is accompanied by the pain of frustrated desires. The enjoyment of such a peace confirms the demands of conscience and renders the mind free for further refinements, whereas the discrepancy between a person's behavior and her conscience creates hostility between the direction of her deepest (but often dim and vulnerable) insight and the appetizing enjoyment of spontaneous, immediately prompting desiderata. The latter enjoyment seems obvious and immediately rewarding. How could the peace of a good conscience compete with it, if that peace (despite its accompanying pain) were not experienced in the practice of a real life? How can a person who has never experienced moral peace be motivated to obey his conscience? Is pure knowledge without feeling enough? Can remorse, the negative feeling that results from discrepancy, suffice to make us obedient to conscience? At least some anticipation of the issuing peace seems necessary to compel us to conscience-abiding practice. Such an anticipation may be found in our empathy with exemplary acts or persons or in an imaginative sympathy with possible actions we could perform; but somehow the practical concretization of conscience's guidance must be sensed and pre-experienced in order to have a convincing insight into the moral truth.

The fundamental issue here is the vast problem of the moral (and, in general, the practical) conditions of truth-seeking theory. Fichte's famous phrase "What kind of philosophy one chooses, depends on the kind of person one is,"[13] is famous, but few philosophers have tried to prove its validity or to determine the limits and conditions of its truth. If philosophy is understood as an activity that remains close to life's existential adventure, it seems difficult to isolate it in the same way as we do with the hard sciences. If important experiences—such as those concerning the meaning of being and the meaning of living, the distinction between good and evil, or that between truthfulness and lies—involve practical engagement and experimentation, no thorough philosophy can disregard the question of its practical—or, in a broad sense, ethical—conditions. A thematization of these conditions must show how, in particular, the basic attitude of real and possible philosophers, their manners of proceeding, their personal purposes, their virtues and vices, their joys and regrets influence their insights.

The antisubjectivistic objection against such an enterprise has its own validity: if philosophy is an attempt to formulate knowledge in a universal language, personal particularities cannot be the final purpose. However, the fundamental union of philosophy with the adventure of a lived existence—a union that can only be lived as a particular and individual affair—is not itself particular: the individuality of a philosophy is as universal as the fact that all philosophers are human, and the universality of philosophy necessarily includes and demands its singularization by adventurous individuals.

Moral Histories

Life is an adventure because its course cannot be predicted. Even in the most traditional context, (1) many unforeseen events occur over which an individual has no control, (2) individuals are unique, and (3) in achieving the task of living meaningfully, they must experiment. Trial and error are necessary, even in morality, and no education can make them superfluous. As we have seen, moral experience includes not only formation and self-training in conscience-led habits, but also the very discovery of a more truthful conscience than the one that is already operative. Moral experiments are ways of acting—as if on a private stage—in which we try out how it feels to follow or modify the commands contained in the ethos of a culture, a class, a church, or our own still searching conscience. Reflection and reasoning are parts of the experimental process; decisions can be made to overcome endless doubting, but a conscience cannot be settled until it "feels right" about an insight that comes from a deeper level than the one that can be verified by calculations or deduction. In this respect, conscience is a good example of a fundamental conviction that grounds, rather than follows from, the reasons that can be given for defending it. Trust—in the broad sense in which it is involved in all the really important transitions of a life—is another example.

The unpredictability of existential adventures makes it extremely difficult to sketch a general pattern according to which a moral life in search of goodness should develop. It is perhaps possible, not only in psychology and cultural anthropology, but also in philosophy, to distinguish different types of moral development, including those that the search for a better practice and a more enlightened conscience can take; but it seems impossible to reduce all these types to the model of a linear development or ideal history.

Many ways, paths, ladders, itineraries, and journeys have been proposed,[14] often as stylizations of the author's own experiments and adventures, but many of them were either too autobiographic to function as universal models, or too general to suffice as guidance for the reader. Hegel's *Phenomenology of Spirit* can be read as an idealized history of the mind, insofar as consciousness, on the way to wisdom, must traverse a series of stages that mirror the stages of the civilization in which it participates. Although the itinerary is much more complicated than I indicate here, it is perhaps not unfair to say that all the stations described in this great treatise—which Hegel himself called his "exploratory expeditions"[15]—represent the developmental stages of one historical idea(l), which can and must be repeated and retrieved on the level of nineteenth century individuals. The history of spirit is understood as a dialectical unfolding (in which the negatives of all positions play a necessary and productive role), unfolding is understood as progress, and progress is interpreted as the victorious self-determination of the spirit, that is, as the center and completion of the mind itself.

Could Hegel's ideal history of the collective and individual mind serve as a model for an exemplary story about the necessary stages of (the practice and theory of) morality? Does the history of western civilization show a pattern of continual progress (which does not exclude periods of loss and decadence or even destruction)? Proponents of an affirmative answer might contrast the enlightened and humane ideas and institutions of the last two centuries with the violence of former ages. Some indulge in horror stories about medieval, or even ancient, "obscurantism" and cruelty, but their knowledge of premodern times is rarely sufficient to back up their claims. Proponents of a negative answer to the question of history's progressiveness can point to the massive violence and indiscriminate cruelty committed in our age against millions and millions of people, its enormous destruction and waste, its mass murder of innocent humans before and after birth, its widespread lack of respect for the dead, its greed for outrageous wealth and absolute power, and so on. Have we become better? And yet, are we not rightly proud of our ideas about universal human rights and our attempts to realize them through education and laws?

Our ethos of equality and human rights offers a good example of partial progress in morality. An accurate description of the entire complex to which our insistence on human rights belongs, cannot be given here, but we can rely on a pervasive conviction that distinguishes our ethos from that of the Italian Renaissance, the English nobility of the seventeenth century, the Dutch merchants of the same time, the medieval knights, or the Roman patricians. Precise historical information and moral sensibility are required to offer correct descriptions of the constellations that each of those and other ethoses characterize. Only when such descriptions are available, we can ask whether the contemporary ethos of equality and universal rights is better than the preceding ones and whether all of them are linked to one another as stages of a single progression. The task of answering these questions is colossal, but we could begin with a few observations about our ethos that call into question any claim of being the best.

Few western intellectuals would deny that the egalitarian and democratic conception of rights is a great conquest, which it would be foolish and evil to give up. The victory of this conception, for which many thinkers, lawyers, politicians, and moralists have fought for centuries, also has less positive aspects, however. As already mentioned, the practice of our time does not impress us by its universal justice, but rather by the enormous dimensions of its worldwide violence, greed, and outrageous corruption at the cost of the poor and powerless. Our epoch is distinct from others in its maximization of political, financial, and cultural power, and its technological possibilities are used to enslave and destroy entire populations. So long as the defense of human rights is confined to the ideals of intellectuals without power (who, moreover, even against their will, participate in oppressive systems), while most of the powerful reduce those ideals to rhetorical devices for concealing their injustice, we have little to boast about.

Another remark that should be made about the ethos of universal rights is that its fascination with right and justice in terms of claims and demands has caused neglect, or even blindness, with regard to principles and virtues that were central and fundamental in other periods and cultures. Not only has the emphasis on individual rights resulted in extreme privatization, with the anarchic consequences that undermine loyalty, friendship, and community, but it has also weakened the worth of honor, style, and decency, the virtues of generosity, compassion, and charity, and the obligations of gratitude and other forms of humility. Exclusive insistence on rights has created an excessive formalism: if everyone has the right to rule one's own life, the content of our obligations is reduced to respect for the right of others to be as autonomous as I am. What we prefer to accomplish within these limits is decided individually in light of self-chosen criteria, such as love of pleasure, power, wealth, beauty, or peace.

A more refined diagnosis of the prevailing ethos must wait until another occasion. Within the context of this chapter, I mention that ethos only to suggest that, as an example of progress, it is a limited and ambiguous one, which (1) in practice is flagrantly unfaithful to itself, (2) in many respects has made things worse, and (3) has suppressed valuable elements of former ethoses. If this tentative interpretation can be confirmed, we still might appreciate the wonderful discoveries and inventions of our own epoch, while at the same time seeing it as only one among other epochs before and besides and after it, each of which has its own partial progresses and regresses. In any case, it seems high time to contest the myth of one history's linear advancement of which we are the fortunate heirs. Equally mythical are reversals of such an eschatology by apocalyptic interpretations of the West or the world as an ongoing history of decadence. Hegel,

Comte, Marx, and Heidegger should not blind us to the multiplicity of disparate and simultaneous histories in which each of us is caught. Awareness of this multiplicity can prevent the excessive simplifications through which even great minds have reduced the past to a preparation of their own situation. The perspective from which they selected their material and projected their judgment was not free but anachronistic. The bench from which they summarized and judged other epochs was made up of their own prejudices.

Stories and Guides

We must return to the question of how the moral aspect of an individual life can be described in the form of a coherent story and whether such a story can be understood in terms of development, progress, regress, wavering, or other categories of movement. On this point, too, a thorough answer demands more preparation than can be accomplished here, but a few remarks can be ventured.

Inculturation and education make us heirs to a heritage in which the results of certain discoveries and creations have been incorporated. Although it might be true that, in some respects, we "stand on the shoulders of our predecessors," the filters through which our heritage reaches us operate in selective ways: some elements are repressed or forgotten; the ones that are conserved, are interpreted and reinterpreted, and when we appropriate them, we continue this process of selection, forgetting, and reinterpretation. In some sense, everyone has to begin all over again. For even though we were never a tabula rasa, once grown up, we are responsible for our ideas and preferences, even if we received them from others. We cannot escape this responsibility by referring to the authority of predecessors or traditions unless we can give convincing reasons for believing in such authorities.

The moral progress of an individual life story depends on many factors, two of which are the following: (1) the refinement of one's own conscience (which might create a conflict with the ethos that prevails in public life or among colleagues and friends); and (2) a growing concordance of the individual's intentions and actions with his progressing conscience (and thus with the originary Desire that tries to express itself in that individual's moral self-awareness). Amelioration is not a necessary process; so long as responsibility plays a role in the history of individual lives, regression or stagnation are equally possible. However, we can sketch a road map for the journey by indicating a few stages of the way to fulfillment of the two conditions just mentioned.

To determine where such a journey begins, we must typify the many situations and attitudes from which various kinds of people in different times and cultures begin their moral journey. The diagnosis of each epoch must then be supplemented with a moral characterization of the past and present of the individual to whom the road map should show the way. Obviously, these requirements imply historical and psychological expertise, but the encompassing perspective is ethical.

Several journeys, based on the experiences and stories of exemplary individuals, have been described by "masters of spirituality" in all moral and religious traditions. Similar developments, although not necessarily in the form of success stories, can be found in ancient and modern dramas or novels, although some of their authors might have been more interested in the aesthetic aspects of their heroes' adventures.

Plato's sketch of an ideal curriculum in the *Politeia* is only one example of an all-encompassing development. In order to show how much courage the ascent to the good demands, he contrasted it with the descent to public and private tyranny recommended by the average ethos of his epoch. Gymnastics, Spartan training, moral askesis, religious, rhetorical, poetic, mathematical, astronomical, and philosophical education represent levels of a formation that makes willing subjects "beautiful-and-good." The transformation of the Greek *kalokagathia* into the Christian ideal of charitable sanctity caused a transformation of the formative process. Compassion, gratitude, and humility became more important than beauty and intelligence, and the union of moral virtues and religious devotion became even more intimate. The intimacy of this union explains why, for many centuries, the moral journey (that is, the practical and theoretical *methodos* of ethics) was thematized mainly in spiritual and mystical literature. Gregory of Nyssa's *Life of Moses*, Bonaventure's *Itinerary of the Mind to God*, Teresa's *Way of Perfection*, and Juan de la Cruz's *Ascent of Mount Carmel* are only a few examples of the Christian (met-)"hodology" that was developed for at least 1600 years. The tradition was not completely abandoned when modern philosophy lost sight of the historical and biographical conditions of individual thought and actions—Hegel's *Phenomenology of Spirit*, Kierkegaard's *Stages on Life's Way*, and the modern bildungsroman from Goethe to Thomas Mann can be interpreted as later versions of the premodern quest for a meaningful life; but few contemporary treatises of moral philosophy pay attention to the peculiar kind of movement that is implied in such a quest.

If a good life cannot be identified as a "state," because it is a continually changing course (even if it maintains an early form, rather than undergoing conversions or revolutions), the subject matter of ethics demands a diachronic interpretation. "To be good" cannot be defined in terms of a here-and-now-present stance. A good life is a specific mode of movement. Goodness is essentially linked with change, transition, transformation, and thus with the temporality of a story and history. Ethics is the study of the moral transformations needed for *becoming* good.

For human beings who are not (yet) perfect, the command "Be good!" cannot mean that one (here-and-)*now* must act in a completely good manner. Regrettably, imperfect people are not able to act perfectly. "To be good now" can only mean that one must do everything needed for becoming as good as possible. Being good is to strive for becoming as good as possible.

What then are the requirements for becoming and thus being good? Since all individuals find themselves in different situations and are gifted with a different set of moral possibilities, it is not possible to give a general description of their points of departure, except that all of them are, to various degrees, under the sway of certain opinions and mores that are not perfect. Yet, some universal rules can be stated, for example: (1) each individual must accept his or her own concrete factuality and possibilities as points of departure; (2) a person must embrace the orientation to perfection contained in his/her own originary Desire; and (3) to be actually guided by this orientation, we must mobilize all our concrete possibilities for an accurate concretization of the originary orientation in the form of a personal conscience and a realistic program of action.

The realization of these guidelines demands self-knowledge and critical self-evaluation (and thus soul-searching skills), imagination, intelligence, models of virtue, experimentation, and so on. All these conditions can be detailed, but the main requirement is that the movement between the point of departure and the target (which—as perfect goodness—is seldom or never realized) remains loyal to the originary Desire.

Each life has its own possibilities, opportunities, and obstacles, but its destiny needs the individual's freedom to adjust it to the erotic movement that must be embraced because it cannot be repressed.

Constancy is the virtue that renders the movement of a life toward its telos good. More than single acts, the underlying dynamics of the entire story determines a life's (relative) goodness. Of course, this does not imply that a life could be good without proving its general progress through concrete actions.

Judging

If history were a continual progress, as many intellectuals of the last three centuries believed, it would be easy to judge former epochs: all of their cultures would be less perfect than the present one. The simplistic schema of a linear progress allows for many complexities, but it makes each past appear as a preparation for the high level of culture that "we" have reached. A progressivist review of preceding history offers a genealogy of the present culture. Since we have integrated the wisdom of the ages, we no longer need to consult with former cultures: we would not find anything worthwhile that we do not already have. In a climate that is "enlightened" by such prejudices, the temptation is strong to see the moral convictions and practices of older times as primitive or barbaric and as far behind our own refinement.

Without denying that many conceptions and practices of the past were immoral and that in some respects we have made progress, I would like to ask here a few critical questions about the standard that is used to judge our own morality and that of other cultures.

The development of a genealogy is most often motivated by the pride of a family that wants to show its noble origins and history. Sometimes it reveals less noble ancestors, bastards, and periods of decline, but the perspective from which the past is remembered is taken from the actual situation. A genealogical history of a culture or one of its branches is equally dominated by the cultural situation that is taken to be the result of preceding developments. All that is told in the story of the past must explain why "we" now are feeling, acting, appreciating, imagining, thinking as we do. The dangers of thus approaching the present and the past are multiple. Not only is it tempting to uncritically accept our position as better than that of any other epoch, but by focusing exclusively on the contributions of former stages to the present culture, we also will miss all those valuable elements that do not fit into our present framework, although this unfittingness might be due to deficiencies of our own. Perhaps we have lost the capacity to appreciate certain forms of goodness and virtue that were central to other times. For example, can we still sincerely admire the Homeric heroes, Roman emperors like Marcus Aurelius, or the ideal of a medieval knight? Are we not seduced into seeing all people of the past as more or less successful or deficient precursors of what is considered a successful person in our western, capitalistic, scientific, technological, rights-celebrating age?

I already mentioned the difficulty of reconstructing the ethos of a culture in which one does not participate. Without a critical distance from one's own ethos, it is impossible to be fair to that which is most proper to other ethoses. In any case, a reconstruction of the past that lacked such a distance would be an enormous anachronism.

Anachronistic genealogies are almost inevitable, but we can mitigate our injustice by combining the formal insight just indicated with the insight that real goodness is not found in the ideal of an unattainable perfection, but rather in the willed and constant movement toward perfection. Another ethos would then be understood and evaluated as a different attempt or experiment at finding out how human beings can be good. We would not presuppose that our own ethos is the criterion but would instead consider it one serious way of trying to be good in addition to and in competition with other ways. While being loyal to our own way, we would perhaps learn from others in order to critically ameliorate our own standard and lives.

For example, we can turn to the use of violence in the time of Pericles, as described by Thucydides, or in the time of Joshua, as stylized in the so-called historical books of the Bible. The horror of these texts is certainly not greater than the horror created by twentieth-century warfare. Slaughtering entire populations is as much a specialty of ours as it was of ancient Greeks and Semites; but we are shocked by the fact that even the writers who report those genocides hardly seem scandalized while we condemn similar mass murders with indignation (and a feeling of superiority). Even if the ruthless elimination of a tribe was a "normal" technique of ancient peoples in war, we cannot declare it decent, but we could try to discover (1) whether it was possible for individual soldiers to see the evil of this practice and to refuse participation in it, and (2) whether, in those times, better-intentioned forces emerged and tried to humanize the common use of violence. Plato's report on Socrates, for instance, presents us with a person who would rather die than commit injustice.[16] Such an attitude might influence the "normal" practice of violence.

We refuse to accept that Joshua's war crimes were prophetic realizations of God's will. But perhaps his ruthlessness can be interpreted as a realistic (that is, at that time unavoidable) attempt at accomplishing a sacred mission. Do we not defend our own war crimes, such as the nuclear bombing of Japan, in a similar way?

Another example of a condemnable ethos that was not condemned by an exemplary person is Saint Paul's attitude toward slavery. In his letter to Philemon, the master of Onesimos, a slave who had attempted to escape, Paul does not protest against slavery, but instead asks that the master welcome his returning slave (who without a doubt will retake his position) "no longer *as* a slave, but as more than a slave—as a dear brother, very dear indeed to me, and how much dearer to you, both as man and as Christian."[17] If we realize that slavery was a constitutive institution of the ancient economy, it becomes obvious that an attempt to abolish it not only would have been perceived as wicked or mad, but also would not have had any effect. What Paul, who calls Onesimos "my child" (verse 10), does is infuse the relationship between master and slave with an inspiration that—as *we* can see—is incompatible with ownership and power over life and death: thanks to Paul's and Philemon's benevolence, the slave must be transformed into a "dear brother" or "son." An oppressive institution is thus transformed in principle: possession is replaced by fraternity, even if it took many centuries before this inspiration was realized in the public and ideological ethos of the society. Whether slavery survives in our culture under other names is a serious question. An accurate answer would require a critique of capitalism, economic colonialism, and political imperialism. Is our morality free from obedience to these inhuman powers and mights?

It is easy, especially for those rich who have never been forced to choose between killing and dying, to condemn the violent practices and convictions of other cultures or times. But it is not so easy to rise above one's own culture by inaugurating a new ethos. The normal outcome of such a revolution is the death of the one who stops obeying and participating in the legal and moral codes of his time. However, between the extremes of zombielike obedience and moral revolution, there are many shades and mixtures of public ethos and personal conscience. Even the hero of a new morality must accommodate his ideals to the real possibilities of the situation.

Once we give up the certainty that a life is good if it obeys the stipulations set for it by the culture, the state, the class, the club, or the church to which one belongs, "good" becomes the term of a lifelong search. To know all that a truly good life implies is so difficult that it demands many attempts and experiments to discover it. These involve us in trials and errors, but relative successes are possible. We revere the heroes of this search: Moses, Socrates, Jesus, Saint Francis, Hammarskjöld, the Dalai Lama, Mother Teresa, and many others have inaugurated new interpretations and movements of Desire, but their success among many has also been accompanied by a weakening of their inspiration.

All attempts at being good are performed in the hope of progress, even if they end in failure. To be fair, it helps to look at those attempts as "not (yet) perfect," rather then condemning them as "(still) bad." With regard to ourselves, we could confess that we are still deficient, although grateful for the good we have received and integrated. From the perspective of our ethos, instead of thinking that our convictions are good and former ones are bad, we should ask (1) to what extent our practice is better, and (2) to what extent our convictions blind us to elements in others' that might be better than ours.

The moral journey is a mixture: we try to be loyal to the codes of our culture, but we remain critically responsible for the acquisition of a true and authentic conscience and its translation into practice. Our genealogy is a multifarious history of different experiments, heroic dramas, and powerful traditions—a rather daunting and bewildering but also reassuring condition for our own adventures.

CHAPTER II

Religion

This book is based on the conviction that the course of each human life is driven by Desire: the Desire of being and becoming good. Desire generates a movement that each human cannot but embrace and fashion in a way of his or her own.[1]

Moved by Desire, our lives are engaged in a multiplicity of erotic constellations and processes, which somehow are gathered into one (multiversal) universe. We experience our universe as both desirable (or not) and provocative (challenging, inviting, demanding, or forbidding). The desirable aspect seems to promote satisfaction, whereas the provocative one confronts us with various kinds of imperatives. With regard to the desirous subject, the contrast between the desirable and the demanding aspect is often translated as a tension between egoistic and altruistic elements: what I desire is good "for me," whereas demands, as coming from someone or something other than me, would be good "for them" or "for the Other." If we accept this language, my satisfaction and the other's exigency may clash with one another and force me to sacrifice one for the other. However, must we deny the possibility of discovering, in some stage of our erotic life, that the various demands with which other beings confront us, on one hand, and our most genuine and proper desires, on the other, converge or even coincide? Could my fulfillment not at the same time fulfill the other's desires?

In any case, each of us must create some order and unity in the many attractive and provocative relations that constitute one's "uni-multi-verse."[2]

In concentrating on the question of what is desirable ("good") for me, we seem to concentrate on my happiness (if happiness indeed is ego's overall satisfaction). How can I strike a most satisfactory balance of egocentric experiences? Utilitarianism is the attempt to justify an ethics that swears by happiness, but it does not pay enough attention to the question of what exactly we desire and why. Often it takes the meaning and content of happiness for granted, without distinguishing between the various levels and dimensions of human desire, fulfillment, and enjoyment.

If we take fulfillment and happiness in a rather superficial sense, the "altruistic" aspects of our universe appear most clearly in encounters with other persons. However, an encounter with human others can teach me that my desiring should not be ruthless and that ruthlessness neither makes me happier nor accords with my most proper and genuine Desire.[3] When I discover that respect and justice are for me also more desirable than my own satisfactions that harm others, I undergo a conversion: my overall striving is summoned to turn away from an "egoistic" way of dealing with my universe in order to adopt another, more inclusive attitude. The other's well-being has then become an important part of my own contentment and (higher/deeper/more genuine) "satisfaction." Devotion to others makes sense, even if we must sacrifice some of our pleasure or "happiness" to take it on. The ideal that is thus introduced comprises both justice and "happiness," as Kant has argued.[4] Not until the meaning of dedication to the other and its desirability are discovered can we also discover our own existence as respectable and as a task that we are obligated to accomplish.[5] That discovery might also awaken us to the claims that many nonhuman phenomena have on me.[6]

Once Desire has learned the respectability of otherness and undergone its first conversion, the universe appears differently. Since the horizon has been disrupted by alterity, I no longer can restrict myself to the question of how to synthesize all my desiderata into one overall balance of proper satisfaction. The universe seems to have fallen apart into a multiverse. And yet, I cannot avoid putting unity and order into my many involvements with all sorts of desiderata.[7] Moreover, my dedication to "the Other" is in fact a dedication to all others (at least the human ones), but how can I be everybody's neighbor and servant?

No ethicist is able to draw a general picture of the ideal synthesis of dedication and true happiness. We can only formulate some general guidelines; for example, the rule that we should learn to desire the other's well-being as part of our personal good, even when it hurts; or that pleasure and "happiness" are bad if they impede meaning; or that well-being (*eudaimonia*) lies in a meaningful, not in a merely "happy" life.

The erotic synthesis must be discovered each time by each individual who tries to be good. Fortunately, we are helped in this task by the communities to which we belong, with their cultures and traditions. Even if these communities themselves have not yet established an ideal form of life, they offer a reasonable point of departure for their members, unless they have degenerated into unruly states of violence. Communities, as well as individuals, are always experimenting with particular kinds of ethoses. If they are mindful, they learn through shifts of feeling and insight, which, we hope, will yield ethical progress, at least in some respect. Saints and prophets are paramount in this process, more so than philosophers, who tend to arrive late; scientists, whose competence lies elsewhere; and journalists, who only echo what others have done, discovered, or invented.

Because precise answers about the right synthesis cannot be given in general, and because no community to which one belongs has the final answer, each of us is, in the end, alone in resolving the question of how this scattered "multiverse" can be arranged as a whole. The standard no longer lies in the desire of an egocentric subject; it is replaced by the law of doing justice to *all* beings (including myself). From now on, my desiring must be measured by that law. If I am really convinced of its force, I will no longer desire anything other than *just* fulfillment (or "satisfaction") and fulfilling justice. Desire is then realized as a synthesis, or rather a coincidence, of goodness and happiness; the opposition between goodness and happiness has been overcome: I now rejoice in the justice that is done (for instance, by me), even if I must suffer for it. As long as my pleasure is paramount, patience and humility are too difficult (except perhaps as provisional strategies for enjoying more pleasure); justice, however, needs humble and patient individuals as a condition for its possibility. Acceptance of necessary displeasure is an integral element of being good (and thus happy).

Faced with suffering and the reality of injustice, we realize that the question of unity and universality is much more complicated than indicated above[8]: not only must I unify the many desires and desiderata that disperse my movement, but I also must embrace a universe in which evil plays a considerable role. How can I, this single consciousness, embrace a scattered, partly unjust, and largely unsatisfactory world? How can the Desire that drives all my behavior and thought not be the source of manifest illusions, if its Desideratum includes acquiescence in a world full of conflict, pain, and evil? What is the originally and ultimately Desired, if it does not fulfill my striving for all that is good and enjoyable, including justice, devotion, and friendship?

The question cannot be rejected in the name of a crusade against totality; for even though we must recognize the impossibility of subordinating human persons as parts or moments to a whole, I am the one who must put order into my being-for-others and their desires in addition to mine. Neither can I stop at the answer that my service to others includes their education to service of others in turn. For although such a propagation of the right attitude is just and necessary, it is not enough. By maintaining the tradition of dedication to others, we do not yet answer the question of *how* we should serve them, *what* we should give them, *what* of their desires and needs we should fulfill, and *when* we should be content about their being and doing. By insisting on devotion alone, we delay such questions. We want the others, just as we want ourselves, to become better than what they and we are here and now; but what does "better"—what do "good" and "well"—in relation to being mean?

If Desire transcends all desires, it reaches beyond all limited instances and kinds of desirability.[9] If being as such is multiple, it collects many limited, and thus finite goods. In that case, erotic transcendence cannot surpass the attractions of a finite multiverse. The ultimate Desideratum could then still be an encompassing horizon, but as the horizon of a finite totality, it would be finite and multiple itself. The alternative would be that the Desideratum is the highest of all goods, but then it too would be finite. As such, it would be comparable, although better than, other goods: a god above or among other gods, demons, heroes, forces, beauties, pleasures. The question of what we should hope for (for others as well as for ourselves) would involve us then in a discussion about the most worthwhile of all goods. Is it justice, friendship, beauty, wisdom, love, property . . . ? Is it a specific combination of such goods? In any case we must then radically modify the description of Desire given in Chapter 4, because the Desired "end" then no longer surpasses the order of finite desires, being simply one (albeit the most powerful desideratum) above others or else the finite horizon of a desirable totality. As for the latter, can such a horizon be anything else than either the (finite) desirability of all the (multiple and thus finite) goods or else the illusion of a paradise in the making?

If Desire is the origin of all movement in human life, it permeates all our feelings and ideas, but why is it then so difficult to get hold of it? During an entire life we try to discover what, in the end and from the very beginning, generates and rules our motivations, but we never grasp it in a clear perception or conception. Does this imply that Desire cannot be delineated, circumscribed, defined, conceived as having limits? Does its transcendence point us toward that which resists all determination because it surpasses the reach of any horizon and thus is infinite? The "width" of the ultimately Desired corresponds to an original void. Are we essentially insatiable because none of all the goods can satisfy our infinite thirst? Does this thirst refer us to a wholly other, unlimited dimension of good?

How can we answer this question? Answering it would be easy if we could compare and choose between the sum total of finite goods, on one side, and the representation or idea of infinite good, on the other. However, we do not and cannot have such an idea because all ideas (or representations or images or experiences) are necessarily finite (as their multiplicity loudly proclaims). The transcendence of Desire points to a "horizon" or "orient" that neither belongs to any totality nor refers to any further horizon. As such, it is neither *a* being nor *the* being of (multiple) beings. It thus appears as nothing: nothing determinate, nothing in particular, and nothing common or universally shared. Is the ultimate Beloved then not extremely imprecise and vague, abstract and uninteresting, completely different from any good or god? Is it only a semblance or perhaps a mask for what infinitely transcends the horizon of all finite desirability?

It is understandable that many people, confronted with the indeterminacy of the originary and ultimate (the originarily ultimate and the ultimately originary), confuse it with the indeterminacy of something like chaos or prime matter, and conclude that eros, in the end, does not lead to anything. They might look down on others who avoid their nihilism by clinging to the idolatry of one or more goods as the highest gods or "values" that make human lives worthwhile. But is polytheism, although more modest, not a more encouraging belief than the disillusioned atheism of the former? Both nihilists and polytheists show tolerance in accepting the absoluteness of the finite, but can they restrict the reference of Desire to such a horizon?

Some philosophers have tried to *prove* that we cannot stop at a finite ground, end, horizon, or totality. Finiteness, they argue, can neither ground nor explain its own existence; the existence of finitude irrepressibly refers us to the infinite. But how can we recognize such a reference (which,

even if it does not promote comprehension, must indicate a decisive difference between all the finite and the nonfinite by which it is transcended)?
How can we distinguish between the finite and the infinite, if the latter
cannot be delineated, determined, and distinguished? How can we separate
that which is indeterminate because of its underdetermined, confused, and
chaotic character, from that which is indeterminable because of its infinite
transcendence? How does the good itself differ from any idea, including all
ideas of any good?

The Christian mystics have answered this question by pointing to the
God who reveals his/her/its all-surpassing and all-encompassing infinity in
the persecuted and suffering humanity of someone who, inspired by and
living for God, is fully devoted to the entire creation. Manifested and present, but utterly obscure, God is the erotic secret of all devotion: Desired
beyond all desirability, God is given in the multiversal giving that dedicates
human beings to one another in the world and thus to God in all things. It
is only within the finite multiverse that we can refer to the beyond: the
God whose transcendent presence is too intimate to be perceived or com-
prehended, the ungraspable, but always sought and thus reached Incomparable to which everything refers and belongs. That this world is scattered
and crucified by innumerable forms of evil intensifies God's hiddenness,
but at the same time it reveals the incredible (and only *credible*) width of a
love that is more than giving: not only generous but also compassionate
and forgiving, patient and merciful.

Can a philosopher learn from such proclamations? Does the experience documented by the mystics express a truth that, in a less self-conscious mode, is lived by everyone who seeks the Good? Can the less divine
experiences that tie us to the world be deciphered as concealing-but-re-
vealing ways of allying all desires with Desire itself? If hypocrisy testifies
to the goodness of virtue, may we then also venture that all idolatry testifies to the irrepressible Desire of the one and only God who is neither separate from the universe nor a god among gods? In which sense can this
God be called the God of all goods or even *omnia* (the all), as Saint Francis did? Surely all things together (*ta panta*) cannot add anything to God's
goodness or being (together with God, they are not greater or better than
God alone), but they are neither nothing nor constitutive elements of God.
Although all desiderata refer to the only Desideratum that does not need
them to be complete (and, in that sense, is the all, *omnia*), the human way
of approaching that fulfillment cannot bypass the multiversal engagement

with the dynamic economy of finite desires. Incarnate passion for the Good itself through loyalty to the world seems to be the concretization of Desire. If the presence of God in the world and its history is indeed realized and symbolized in a crucified but absolutely devoted body, if all finitude is the spatiotemporal expression of the infinite itself, and if the proliferation of evil can neither destroy nor absolutely obscure the original and eschatological simplicity of God-in-all-things, the ultimate Desirable does not compete with the many desires that, if left to themselves, can only war with one another. Desire simplifies life by releasing an endless variety of courses and devotions as versions of one unifying Devotion, which is as much corporeal and earthly as it is divine.[10]

The fulfillment of Desire has then always two seemingly contradictory aspects: (1) since it absolutely transcends all desiderata, it empties itself of all plenitude through a radical *kenosis*, but (2) as the Desire of all desires, it frees all commitments to finite desiderata from their frustrating self-obsession. Only this freedom enables us to enjoy finite fulfillments without ambivalence and to suffer their factual or threatening absence with equanimity. Even injustice, contempt, and hatred—although they might be even more incomprehensible than the infinity of the Good—cannot ruin the peace of being united and one by being passionately involved in those desires that Desire adopts to realize its love of the world in God.

The Just

How does a man or woman live, whose Desire has become worldly by permeating all passions and actions? What happens to our desires when they are oriented to the all-inclusive but different Desideratum? When do we speak of a saint?

Many courses, careers, characters, styles, and professions are possible within the scope of human perfection; all of them show peace, although none of them is without lack. Each individual can achieve only one among numerous possibilities of life. Nobody can pay attention and do justice to all the persons, animals, things, works, institutions, and imperatives that deserve it. One's range of dedication and service remains extremely limited in comparison to the needs of the universe. If ethics were a question of isolated individuals and not of the entire humanity in its history, the gap between "is" (what we are) and "ought" (what we should achieve) would be so enormous that moral and ethical courage would become rare. Why bother if only so much can be done to establish justice, even by saints?

Even saints cannot overcome all neglect and violence: participants in a history that is already full of violence and injustice, they cannot but select some human and other beings and interests to which their life (and death) will be devoted. Who is going to serve the others whom they cannot reach?

Each dedicated life is caught in a small world where its goodness is experienced. The forms of evil that populate that world are attacked but not necessarily annulled by living goodness; the combat is often exacerbated and this might add new violence—the sword instead of peace—to the situation. A saint might cause bloodshed: the martyrs' own and that of their followers or enemies. Does devotion to justice justify so much suffering? Does Desire deserve praise if it causes disasters by becoming a worldly force? Is holiness an enemy of peace?

Since Homer and Plato, death and mortality have played an essential role in ethics because a life cannot be truly good if it refuses to die for goodness. To be (or become) good is absolutely good, more good than all nongood (evil, vain, empty, merely pleasurable) existences. If the choice of being/becoming good is met with persecution, the latter cannot be a reason for giving up. Devotion includes the acceptance of eventual martyrdom. Betrayal destroys the last vestige of goodness in all hypocrisy: apparently this life had another motivation than the one that was suggested by its dedicated behavior.

If becoming good presupposes dedication to a small constellation or world of related persons, animals, vegetation, houses, things, and networks, this does not cut such a constellation off from solidarity with humanity as a whole; every moral community is experienced as part of the human universe in its many geographic, cultural, and historical varieties. However, it does mean that each individual has a milieu of his or her own, a place and time where this unique person has to be for others in honoring and doing justice to those that determine one's unique chance of a good or bad or mediocre life. Can philosophy say anything about the reasons why your or my or another's life has to be lived here, in this part of the world, and now, in this period of history? In religion, election and vocation are fundamental for the task that particular groups, peoples, or individuals (for example, kings, prophets, judges, fighters) must achieve. Could philosophy

learn from that perspective in order to understand why we cannot be dedicated directly to humanity as a whole, but only to smaller communities:
the constellations to which one is assigned by birth and education, and by
the adventures that happen to shape one's course of life? Although individuality cannot be reduced to a particular formation of space and time, the
unique constellation of each individual's "small world" may be interpreted
as a crystal in which the moral aspect of world history and universal solidarity is mirrored. From the perspective of religion, this crystal represents
the place and time (the present) where a human person meets with the
Beloved. It is God's incognito as in-and-for-and-with the world.

The Thinker

After this general—too general—sketch of a just person, we could
try to specify justice by characterizing the goodness of persons according to
their vocation or the roles they perform within the society, the state, the
church, or any other public constellation. To do so is the task of an ethics
of the professions, if we take "profession" in a broad sense, which also includes states of life and belonging to a social class. As an illustration of
such an ethics, we can try to draw a general—too general—picture of the
moral attitude and behavior of persons who are so much dedicated to
thinking that we may characterize them as "thinkers." Without any pre-
tension to completeness, I would like to finish this book with a few indications about the ethical aspects of thinking as concretized in the tasks of
professional (or vocational) thinkers.

Thinkers are mainly found among philosophers, theologians, math-
ematicians, and theoreticians of literature and the sciences. A few of them
live an isolated life, like mental hermits who need their distance to better
think about the issues they consider; most, however, do their work within
the communicative patterns of academic or learned associations. In order
to specify their ethical involvement, we need to analyze their scholarly tasks
and the institutions in which these are accomplished (for example, the system of hiring, the reviewing processes, the emergence and recognition of
authorities). Once the tasks and factual practices of thinking are clarified,
we can illuminate them from the perspective of ethics, which then may result in a list of good and bad attitudes, duties, and rights.

Here, my main paradigm is the thinker about moral issues, or—
more generally—the philosopher. How should a philosopher—especially

an ethicist—search, analyze, synthesize, evaluate, and criticize the issues under consideration, including the thoughts of other philosophers? How should thinkers communicate? When is a discussion decent and when does it become unfair? But also—on a more fundamental level—how should a thinker relate to the reality, feel about it and approach it? If thinking is an activity that demands the input of the entire person, which moral qualifications make this activity a good, not an evil or slovenly, one?

Such questions must be supplemented by questions about the institutional aspects of the philosophical "business," which is as much a social and historical affair as the activities of "Wall Street" or "the government," although philosophical communities are less regulated by legal and political sanctions.

If the principle of correspondence, argued for in this book, is essential for a good attitude with regard to being, thinking itself must accord with it. Instead of avoiding all involvement with its issues, looking at them from a superior, judging and manipulating distance, thinking should respond as adequately as possible to all that surprises the thinker according to its own mode of appearance. Thinking itself is an engagement with the thinkable that invites a thinker to admire, abhor, love or hate, absorb or attack, enjoy or explore it. An encouraging smile, for example, or a stern warning cannot be treated as interesting objects, but neither can they be reduced to some proposition in the standard form of predication. A thinker who considers the smiling face that greets her is already involved in a personal relationship that structurally and dynamically differs from the "unengaged consideration" that from Descartes to Husserl was seen as an ideal basis for philosophy. True, a certain distance is necessary for unbiased and critical thinking, but (1) this distance may never destroy or eliminate the engaging phenomenon (the smiling that engages the thinker); (2) the thinking distance must be combined with the most adequate response to the smile; and (3) this combination is possible only if the thinker is able to think "laterally": from aside, approaching the relation of address (the smiling) and response in such a way that the emerging relation inspires interest (for example, joy of being addressed at all and curiosity) without seducing the charmed thinker to thoughtless abandonment. As long as the thinker thinks, abandonment is out of the question, but one can choose to stop thinking in order to smile back and indulge in pleasantries. In talking, a thinker experiences the same twofold of involvement and distance: while addressing someone who addresses me, I can reflect upon the words we are

using, the style and the accompanying gestures, and so on, but such reflection remains lateral; otherwise it would suppress the communication by
objectifying my interlocutor.

A philosopher, like a medical doctor or a psychoanalyst, is obligated
never to reduce another person to an object but always to embed his or her
thought in the basic respect to which all communication owes its decent
character. The chiastic asymmetry of mutual reverence, described in Chapter 6, must rule all discussing, teaching, writing, inviting, presenting, and
celebrating.[11] If the "business of philosophy" may be interpreted as a "republic of thoughts"(more or less similar to the *république des lettres* of the
seventeenth and eighteenth century), the leaders of this republic (organiz-
ers of congresses, governors and judges of journals and publishing houses)
must make the application of that rule and the realization of appropriate
correspondence possible and attractive. Does the dominant ethos of today's philosophical world correspond to such a picture of a respectful and
diaconic community? Does it testify to an eros that gathers its members
into a common search for that which is so genuinely true and good that it
inspires them to mutual devotion or even friendship? What could that be?
How must the ultimately desired and searched for beloved be in order to
inspire more than an objective, thematizable, anonymous "truth"? To bring
thinkers together in mutual service and dedication—or even friendship—
the gathering must at least be "in-spired." Does this (in-)spiration, this life-
giving breath, come from a spirit? A Spirit that devotes the thinkers to one
another on their various paths to the sought? A nonhuman fountain of life
that sanctifies them through a passion for the unique Good, which, although totally Different, does not lack anything of all that can be desired
because it already has it and gives it by way of foretastes? If philosophy is
the attempt to discover and meditate on traces and shadows of that which,
in the end, matters, it cannot avoid entering into the realm of religion,
even if thinking cannot embrace or deduce it. Hope, accompanied by
trust, reaches further—and fortunately they are stronger—than argumentation. If trust and hope fade away, how would we be able to continue
searching despite the overwhelming evidence of darkness and injustice?
Only the clear obscurity of Grace in the dusk and dawn of our universe
can save the ongoing quest for truth.

Notes

INVITATION: FROM "KNOW YOURSELF!" TO CORRESPONDENCE

1. Cf. G. W. F. Hegel, *Enzyklopädie der philosophischen Wissenschaften* (1830), §377; and Adriaan T. Peperzak, *Selbsterkenntnis des Absoluten; Grundlinien der Hegelschen Philosophie des Geistes (Spekulation und Erfahrung II, 6)* (Stuttgart-Bad Cannstatt: Frommann, 1987), 36–37, 79–90, 125–65.

2. "*Mēden agan!*" Another proverbial, or perhaps ritual, apophthegm attributed to several ancient authors, even to the Delphic Apollo himself. Cf. Pierre Courcelle, *Connais-toi toi-même de Socrate à Saint Bernard*, 3 vols. (Paris: Études Augustiniennes, 1974–75), 1:11 ff.

3. Pindarus, Pythian Ode II, 72.

4. Aristotle, *On the Soul*, III, 8 (431b 20–22).

CHAPTER 1

1. Descartes, *Discours de la méthode*, AT VI, 62: "et ainsi nous rendre maîtres et possesseurs de la nature."

2. Cf., e.g., Etienne Gilson, *Étude sur le rôle de la pensée médiévale dans la formation du système cartésien* (Paris: Vrin, 1930). Neither Descartes, nor Spinoza, Leibniz, Kant, Hegel, or Schelling, are understandable without acquaintance with the medieval and modern scholasticism that they received most often in a second- or third-hand version, especially through postmedieval manuals. Many interpretations of the modern classics are anachronistic as a result of their interpreters' unfamiliarity with the scholastic tradition from medieval Augustinianism and Aristotelianism to the Wolffian scholasticism of the eighteenth century.

3. For more on the actual situation of ethics, cf. my *Before Ethics* (Amherst, Mass.: Prometheus Press [Humanities Books], 1998), 1–14, 102–18.

4. The ancient ideal of wisdom remained, throughout its Greek, Jewish, Roman, Christian, and modern transfigurations, the philosophical goal of Descartes, Spinoza, Leibniz, Malebranche, Kant, Fichte, Hegel, and Schelling. See, e.g., Descartes' *lettre-préface* to the French edition of his *Principes de Philosophie*. An interpretation of Descartes' method as integral to his search for wisdom can be found in my "Life, Science and Wisdom According to Descartes," *History of Philosophy Quarterly* 12 (1995): 133–53; also in *The Quest for Meaning* (New York: Fordham University Press, forthcoming in 2003).

264   *Notes*

5. For many years, I have gathered materials and thoughts about "a diagnosis of our time," but the task showed itself to be more and more impossible. Only a genius can perhaps accomplish it in a satisfactory way. In any case, several limitations must be accepted, which will restrict the relevance of any result. What strikes me in the philosophical attempts at giving a diagnosis of western civilization and its philosophy that I have read is their oversimplification, often fostered by a rather narrow and biased selection of illustrative facts. Although I have not altogether abandoned the project of writing about some key aspects of the actual world in relation to its own heritage, by way of a possible guide for orientation, such an investigation cannot be reduced to an introductory section of this (partial) Ethics.

6. Another way of preparing or warning the reader with regard to the methodological features of the text that follows would consist of a more or less autobiographical story about the teachers, works, and philosophers with whom the author has conversed through learning, struggling, assimilation and rejection, discussion, and transformation. Even then, the latter's work would show that he gave a personal—although not necessarily original—twist to the method(s) he deemed promising.

7. Of course, many other (Stoic, Ciceronian, Augustinian, and other) elements are retrieved in Aquinas's *Summa Theologica*, but they are adjusted to the indicated framework.

8. Cf. Aquinas, *Summa Theologica*, Iª IIªᵉ, qu. 1–5, 6–21, 22–48, 55, and IIª IIªᵉ, qu. 49–54.

CHAPTER 2

1. Cf., e.g., Kant's concentration on law and duty as the principles of ethical practice and theory.

2. Since Plato, the comparison of a good life with the achievement of a task or "work" has been helpful in the analysis of the ethical, but it has also seduced many authors into overlooking the fundamental difference between making (*poiēsis*) and behaving (*praxis*). In a civilization that considers work and being busy the normal fulfillment of human time, the danger of confusing *poiēsis* and *praxis* is especially threatening, for example by ranking all forms of contemplation below productivity.

3. Aristotle, *Nicomachean Ethics*, 1140a1–23, b3–7. Cf. 1094a3–6; 1139b1–4; 1178b18–21.

4. Cf. Emmanuel Levinas, *Totalité et Infini* (The Hague: Martinus Nijhoff, 1961), 79–90, 131–36; translated by Alfonso Lingis as *Totality and Infinity* (Pittsburgh: Duquesne University Press, 1969), 107–17, 158–62. In further references to *Totalité et Infini*, I will cite the pages of the English edition in parentheses following the pages of the French edition.

5. Cf. below, Chapter 4.

6. Plato's and Aristotle's use of *kalos* ("beautiful") and its association with *agathos* ("good") shows that for them the ethical and the aesthetic aspects of human behavior are much less distinct than for us.

7. Cf. Martin Heidegger, *Sein und Zeit* (Tübingen: Niemeyer, 1927), 50–53; Françoise Dastur, *Death: An Essay on Finitude*, trans. John Llewelyn (London: Athlone, 1996); Emmanuel Levinas, *Totalité et Infini*, 201–17 (226–39); and my own *To the Other: An Introduction to the Philosophy of Emmanuel Levinas* (West Lafayette, Ind.: Purdue University Press, 1993), 186–90.

8. Cf. his letter to Menoikeus, 125: "Death, the most dreaded of evils, is therefore of no concern to us; for while we exist death is not present, and when death is present we no longer exist." Epicurus, *Letters, Principal Doctrines, and Vatican Sayings*, trans. Russel M. Geer (Indianapolis: Bobbs-Merrill, 1964), 54.

9. Cf. Descartes, *Lettre-préface* for the French edition of *Les Principes de la Philosophie*. Cf. *Oeuvres philosophiques de Descartes*, ed. F. Alquié (Paris: Garnier, 1963–73), 3:779–85.

10. Ethical judgments about topics such as abortion, euthanasia, biogenetic research, and experimentation with embryos remain inadequate if they are not based on an ethical diagnosis and critique of the technological and ideological culture of our age. Since such a diagnosis presupposes a host of historical and sociological research, a philosophical ethic remains formal so long as it has not integrated the results of that research. This does not mean that ethicists should wait until the social sciences have done their work, for scientific research itself needs a philosophical analysis of the ethical perspective to know what it should investigate in order to design a map of ethically relevant facts and structures.

11. A "master and owner of nature" cannot accept that nature makes him uncertain by playing tricks on him. All facts must be certified, controlled, produced, or repressed at will.

12. Cf. Plato, *Phaedo*, 67b–c and 68a.

13. Heidegger, *Sein und Zeit*, §53.

14. Levinas, *Totalité et Infini*, 211–12 (234–35).

15. "*Conatus essendi*," as Levinas, borrowing this expression from Spinoza, often says.

16. Cf. Theognis 425–28. Epicurus refers to these verses in his letter to Menoikeus, 126–27a (see note 8), but calls them much worse than foolish "not only because life is desirable, but also because the art of living well and the art of dying well are one." His argument is simple: "If a man says this and really believes it, why does he not depart from life?" (55). However, this argument neglects the possibility that a "departure from life" might be the beginning of a life in Hades as well as the possibility that suicide is a terrifying sin.

17. Jeremiah 20:14–18; Job 3:3–16.

18. In the case of Jeremiah and Job, it is clear that their laments represent intermediate phases of their struggle for hope and acceptance.

19. Socrates, *Gorgias*, 469b–c, 474c, 479c–d, 509b–c, 511a.

20. The dramatization of death by several twentieth-century philosophers invites an analysis of the mentality that characterizes their culture and its relations to religion and secularity. Psychoanalytic and sociocritical observations about their

fascination with death could contribute to a philosophical diagnosis of their time, which then would confirm the circularity (or "spirality") of any ethics of mortality.

21. Cf. Fyodor Dostoyevsky, *The Brothers Karamazov*, trans. Richard Pevear and Larissa Volokhonsky (New York: Knopf, 1992), book 5, *Rebellion*, 245.

22. Cf. David Hume, *A Treatise of Human Nature*, book 3, part 1, "An Enquiry Concerning the Principle of Morals," section 1 and appendix 1.

23. From Aristotle to Hegel, the unavoidability of immediacy and the priority of intuition with regard to discursivity has been recognized, and phenomenology has methodically explored this priority. That true intuitions presuppose purification is often forgotten, however. See below, Chapters 9 and 10.

24. Cf. Peperzak, *Before Ethics*, 1–14.

25. Paradigmatically expressed by Hegel in his inaugural address at the University of Berlin on October 22, 1818: "To begin with, I may not demand anything else from you then trust in *Science, faith in Reason, trust and faith in yourself*" (*Gesammelte Werke* [Hamburg: Meiner, 1968 ff.], 18:18).

26. For more on the relations between faith and philosophy, see my *Reason in Faith* (New York: Paulist Press, 1999) and *The Quest for Meaning* (New York: Fordham University Press, forthcoming in 2003).

CHAPTER 3

1. Martin Heidegger, *Sein und Zeit* (Tübingen: Niemeyer, 1927), §40, 50–53; *Wegmarken, Gesammtausgabe*, ed. Friedrich-Wilhelm von Herrmann (Frankfurt am Main: Klostermann, 1976), 9, 111–18.

2. Cf. Spinoza, *Ethica*, III, propositio VI.

3. Among the innumerable expressions of this *Amen*, one may emphasize Nietzsche's *Also Sprach Zarathustra* or Rainer Maria Rilke's *Sonette an Orpheus*.

4. Cf. Peperzak, *Before Ethics* (Amherst, Mass.: Prometheus Press [Humanities Books], 1998), 15–24.

CHAPTER 4

1. Aristotle, *On the Soul*, III, 8 (431b20–22).

2. Aristotle, *Nicomachean Ethics*, I, 4–5 (1095a14–1096a3).

3. A plea for not separating philosophy from life as an adventure of spirituality can be found in my *Reason in Faith* (New York: Paulist Press, 1999).

4. Of course, the similarity among the above-mentioned philosophies in this respect does not abolish profound differences between their interpretations of the human eros.

5. From Plato's *anamnesis* and Aristotle's *nous* to Kant's a priori and Hegel's necessary immediacy (*Unmittelbarkeit*), this phenomenological principle has been recognized explicitly by all philosophers, including rationalists, empiricists, and pragmatists. Those who swear by argumentation alone are building on quicksand.

6. Goethe, *Faust*, II, 6875–76: "Was wollen wir, was will die Welt nun mehr? Denn das Geheimnis liegt am Tage."

7. A radical phenomenology of *Angst* cannot be found in a phenomenology of mortality. The trembling that is caused by the imminence of death feels different according to the meaning (or the lack of meaning) expressed in it. Cf. above, Chapter 2.

8. Cf. Levinas, *Totalité et Infini* (The Hague: Martinus Nijhoff, 1961), 3 ff.; translated as *Totality and Infinity* (Pittsburgh: Duquesne University Press, 1969), 33 ff.

9. Cf. Aristotle, *Nicomachean Ethics*, I, 1 (1094a1–5).

10. Cf. Aristotle, *On the Soul*, III, 10 (433a10 ff.).

11. See *Dictionnaire de spiritualité ascétique et mystique, doctrine et histoire*, eds. Marcel Viller et al. (Paris: Beauchesne, 1937–55), I, col. 166–69 and III, col. 99–103.

12. See below.

13. Cf. Emmanuel Levinas, *Totalité et Infini*, xv; *Totality and Infinity*, 27.

14. "Be aware of the end" (Aristotle, *Nicomachean Ethics*, I, 10, 1100a11–12).

15. Cf. Immanuel Kant, *Grundlegung zur Metaphysik der Sitten*, Ak 4:434–35.

16. Cf. Plato, *Symposium*, 210e–211e.

17. Cf. Plato, *Politeia*, 504d–509b. For the synonymy of "beautiful" (*kalos*) and "good" (*agathos*), see, e.g., 507b.

18. Here ethics and philosophical anthropology intersect with metaphysics, insofar as the latter thinks the unity-in-difference of the "source" (*bpgè*) or "the One" with the totality.

19. Cf. Chapter 3.

20. Cf. Kant, *Grundlegung zur Metaphysik der Sitten*, Ak 4:418.

21. To what extent is it possible to reduce the differences between the ethical theories of Aristotle, Wolff, Kant, hedonism, and so on, to their intuitions with regard to "success" taken in its deepest and most encompassing sense?

22. Cf. Plato, *Symposium*, 206a ff.; *Phaedrus*, 244a ff.

CHAPTER 5

1. Aristotle, *Nicomachean Ethics*, II, 1–2 (1103a18–1104b3), and II, 4 (1105a17–1105b18). See also below, Chapter 9.

2. Aristotle, *On the Soul*, III, 8 (431b20–22). See also above, Chapter 4.

3. Certainly, all history and all studies of other cultures (e.g., Bantu, Japanese, Chinese) presuppose sympathy and "empathy": feeling, perceiving, and imagining *with* and *as* participants in that culture; but such a solidarity remains distant, reserved, and reconstructive. Identification would demand a conversion so radical that it can only be exceptional.

4. Cf. my "Over waarheid," *Tijdschrift voor Filosofie* 44 (1982): 3–51; and "A la recherche de l'expérience vraie," *Archives de Philosophie* 29 (1966): 348–62.

5. To recognize the power and the chances of enlightenment we owe to our traditions creates problems for the modern tradition of reason's autonomy. Cf. my *Reason in Faith* (New York: Paulist Press, 1999).

6. Cf. Levinas, *Totalité et Infini* (The Hague: Martinus Nijhoff, 1961), 168 ff.; translated as *Totality and Infinity* (Pittsburgh: Duquesne University Press, 1969), 194 ff.

7. The last three questions dominate the following pages, whereas an answer to the first question is broached in Chapter 6.

8. Descartes, *Discours de la méthode*, AT VI, 62: "et ainsi nous rendre comme maîtres et possesseurs de la nature."

9. See "*Natur*" in *Historisches Wörterbuch der Philosophie* VI, col. 421–41, for *physis* in ancient Greek philosophy and col. 441–82, for the further history of *naturall naturel Naturl naturaleza*. See also Hans Leisegang's *Physis* in *Paulys Real-Encyclopädie der classischen Altertumswissenschaft* I (1941), col. 1130–64.

10. Cf. Aquinas, *Summa Theologica*, I^a II^{ae}, qq. 93–94. Of course, "*naturale*" is synonymous with "essential" and not with the modern "natural" or "biological."

11. Cf. Hegel, *Philosophie des Rechts*, note to §258 Remark and Nietzsche, *Genealogie der Moral*, I, 13.

12. See note 8. I presuppose here that "earth," "world," and human history, as investigated by the social sciences, can be understood as an extension of Descartes' "nature" or—in Hegel's words—as a "second nature." For the history of this expression, see *Historisches Wörterbuch der Philosophie* VI, col. 484–94; and for Hegel's use of "second nature," see my *Modern Freedom* (Boston: Kluwer, 2001), 185–87.

13. When Socrates stated that a true poet is capable of writing comedies as well as tragedies (*Symposium*, 223d), and when Plato showed himself to be such a poet by staging both kinds of drama in the *Politeia* and other dialogues, they did not promote any desperate or cynical world vision, but rather tried to measure the heights and depths of human lives and history.

14. Cf. Miguel de Unamuno's *Del sentimiento trágico de la vida en los hombres y en los pueblos* (Madrid: Renacimiento, 1912).

15. Aristotle, *Nicomachean Ethics*, 1094a24, 1106b28–35; cf. Plato, *Philebus*, 194a.

16. "Objectivity" encompasses, in this context, not only nature, but also the historical world of institutions and customs that Hegel characterizes as "second nature." Cf. his *Encyclopedia* (1830) §§483–552.

17. Cf. below, Chapters 6 and 7.

CHAPTER 6

1. Aristotle, *On the Soul*, I, 1 (402a22–403a3); II, 1–3 (412a3–415a10).

2. I have expressed my debt to Emmanuel Levinas' writings in *To the Other* (West Lafayette, Ind.: Purdue University Press, 1993) and *Beyond: The Philosophy of Emmanuel Levinas* (Evanston, Ill.: Northwestern University Press, 1997).

3. This sentence anticipates the crucial thesis for which this and the following chapters make a case. Desire must learn that the appearance of authentic duty coincides with the genuine desirable, but this learning involves it in a profound conversion.

4. I use the words *intersubjective* and *intersubjectivity* in contrast with *social(ity)* and *communal(ity)* to name face-to-face relations in which at least one person is turned toward another person. For the meaning of the latter expressions, see below.

5. On friendship see, e.g., the *Routledge Encyclopedia of Philosophy* (New York: Routledge, 1988), 3:794–97; and *Historisches Wörterbuch der Philosophie*, II, col. 1105–14.

6. I will not dwell here on the differences, but see my *To the Other*, 166–84; *Beyond*, 121–30; and *Before Ethics* (Amherst, Mass.: Prometheus Press [Humanities Books], 1998), 42–73.

7. Does the text here slip from a Husserlian style of phenomenology into a more Hegelian one? Or—worse—does it replace phenomenology with "telling stories"? Quasi-genetic or -genealogical "stories" do not describe concrete behavior but try to reconstruct it by distinguishing elements and layers that, if developed in isolation, lead to unavoidable contradictions. The modern discussion about the necessity of escaping from a "state of nature" is a good example of such a quasi-story. Similarly, one can ask what being faced by someone means by contrasting it with the behavior of an ego that has eyes and ears only for conquerable phenomena. For such a persona, another's face appears as a contradiction or—if it is allowed to shine—as an interruption and as a demand of attitudinal change.

8. Cf. Peperzak, *Before Ethics*, 27–36.

9. Coincidence does not entail identity. I am not speaking here about the contents or meanings that are expressed by your and my voice, but only about the formal features of the audible addressing that creates an interpersonal relationship.

10. While trying to think what the consequences of absolute egoism (or "narcissism")—which, to some degree, is a universal inclination—would be, I am not suggesting that any human being *in concreto* is totally obsessed by the monopolistic desire of mastering and possessing the universe. Seen from the perspective of a monopolistic (albeit imaginary) individual, which a genealogical phenomenology may isolate as a *provisional* abstraction, the other's emergence in "my" world is the revelation of "You shall not kill!"

11. Here I take issue with Levinas' insistance on the nonreciprocity of the primordial ethical relationship. In *To the Other*, 172–74; and in *Beyond*, 126, 169, I argue that its asymmetry does not contradict but implies reciprocity.

12. For other aspects of human freedom, see Chapter 8.

13. The international Hegel scholarship of the last fifty years has sufficiently proved that Kojève's historicizing interpretation of Hegel's dialectic of "master and slave" does not have much to do with Hegel's dialectic of self-consciousness, as explained in his *Phenomenology of Spirit* and *Encyclopedia*. (See my *Modern Freedom: Hegel's Legal, Moral, and Political Philosophy* [Boston: Kluwer, 2001], 142–58.) However, both the Hegelian and the Kojèvian version of the "story" are analyses of a dimension that I contrast here, as "economic" (in a broad sense of the word), with the dimension of morality. While the "economic" aspects of intersubjectivity are based on needs and desires for power and possession, the moral dimension has

another principle, although historical concretization of the latter cannot avoid compromises with the often violent realizations of the economic dimension.

14. Cf. Levinas, *Autrement qu'être ou au-delà de l'essence* (Boston: Kluwer, 1974), 94–102 (75–81 of Alphonso Lingis' translation, *Otherwise Than Being or Beyond Essence* [The Hague, Martinus Nijhoff, 1981]).

15. Cf. Plato, *Alcibiades*, 128d ff.; *Apology*, 29e, 32d; *Phaedo*, 107c.

16. See also below.

17. Cf. Aristotle, *On the Soul*, II, 1 (412a3–413a10). Without a spiritual soul (its "form"), a "human" body would be a corpse, essentially different from any living body.

18. Cf. Kant, *Kritik der praktischen Vernunft*, Ak 4:434–35.

19. Kant, *Grundlegung der Metaphysik der Sitten*, Ak 4:401 (note); and *Kritik der praktischen Vernunft*, Ak 5:72–82.

20. Kant, *Grundlegung der Metaphysik der Sitten*, Ak 5:429.

21. Your "height" converts my desire into caring for you (cf. note 15).

22. If we take Kant's hyle-morphic distinction between the (rational) *form* and the (sensible) *matter* of morally good behavior seriously, his formalism is much closer to Aristotle's analysis of the ethical virtues than is commonly noted. In any case, it excludes a dualistic interpretation.

23. Cf., e.g., Chapter 5.

24. Cf., e.g., Rainer Maria Rilke's *Sonnette an Orpheus*. See also the next section on Art.

25. Compare Martin Heidegger, "Bauen, Wohnen, Denken" and "Das Ding" in *Vorträge und Aufsätze* (Pfullingen: Neske, 1967), 2:19–55.

26. Compare Heidegger's retrieval of Hölderlin's religious poetry with the renewed interest in Christian mysticism.

27. In Aristotle's ethics, *hoti deon* is much closer to *hoti kalon* than is Kant's and our understanding of duty. Cf. above, Chapter 2.

28. Cf. Chapter 5, note 12.

29. When Heidegger, in *Unterwegs zur Sprache* (Pfullingen; Neske, 1959), 254–56, says that *die Sprache spricht*, he does not deny that speakers are "necessary conditions" for the existence of language, the (trivial?) truth of which I state here polemically against hypostatizing interpretations against which Heidegger himself warns (226).

30. For an analysis of Gabriel Marcel's "*fidélité créatrice*," see his *Position et approches concrètes du mystère ontologique* (Paris: Vrin, 1949), 76–79.

31. It is this distance that enables individuals to ask questions about the fundamental relations between the community of which they are parts and their individual destiny.

32. Hegel integrates and sublates the modern discussions about the foundations of the state by subordinating the choosing or "arbitrary" moment of the will (*die Willkür*), which is the principle of Rousseau's *volonté de tous*, to the rational will (*der freie Wille*) which, as practical reason, is the principle of the universal or

common will (Rousseau's *volonté générale*). This enables him to distinguish, as well as to unite, the political and the contractual aspects of the community. See his *Grundlinien der Philosophie des Rechts* §§5–21; and my *Modern Freedom: Hegel's Legal, Moral, and Political Philosophy* (Boston: Kluwer 2001), 191–217.

33. Aristotle, *Politics*, I, 1 (1253a26–29).

34. Kant, *Zum ewigen Frieden*, Ak 8:366.

35. See above, Chapter 3 and Chapter 5.

36. See above, Chapter 5, and below, Chapter 9.

37. Kant, *Grundlegung zur Metaphysik der Sitten*, Ak 4:399 and 418.

CHAPTER 7

1. The statement that "God" can refer neither to "a being" (or entity) nor to the being that—in some sense—is common to all beings presupposes that God is neither a part (not even the summit) of any universe or totality (which, as composite, is necessarily finite), or its substance, essence, subject, or being. This old and traditional truth is often forgotten in attacks on and defenses of "ontotheology."

2. In one of his descriptions of the other's face, Levinas used Sartre's expression "*un trou dans l'être*" to evoke its otherness and exceptionality with regard to the "being" that gathers all beings in one totality. Elsewhere, he uses Aristotle's *thurathen* (from the outside) to express the face's "unworldly" character.

3. On the analogy or univocity of being, see *Historisches Wörterbuch der Philosophie* I, col. 215–27.

4. Descartes, *Discours de la méthode*, AT VI, 62. See above, Chapter 2.

5. See Chapter 4.

6. Thus I am also responsible for the entire constellation in which I find myself, as determined by many circumstances and actions that I have not inaugurated.

7. Cf. Plato's or Socrates' care for oneself (*meletē tou heautou*), referred to in Chapter 6, note 15, and the splendid title of Ricoeur's book *Soi-même comme un autre* (Paris: Du Seuil, 1990).

CHAPTER 8

1. Pp. 48–49. See also pp. 17–18.

2. "Ich kann, denn ich soll." In one of his *Xenien* (n. 294: *Ein Achter*), Schiller parodied Kant's moral philosophy in the following words:

"Auf theoretischem Feld ist weiter nichts mehr zu finden,
Aber der praktische Satz gilt doch: Du kannst, denn du sollst!"

(On the field of theory nothing further can be found,
But the practical thesis remains valid: You can for you must).

Cf. *Kritik der reinen Vernunft*, Ak 3:524–25; Kant, *Kritik der praktischen Vernunft*, §6 *Anmerkung*, Ak 5:28–30, esp. the end: "that he can (*kann*) do something [scil. perform a morally good but extremely difficult act] because he is aware that he ought (*soll*) to do it. He thus knows in himself the freedom which otherwise [namely, without awareness of the moral law] would have been unknown to him" (30); and 159: "that one *can* because our own reason recognizes this [duty] as its commandment and says that one *ought* to do it." See also Kant's, *Grundlegung zur Metaphysik der Sitten*, Ak 4:452–53; *Metaphysik der Sitten*, Ak 6:380; *Zum ewigen Frieden*, Ak 8:370; and *Religion innerhalb der bloßen Vernunft*, Ak 6:45.

3. The reduction of all demands to debts would suggest that duties are the consequences of a person's prior wrongdoing; it seems to associate the concept of duty with the concepts of compensation and punishment and tends to a contractualistic conception of morality.

4. Often translated as *choice*. For a good synthesis of Aristotle's analysis of this concept, see *Historisches Wörterbuch der Philosophie*, VII, col. 1451–58.

5. See Chapter 9.

6. See above, Chapter 5, note 12.

7. "Theological" is here taken in a sense that encompasses the typically religious (Jewish, Christian, Hindu, etc.), as well as the Greek and "natural" or "ontotheological" meaning of this word. Much of theology in the latter sense was already developed by the "pagan" Middle- and Neoplatonists.

8. Cf. Plato, *Apologia*, 31d, 40a; *Alcibiades*, 103a; *Euthydemus*, 272e; *Phaedrus*, 242bc.

9. Through the *epithymiai* and *pathē* analyzed by Plato, Aristotle, and the Stoics, and the *sinnliche* or "*natürliche*" *Neigungen*, of which Kant speaks, I understand the entire realm of human affectivity, which deserves a much more precise mapping than I can provide here.

10. Cf. the second book, titled *Dialektik der reinen praktischen Vernunft*, of the first part of Kant's *Kritik der praktischen Vernunft*, esp. Ak 5:110–19.

11. See Chapter 2, note 8.

12. See my *Modern Freedom: Hegel's Legal, Moral, and Political Philosophy* (Boston: Kluwer 2001), 91–95.

13. Both Kant and Hegel appealed to the existing ethos of their society, but they failed to prove that this ethos was a good standard for the evaluation of all human behavior. In other words, they replaced philosophy with faith in the authority of a contingent historical configuration.

14. Cf. Aristotle, *Nicomachean Ethics*, I, 7 (1097b22–1098a20).

15. Cf. Aristotle's discussion in *Nicomachean Ethics*, I, 9–10 (1099b–1101a22).

16. Cf. note 10 of this chapter.

CHAPTER 9

1. On the relations between *amor*, *connaturalitas*, and *convenientia*, cf., e.g., Aquinas, *Summa Theologica*, I^a II^{ae}, 26, 1, 3: "Omnibus [rebus] est pulchrum et

bonum amabile [as Dionysius writes in *De divinis nominibus*, cap. 4], cum un-aquaeque res habeat connaturalitatem ad id quod est sibi conveniens secundum suam naturam." On the role of *connaturalitas* in knowledge, see P. Rousselot, *L'intellectualisme de Saint Thomas* (Paris: Beauchesne, 1924), 2nd ed., 70–72, 202–3, 212–14; J. F. Dedek, " *Quasi experimentalis cognitio,*" *Theological Studies* 22 (1961), 357–90; and Andrew Tallon, *Head and Heart: Affection, Cognition, Volition as Triune Consciousness* (New York: Fordham University Press, 1997).

2. Cf. the articles *Ascèse* and *Katharsis,* in *Dictionnaire de spiritualité escétique et mystique, doctrine et histoire,* eds. Marcel Viller et al. (Paris: Beauchesne, 1937–55), I, col. 936–90, and VIII, col. 1664–90.

3. See above, Chapter 5. By emphasizing the necessity of (self)purification, I do not intend to deny the role of spiritual guides. Both roles were emphasized by most ancient philosophers—as Pierre Hadot has shown abundantly—as well as the Christian classics of philosophy, theology, and spirituality.

4. See note 2 above and *Reinigung,* in *Historisches Wörterbuch der Philosophie,* VIII, col. 531–53.

5. See my *Platonic Transformations* (Lanham, Md.: Rowman and Littlefield, 1997), 133–48.

6. If a human body includes a human soul (because its loss of animation would change it into a corpse, which is *substantially* different), it is obvious that it is also essentially and substantially different from an animal body.

7. Plato, *Politeia,* 519d.

8. Aristotle, *Nicomachean Ethics,* II, 1 (1103a24–1104a25). If living a good life must be learned by living well, this can only mean that one performs the most difficult experiment as well as possible, i.e., that one maintains the right direction, while approaching, in trial and error, the ideal. It is a pity that Kant did not thematize the Desire or *erōs* that precedes and surpasses the universe of conflicting inclinations, because it is their transcendental origin. However, in the *Dialektik der praktischen Vernunft,* Kant implicitly appeals to it when he states that goodness and happiness ultimately *must* be united. Cf. Kant's *Kritik der praktischen Vernunft,* Ak 5:110–19.

9. Kant, *Glückseligkeit.* Cf. *Kritik der reinen Vernunft,* Ak 3:523.

10. See Chapter 4.

11. See also Chapter 4 and Chapter 6.

12. Besides suggesting that which finalizes all ends, the Dutch word *einder* is a synonym for *horizon,* but *horizon* does not express that which, in addition to encompassing all ends, is also responsable for their desirability.

CHAPTER 10

1. Plato, *Politeia,* 514b (*periagein,* also in 515c), 516c (*metabolē*), 518c (*strephein*), 518d (*periagōgē,* also in 518e and 521c), *metastraphēsetai,* and *metastrophē* (525c, 532b8).

2. Plato, *Phaedo*, 118a.

3. Plato, *Phaedo*, 67bc, 68a, 98b, 114cd.

4. Aristotle, *Nichomachean Ethics*, I, 5 (1095b14–1096a11).

5. Nietzsche, *Also Sprach Zarathustra*, I: *Von den drei Verwandlungen*.

6. See my *Before Ethics* (Amherst, Mass.: Prometheus Press [Humanities Books], 1998), 28–40.

7. See the articles *Échelle spirituelle* and *Guides spirituels*, in *Dictionnaire de spiritualité ascétique et mystique, doctrine et histoire*, eds. Marcel Viller et al. (Paris: Beauchesne, 1937–55), IVi, col. 62–86, and VI, col. 1154–69.

8. See note 7.

9. The entire *Politeia* is structured by the movement of ascent and descent.

10. Aristotle, *Nicomachean Ethics*, II, 1 (1103a14–1104a25); *Politics* VII, 14 through VIII, 7 (1332b12–1342b35).

11. Cf. *Dictionnaire de spiritualité*, XVI, col. 1200–1216.

12. Cf. Descartes, *Meditationes de Prima Philosophia*, II, end of first section (AT VII, 24: "punctum . . . quod esset firmum et immobile . . . si vel minimum quid invenero quod certum sit et inconcussum") and section 4 (AT VII, 25: "ut ita tandem praecise remaneat illud tantum quod certum est et inconcussum").

13. Fichte, *Versuch einer neuen Darstellung der Wissenschaftslehre: Erste Abteilung* (the so-called *Erste Einleitung in die Wissenschaftslehre*, Jena 1797): "Was für eine Philosophie man wähle, hängt sonach davon ab, was man für ein Mensch ist." That Fichte here does not defend any relativism but instead summarizes his argument that a true philosopher must reject "realism" and choose "idealism" in the name of freedom and morality, is explained very well by Luigi Pareyson in "Die Wahl der Philosophie nach Fichte," in Franz Wiedmann, ed., *Epimeleia: Die Sorge der Philosophie um den Menschen* (Munich: Pustet 1973), 30–60.

14. From Parmenides through Plato and Bonaventura to Kierkegaard and Heidegger. Cf. also notes 7 and 11.

15. Cf. Karl Rosenkranz, *Georg Wilhelm Friedrich Hegels Leben* (Berlin, 1844; photographic reprint by the *Wissenschaftliche Buchgesellschaft*, Darmstadt, 1969), 204.

16. Socrates, *Gorgias*, 478e, 479cd, 509b–d, 527b–d.

17. Saint Paul, *Philemon*, verse 16.

CHAPTER II

1. See Chapter 4.

2. See Chapter 7.

3. See Chapter 6.

4. Kant, *Kritik der praktischen Vernunft*, Ak 5:110 ff.

5. See Chapter 7 and Chapter 8.

6. See Chapter 6.

7. See Chapters 4 and 7.

8. See Chapter 7.

9. See Chapters 4 and 7.

10. Cf. my "La référence érotique des négations théocentriques," in M. Olivetti (ed.), *Theologie négative* (Padova: CEDAM, 2003), 83–94.

11. See Chapter 6.

Index

In this index "f" after a number indicates a separate reference on the next page, and "ff" indicates separate references on the next two pages. A continuous discussion over two or more pages is indicated by a span of numbers. "Passim" is used for a cluster of references in close but not consecutive sequence.